RAMBLES
WITH MY
FAMILY
(STARTING IN CHINA)

WENDY MAITLAND

Published by Wendy Maitland
Wendy Maitland ©2015

ISBN: 978-1-911412-44-1
iBooks: 978-1-911412-51-9
Kindle: 978-1-911412-52-6

Printed by Dolman Scott
Ltd www.dolmanscott.co.uk

AUTHOR'S NOTE

When I was asked by Dr Peter Liddle (Director of the Second World War Experience Centre in Leeds) to write an account of my experiences during the war in China and Burma, it started me off on this memoir, and when people reading the wartime account wanted to know what happened next, the story gradually expanded itself into this book as I went on writing.

The first two chapters are reproduced from my original account, written (as far as I was able to) in the documentary style requested by Dr Liddle: just plain facts, avoiding any personal, emotional or humorous observations. After several attempts, I found it was impossible to remain impersonal when describing so many dramatic events, and Dr Liddle, understanding my frustration, then allowed me to write more freely while keeping to the documentary style as much as possible.

The map accompanying the wartime story was drawn by my sister Ros, who has been very supportive and encouraging all through this process, checking the narrative for accuracy and occasionally adding her own comments, which are always illuminating. My thanks to Ros, and also to my husband Charles and daughter Louise, who have been great allies and motivators.

Then there is Sue Daly: writer, photographer and film maker extraordinaire, who arrives on a bicycle to help me assemble photos or pieces of writing. And special thanks to Vivien Lipski who very patiently edited my first drafts, and gave me confidence to press on with the telling of this story.

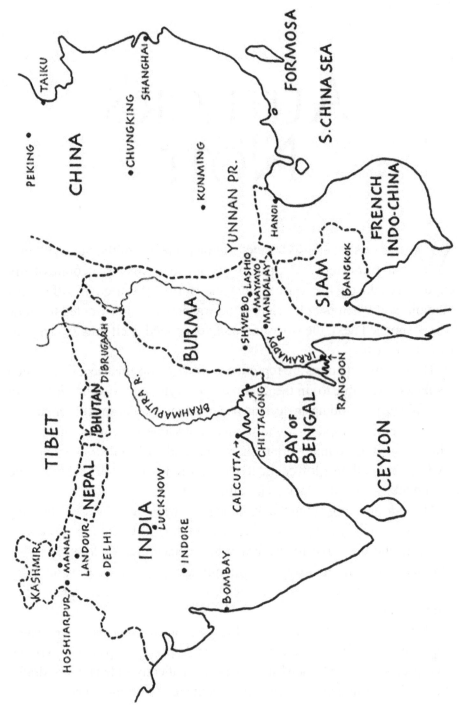

CONTENTS

CHAPTER 1

In order to provide context and historical accuracy for the wartime events, I have needed to refer to my parents' diaries and notes, so the story includes these with my own memories until my clear impressions as a child develop sufficiently to stand on their own. At the beginning of this account my parents were twenty-eight and twenty-nine; Father was very tall at six foot four, while Mother by contrast was barely five foot and petite. They were both Londoners.

I was born Margaret Crowther Craddock in September 1938 at the London Hospital where my father had trained as a doctor some years before, while mother was a nurse from University College Hospital. My middle name Crowther was bestowed on me in honour of my parents' friendship with Bishop Crowther, an African colleague of theirs in Nigeria. They were missionaries, now having returned from their mission in Zaria, Northern Nigeria, for the birth of their first child to take place safely in England. It was not thought suitable, then, for children of Europeans either to be born or to live in Nigeria, which was commonly referred to as the 'White Man's Grave'. Since this made it impossible for them to return to Nigeria after my arrival, the Church Missionary Society decided to send them to China instead. Japanese forces had already invaded China at this time and a state of war was in progress.

After an epic journey west from England, crossing the Atlantic and Canada, then by ship again across the North Pacific and Yellow Sea, our little family duly arrived by steamer at the Chinese port of Taiku in March 1939. There we were confronted by Japanese soldiers terrorising the arriving passengers with fixed bayonets, which they were jabbing into luggage and belongings, so that when they came to my carry-cot covered in a blanket I was very nearly dispatched, but for Mother's quick thinking in grabbing the arm of the soldier before it descended on me. We then proceeded on to Peking by train without further incident.

My parents' first task in China was to learn the Mandarin language before they could take on any medical or missionary work. So they were enrolled in the Language School at Peking University, which was a full-time course lasting for a year, taught by Chinese scholars who spoke no English. While they were fully occupied doing this, I was cared for by a Chinese amah called Wang Nei Nei. I remember clearly, though I was very young, being taken by Wang Nei Nei each day to the city square, where we passed many happy hours watching the activities of flocks of pigeons that swooped and whirled around us. They had whistles tied to their tails, which made a charming noise when flying such as could enthral a small child, and I remember being fascinated by this and pointing and exclaiming in Mandarin, which quickly became the most natural language to me, as we all spoke it at home so my parents could practise together.

Wang Nei Nei was a small round woman dressed plainly in black tunic and trousers. She had tiny black-slippered feet on which she seemed precariously balanced, but walked unhesitatingly with quick short steps like a clockwork doll. She was kind, gentle and infinitely patient. My memories of her recall a sense of complete serenity.

It was at this time that my father decided I didn't look or behave like a Margaret; in his opinion I was more like a Wendy, so my name was changed. Later, when I asked him about this, he said I was too much of a fairylike creature to be a Margaret!

When the year in Peking came to an end and my parents were competent in Mandarin, we set off on our first posting which was to the city of Kunming, a long way south in Yunnan Province, a month's journey by train and ship via Shanghai and Hanoi. The Japanese were bombing the Indo-Chinese border which we had to cross by train, and had destroyed a rail bridge while a train was crossing a few days previously, killing many passengers, so my parents were anxious. After this incident the trains ran at night to avoid being spotted from the air and, even so, were sometimes obliged to hide in tunnels. So the threat from bombing was replaced by a real fear of suffocation from poisonous fumes building up in the tunnel. However, those who succumbed to unconsciousness came round when the train emerged into fresh air again. My parents and myself were the only European travellers on the train as it laboured cautiously through each night until, at last, on the fifth day after leaving Hanoi, it reached Kunming safely at four o'clock in the morning.

After finding our way by rickshaw to the hospital and staff quarters and at last being able to rest and sleep peacefully, we then discovered that our Pekingese speech was regarded as quite foreign in that part of China, and we would need to learn Yunnanese in order to speak correctly and be properly understood!

The city of Kunming itself caused some dismay to my mother on first arriving and seeing how primitive and dirty it was after Peking, with a pervading stench from open drains which steamed with human and pig excrement, and a general air of squalor. But these sensations were soon forgotten in the warmth of welcome received from the hospital staff and resident CMS missionaries, who were delighted to see new faces and lost no time in showing us to our house. This was large and rather grand in a Georgian style, entirely surprising for a missionary house in China, and my mother was amazed and overjoyed. It was to be my parents' first proper home since they had married four years before, and at long last they would be able to unpack and display their wedding presents, which had been crated and forwarded from England despite the exigencies of war. Among the proudest of possessions was a carpet bought at a Harrods' sale, and mother's piano.

My father was appointed Professor of Medicine at Kunming General Hospital, and Mother was happily entertaining large numbers of guests with a Chinese cook and housemaid. Her transition from the Peking form of Mandarin to Yunnanese caused much amusement and confusion in trying to explain menus and other instructions to the house staff. These were balmy days, while the Japanese were engaged in consolidating their hold elsewhere in the country, but they were gaining ground fast.

After just a few months in Kunming, on a bright cloudless afternoon in 1940, we suddenly heard the noise of aircraft and a formation of twenty-seven Japanese planes appeared overhead. Within moments, bombs rained down from the planes, but were not aimed at our part of the city and the hospital was spared, but was soon put on alert to receive casualties. After this initial raid, a short respite was gained as the weather changed to rain and mist in that part of the country. Luckily for us, the Japanese needed clear conditions for flying; this allowed a little time for contingency planning.

As the bombing raids resumed, a system of graduated warnings was set up so that as soon as the planes left their bases in Siam the first warning gongs would sound. If the planes entered Yunnan Province, the next warning was given, which consisted of a bright red ball hung from the tallest building in the city for all to see. This was called a '*chin-pao*'. Then, if the planes were seen to be flying towards our city, there was a final warning called a '*chin-chi-chin-pao*'. This was a great crashing of gongs up and down every street, which no one could miss unless they were stone deaf.

One morning, the *chin-chi-chin-pao* started with its great fury of sound and my parents hurried off to make sure all the patients in the hospital were placed underneath their beds, as was the drill for direct raids. Father stayed at the hospital to give heart to them and to the staff, while Mother collected me and one of the missionary women who was too scared to think what to do, and was looking for a safe place to put her typewriter!

As the planes were very close at this stage, there was no time to dash for a shelter and we all squeezed into the under-stairs cupboard in our house. The next moment, Father, coming to check on us, arrived breathless and was appalled to find us crouching under the stairs. He grabbed us all and pushed us out into the garden and into a slit trench, which was in the process of being dug. This was no more than four foot deep, and we all tumbled in as the first bombs fell. A very large dog belonging to one of the missionaries flung itself in on top of us, and there we all were, flailing about, trying to keep our heads below ground level.

At that moment a massive explosion blasted our ears and rocked the entire area around us like an earthquake. Stones and bricks and pieces of earth and debris and branches of trees rained down on us, seemingly without end. We could not see each other; the air was black and dense and the earth went on shaking as more bombs fell and everything around us seemed to be disintegrating. After a very long time in a state of complete rigidity, unable to move or think or speak, as the stones stopped falling and the air cleared a little, I pulled myself up and peered out. The world had changed in that instant of time while the bombs fell, and all I could see was a smoking wasteland.

During the period of misty weather just a short time before, when plans were put in place for defence of the city against attack, the British Embassy had advised its nationals to paint Union Jacks on the roofs of their houses in the belief that Japanese planes would avoid them. However, this tactic appeared only to serve as a target identification mark and the bombers zoned in on the painted flags. Our house had taken a direct hit, and nothing remained of it except a few tottering walls and great mounds of smashed timber and furniture thrown together with wrecked bricks, over which a choking canopy of dust rose and fell. Everywhere we walked our feet crunched on glass as we looked for anything that might still be left intact or worth retrieving. Of the mother cat with kittens, asleep on a bed upstairs before the bombs fell, there was no sign. Mother's piano had disappeared too, but it was the fate of the cats that upset me the most.

The hospital had also been hit and most of the staff had fled in panic, leaving father and a CMS nurse to treat the casualties and run things generally, cooking food for the patients as well as pumping water and keeping the hospital open.

Meanwhile, it was thought sensible for Mother and me, with two Chinese maids, to leave the city and drive out to a small place called Laokai, where the mission had a holiday cottage on a quiet lake, which was unlikely to draw attention from bombers, and where we could be housed safely for the time being. Mother was six months pregnant with a second child when all this was happening, and I was not much more than two years old, surprisingly able to remember quite a lot of what was going on.

No sooner had we settled into the little cottage, thinking ourselves safe after one blissful night of calm, when early the next morning gongs sounded from the city and bombers appeared over Laokai. Mother was advised to gather up a few necessities and take to the hills above the lake. She brought binoculars as one of her necessities and with these we were able to observe from our elevated position the ongoing, systematic destruction of Kunming and its surrounding districts, this whole region having strategic importance for the Japanese. Of course, we were in a state of great alarm about Father and what was happening at the hospital. But later, when the planes had droned off back towards Siam and the coast was clear, we could go down to the cottage and, joy of joys, a messenger arrived to give us news that Father and the hospital were safe.

A pattern then started to emerge as the bombers returned each day to pound the city, and we settled into a routine of leaving the cottage early to hide up in the hills until evening, when we knew the planes could not return in the dark. It was a severe temptation to go back down to the cottage earlier if the bombing eased, but a formation of planes could be followed by another and another, and Laokai was right under the flight path.

We began to feel safer as each day passed without incident, but then one morning when we had settled down with other villagers for another day out on the hillside, the planes appeared as usual, but this time they were flying low and making straight for us.

I remember this very clearly as it was so terrifying and unexpected. We had never thought it possible that the Japanese would attack defenceless women and children exposed on an open hillside, and were quite unprepared as machine guns opened up on us from the air. The noise and bedlam all around was sudden and horrific. I remember seeing the earth spurting up in a line coming towards where we were cowering, as streaks of metal seared into the earth with a ferocious mechanical stuttering sound; it seemed to me like a giant sewing machine stitching up the earth and us with it. I thought I must not move or make a sound as I waited for the hideous crazed drilling to hit and stitch us into the ground. That is what it felt like. I must have been too shocked to register what happened to the other people, as I have no recollection of the aftermath of this attack, only that it subsided after some considerable time and, to my great astonishment, Mother and I were unharmed.

After this, we decided it might be less frightening to spend daytimes in the cottage and risk being bombed, than face more attacks on the hillside.

This decision, however, soon proved to be academic, as another twist in our fortunes was about to happen.

Father was still at his post in Kunming, attempting to keep domestic and medical services at the hospital running as normally as possible, while casualties continued to pour in from the relentless bombing raids. As if this was not enough of a challenge, one evening a colonel of the Kuomintang (Chinese National Army) arrived at the hospital in a manic state and went berserk among the staff and patients, which, as he was heavily armed with a variety of weapons, was a very dangerous situation. Father attempted to reason with him but this seemed only to provoke the man, further enraging him, so Father then tackled the colonel physically and removed his weapons, at the same time giving him morphine to calm him down. This was an instinctive action, but it was a serious offence to disarm an officer of the Chinese Army as it would cause immense loss of face to the man concerned, which could not be tolerated under any circumstances.

Consequently, in no time, the hospital was surrounded by National Army soldiers demanding that Father be handed over to them or they would burn down the hospital. But before they had time to post guards on the exits, one of the CMS nurses, with great presence of mind, assisted him to escape out of a back door and directed him to the temporary refuge of an American YMCA worker's house nearby. It was clear this was not going to be safe for very long, as the soldiers were becoming increasingly excited and had been joined by a mob, which spread out to search for Father in the neighbourhood of the hospital.

A plan was quickly put into action by the courageous YMCA worker, who hid Father in his car and sped away with him out of Kunming, driving to a place called Laotzu in rural Yunnan, where some missionaries of the China Inland Mission were stationed and, it was hoped, would shelter Father until a further plan could be hatched.

Meanwhile, Mother and I remained in the cottage on the lake, completely oblivious to these developments until the same CMS nurse who had rescued Father came to tell us what had happened, and that we would have to wait there and hope for the best as there was nothing else we could do at that stage. Later, as it was getting dark that evening, there was suddenly a lot of shouting and marching of feet outside the cottage and, when Mother went to investigate, all the lights were abruptly turned off and the door was locked from the outside. We felt very frightened, imagining that soldiers had come to take us hostage in retaliation for failing to catch Father. After several hours of listening and waiting in the dark, we became increasingly fearful of our fate when there was the sound of a key turning in the lock, and we imagined the worst. But to our amazement, friendly voices greeted us, explaining that soldiers from the local Yunnanese Army had come to guard us against capture by the Kuomintang!

Although we should have been reassured by this and the sight of our guards laughing and chatting and eating rice outside in the courtyard, our nerves were too jangled to be able to sleep very much that night, and then just before dawn there was another disturbance outside. One of the Chinese doctors from the hospital in Kunming, Dr Yu, had driven up in a very agitated state, saying that we must leave with him immediately as we were still in great danger. Moreover, he was on his way to Laotzu from where Father had sent an urgent message for surgical instruments, which were needed in all haste to save the life of the brother-in-law of the British Consul, who for some unexplained reason was also in Laotzu, where no hospital or other medical facility was available in such an isolated place.

It was a very strange story. The British Consul in Kunming was called Mr Prideaux-Brune, and his brother-in-law was a Professor Urquhart, whom my parents had first met in Peking at the university. So when they went to Kunming they already had this connection with the Consul's family, who visited and dined with them on many occasions before the bombing started.

It appeared that Professor Urquhart, on a visit to the Consul, had been injured in a bombing raid, and to escape further danger had been moved to the countryside at Laotzu, where the CIM missionaries were looking after him and tending his wounds as best they could without medical help. By the time Father arrived, a leg injury had turned gangrenous and amputation of the leg was the only way to save him. So that was the reason for Dr Yu's urgent summons to bring amputation instruments.

With our meagre belongings, Mother and I duly accompanied Dr Yu, which, despite our weariness, was a happy surprise, because we would be reunited with Father. It took all day to reach Laotzu and the journey was an ordeal of acute discomfort and reckless speed over primitive roads, but at last we saw Father waving to us from the CIM house and we had arrived safely. Sadly, it proved not such a happy arrival as he soon gave us the news that Professor Urquhart had already died, and the most urgent task now was to get him buried, as the custom in China did not allow for any leisurely funeral preparations.

Chinese people, in anticipation of such events, had their coffins made ready, well in advance of any expectation of death. It was quite normal for a coffin to be seen standing on end in a room used every day by the family, almost as part of the furniture, as these were often very ornate and richly decorated. But in this case no coffin was to hand, and Father, with Dr Yu and the CIM missionary Mr Allen, had to go on a tour of the village to find someone who could be persuaded to sell their coffin. As well as this, a burial site had to be bought from a landowner where it would be in the correct position, so that Professor Urquhart's head would be facing in a propitious direction according to accepted custom. Ultimately, a very fine site was achieved, facing west to some splendid mountains, of which it was felt the Professor would have approved.

Meanwhile, the only room in the CIM house that had space enough for my parents and me to lie down and sleep was the room accommodating the Professor's body, which we had to share. When it came to fitting him into his coffin the next day, a major snag was encountered in that it was a Chinese coffin made to measure for a Chinese man (in this case the Mayor of Laotzu), while the Professor was over six foot in height. So he had to be folded up to fit, which was not entirely dignified, but the best that could be done in those strained circumstances. What happened to Mr Prideaux-Brune, the British Consul, either then or subsequently, we never heard.

We were now, after all these adventures in escaping from Kunming, nothing more than fugitives or refugees, having to rely on the kindness of the Allens at the CIM house for shelter, and trying to stretch out the pitiful amount of cash we had left to buy food. Even had we the means, there was very little to buy in Laotzu, which had no fresh milk and not much of anything else. The Chinese villagers, who were accustomed to hardship, were themselves struggling to survive. Nothing was getting through from Kunming, or anywhere else, and we knew we had to leave somehow and reach a place where we could be safe in time for the new baby due in three months. Father had grown a beard as disguise for our next fleeing attempt.

We had one crucial contact. She was the wife of an intelligence officer attached to the Embassy and had been a patient of Father's in Kunming. To escape the bombing of the city, she had discovered that it was possible to fly out of Kunming and across the border to Burma in an American plane which regularly did the trip from Chongqing in the north. So it was arranged that we would secretly rendezvous at the very primitive airport in Kunming and fly out on this plane. Having got this far by various means and in a considerable state of nervous exhaustion, there we were on 31 October 1940 waiting for the plane to arrive from Chongqing and rescue us. But, to our dismay, we then heard that it had been shot down that morning by Japanese fighters while on its way, and all on board had been killed, including the pilot. This was a blow, and all we could do was retreat to the ruins of our Kunming house to hover there until the next day and another attempt by an American Dakota to get through.

After waiting all day at the airport, a plane at last shimmered into sight just as dusk was falling and Japanese attackers would not be so much in evidence. A coolie with a hurricane lamp guided the plane in. But before we could get on board, the two American pilots who were in charge said they were carrying the body of the dead pilot who had been shot down, and a full ceremony of American formality must first take place for the offloading of the coffin and flag. At last, at about 10 p.m., we were able to board and found ourselves quite spaciously accommodated, as there were only a few other passengers, the rest having cancelled due to the Japanese atrocity of the previous day. We were told that after shooting down the plane, Japanese soldiers on the ground had machine-gunned the survivors of the crash. So it was not encouraging.

All the same, after two and a half hours flying in total darkness in the cabin (so the plane would be less visible to any watching Japanese) and Mother very fidgety about this, peering out of the window to try and spot any sight of enemy planes creeping up, we finally arrived safely at Lashio in Burma sometime after midnight. Checking on our further plans, the American pilots were appalled to find that we had nowhere organised to go to, and no bedding-rolls or chop-boxes, without which respectable people did not travel, but they very generously gave us green blankets out of the plane and found us a place to sleep for the rest of the night.

In the morning, all of us were commanded to appear at the office of the British Resident in Lashio immediately. Our night flight over the mountains, out of China into Burma, had been done without official authorisation and we were all to be reprimanded.

Before leaving China, Father already had a plan to put into action when we reached Burma. The ruthless expansionist aims of the Japanese, which were obvious for all to see in China, convinced him that war with Japan was inevitable and British forces would be fully engaged very soon. In his judgement, this was not a time for him to be pursuing missionary work, and instead he had decided to offer his services to the British Army in Burma.

There were two garrison units of the British Army in Burma then: the Glosters and the King's Own Yorkshire Light Infantry. Army HQ was in Rangoon, 530 miles away from Lashio, so Father arranged an interview and took the train which ran via Mandalay to Rangoon. He was accepted and commissioned to start work immediately as Medical Officer to the Military Hospital in Maymyo, a hill station forty miles east of Mandalay. In addition to this medical appointment, his fluency in Mandarin led to him being given an additional role as an interpreter for Chinese workers employed by the army.

Despite this sudden elevation in status for Father, when my parents first arrived in Maymyo their total assets amounted to about seven annas (roughly one shilling), as their salary was paid by CMS into an account at the Shanghai Banking Corporation and, due to the dislocation of war, could not be accessed. But once again we were taken under the wing of missionaries, this time at the American Baptist Mission Rest House, where a very dear and very large, affectionate woman called Mamma Guis (an American of German origin) welcomed us under her roof, feeling great compassion for Mother who was very near to her time for having the baby. Mamma Guis went into action, organising everything that might be needed.

A young Burmese woman called Ah Pu was taken on as a nanny for me, and very soon all of us were moved into a house of our own called Fernside; one of the old colonial-style houses with a wide veranda giving on to vast swathes of lawn and shady jacaranda trees. This seemed like paradise after all that we had been through in the past few months. As it was a government house for the use of government officers (which I suppose is what Father now was), a full staff of servants was supplied to run the house and garden. The garden was a joy and delight for me, the first garden I could remember as being 'ours', and the gardeners were my friends. I was absorbed all day by their activities. At first light each morning, when dew was still wet underfoot, the gardeners picked flowers which were carried into the house to be arranged by them in numerous vases in the hall and main rooms before breakfast. Later, I would go with them to the hutches where we kept baby rabbits as pets and these were carefully lifted out onto the lawn to be played with, while the gardeners watched and made sure none of them hopped too far away.

So it was that we approached New Year 1941 in this state of temporary euphoria. One of the final and most ironic events of the closing year was the surprise arrival of a cable from the Kuomintang Foreign Minister in China. Addressed to Father, it urged him to return to Kunming with all speed, where his services were much needed at the hospital. A full apology was offered for the incident with the Chinese colonel, who had turned out to be a dangerous homicidal maniac and had been suddenly retired!

The other event of that time came soon after New Year with the apparently effortless arrival of my sister Elaine, who I was very pleased with at first. But it never occurred to me that the baby was going to be a permanent part of our family. I quite thought that she would go to someone else after a few days. She was doll-like and docile most of the time, but also could make a fearful amount of noise, especially at night, which I found very annoying. It was a shock when I found out that she was staying regardless, and that our family was not going to remain in its previous intimate form with just my parents and me. I couldn't see why we needed anyone else when things were perfect with just the three of us.

Ah Pu, however, was sensitive to these feelings of mine and devised ways to include Elaine and me together in harmonious activities. The most charming of these took place each evening when we went for a walk along paths and lanes near the house, Elaine in her pram pushed by Ah Pu, while my assortment of baby rabbits came along in the pram too, dispersed among the covers quite unperturbed, like fluffy toys.

I had my third birthday during this idyllic time at Maymyo and the memory of it remains sharp. We had a lot of friends by then among army and other expatriate families, so my birthday party was quite a lavish event with a large number of children invited. Out on the lawn we had a carousel, chute, swings, a see-saw, and pony rides to entertain the children with their mothers and nannies. It was the best fun I'd ever had and the next morning, as soon as there was a glimmer of light outside, I ran out to the garden playground again. There had been a heavy dew and the garden was misty and grey in the early morning, shrouding the lawns where the playground had been. But on looking closer, it had vanished! There was not a sign of it left. I didn't know that it had been hired only for the day and the same evening, after I had gone to bed, all had been dismantled and taken away. It was an immense disappointment to find it all gone, and that it had never been meant to stay. I had thought the playground was a birthday present, and birthday presents don't usually get taken away after the party.

Life continued however without missing a beat, and Ah Pu invented new diversions. She was an intelligent girl, from the Karen tribe, slender and graceful in her white *aingyi* (blouse) and *longyi* (coloured sarong-style skirt), her shining black hair swept up with a flower tucked in at the side. She was a Christian and always dressed with particular care on Sundays when she went to church. Touchingly, she called my parents Mummy and Daddy and attached herself to our family as one of us.

CHAPTER 2

This period of peace and tranquillity was like the false calm at Kunming before the bombs started falling. We had been in Maymyo for just over a year and despite the forebodings felt by my parents after their experiences with the Japanese in China, Mother was making new curtains for our house and pressing on with life as normally as possible. She was very pleased to find lilac fabric (her favourite colour) in one of the shops, and was about to hang the new curtains when the phone rang. It was Father calling from work to say that the Japanese had attacked Pearl Harbour the day before, 7 December 1941, and Mother was to lose no time in putting blackout on the windows and instructing the gardeners to dig a trench for a bomb shelter. Again. Within a matter of days we were seeing the same formation of Japanese planes overhead that we had grown used to before, always twenty-seven, and always the same tense waiting to hear how close the bombs were falling. But, despite daily air raids and the discomfort and tedium of sitting crammed into the trench for an uncertain amount of time each day, we did not have any close hits.

After about a month, news came that Singapore had fallen to the Japanese, with many casualties and prisoners taken. Father was convinced that Rangoon would be next if reinforcements were not sent out immediately to block Japanese forces from invading Burma, but they were advancing at such a rate it seemed a slim hope that units could be mobilised from Britain in time. With this dire outlook in mind, he became very busy and preoccupied at work, putting in place a network of plans for medical

15

services to meet what he saw as a certain prospect of heavy casualties, both military and civilian.

In early February 1942, the British Governor in Burma, whose name was Mr Dorman Smith, made a broadcast to residents saying, 'Let there be no panic. Rangoon will be another Tobruk and will not fall.' The next day, all the senior government officials, including the Governor himself, began evacuating their families by air to India. There were no plans announced for any other personnel or families to get out. Mother had a friend with three young children, who discussed the possibility of trekking out over the mountains to India with elephants to carry them and their luggage! Finally, in the first week of March, Rangoon fell. Army personnel were served with notices that a convoy of lorries and cars would leave Maymyo on Thursday, 14 March, to drive north 120 miles to Swebo, where planes would arrive for transport to India. The convoy would take 80 women and children, with husbands to volunteer as drivers. Many of the women were pregnant and there were a lot of small children and babies, so Father was to escort the convoy as far as Swebo to provide medical assistance if needed. He was then to return to Maymyo without us.

Mothers joining the convoy were told to pack one bag per family, just with essentials. So these bags were mostly filled with nappies and dried milk for babies. Mother looked round at the possessions she had managed to collect at Fernside. Friends coming over from Kunming had kindly brought with them a few of my parents' wedding presents salvaged from the bomb site, and these now looked forlorn. All had to be left behind once more. But, worst of all, we had to leave Ah Pu, who was heartbroken and could not believe her family would abandon her. Our Burmese servants promised to look after the animals as, apart from the rabbits, we had Siamese kittens and two spaniels called Jasper and Max. Thomas, the cook, assured Mother that he would stay with Father whatever happened.

We set off for Swebo about midday on that Thursday, 14 March 1942. Father was driving us in our own car, which was a Ford V8, and we had three elderly nuns with us. There were about 20 cars and several lorries in the convoy as we arrived at the Ava Bridge over the Irrawaddy River around 4.30 p.m. The convoy started to cross and was about halfway over when a familiar ominous sound reached us: Japanese planes in their bombing formation, flying towards the bridge. A policeman who was in charge of the convoy gave the order to abandon vehicles, and we all scrambled out somehow and down the river bank to get under the arches of the bridge. The poor nuns in their long habits had a hard time of it. But the extraordinary thing was that the planes took no notice of our convoy exposed on the bridge, and instead flew on. Maybe the bridge was needed to stay intact for the Japanese advance later on.

By late evening, having gradually descended from the cool altitude of the hills, we arrived at Swebo, which was a ramshackle, sweltering place, miasmic with heat and mosquitoes, and no sign whatever of any serviceable landing strip or likelihood of planes appearing. By now, the stress and distress of hot hungry children and frantic mothers was beginning to reach crisis point, and somewhere had to be found for the night, along with safe drinking water and food supplies.

Father and two other officers went to buy supplies and arrange the only possible accommodation, which was in some old Sepoy barracks containing primitive beds of wooden frames with ropes woven across, fifty of these to a room, with straw mattresses. These turned out to be swarming with bed bugs, and a very fractious night was endured in these conditions, with loud wailing and screaming going on almost continuously as exhausted children could not settle and mothers became increasingly distraught.

In the morning, Father decided he was taking us back to Maymyo straight away. The other families were given a choice: whether to stay and see if the airlift promised by the authorities would materialise, or return to Maymyo and take their chances.

When we arrived back in Maymyo, we were told that a train was leaving the next day for Mandalay in a second evacuation attempt and this was the only hope for those still left behind. We had no other way out and Father took us to the station on that terrible day of utter dejection and desperation, Mother clutching the bag of supplies with Elaine in her arms, while I was clinging onto her skirt and my panda, which was the one toy I had chosen to take with me. Only one toy was allowed per child.

When Father didn't get onto the train with us, I could not understand what was happening. Then, as realisation set in that he wasn't coming with us, I was incredulous and terrified and overcome with grief at leaving him behind. It seemed more than I could possibly bear. I did not know that of the fathers who stayed behind in Burma at that time very few would ultimately come out alive, but I must have sensed this, and the parting has remained with me as one of the most desolate moments of my life. I looked out of the window at him as the train pulled away and he looked utterly desolate himself. I carried this last glimpse of him in my mind: a very tall, lean, fit and tanned man with black hair and intense dark eyes, looking strained and drained. But he could not come with us as there was going to be a lot for him to do in the coming months and years of war in Burma. He was just thirty-one years old, and Mother was thirty-two.

She, always practical in situations like this, was preoccupied with making sure our drinking water container was to hand with other essentials for the journey. Her sense of calm and orderliness was consoling and steadying. Our precious drinking water supply was not sufficient for making up babies' bottles, however, and when we stopped at a station, she went to ask the engine driver for boiling water from the engine. This looked oily and disgusting, but it was boiled and therefore must be thought to be sterile!

The train crawled south towards Mandalay, which meant we were travelling down into the path of the Japanese advancing up from Rangoon, instead of away from them. But the orders were for us to go there and await further instructions. The train was full of retreating families but, unlike us, many had fathers with them if they were civilians not needed to stay behind for the war. After reaching Mandalay, the train changed direction, turning north-west, away from the Japanese. It then rattled on infinitely slowly for the rest of the day, finally arriving at none other than that hideous place Swebo, all over again. However, there was now a landing strip of sorts dug out of the surrounding jungle, and planes were coming in from India. But the new landing facility had attracted Japanese bombing raids, so our rescue planes had to contend with bombs or attacks by Japanese fighters. Sometimes they could not come in at all for a whole day or days at a time.

Everyone had to be weighed in preparation for getting onto a flight, to make sure the American Dakotas were not overloaded. Mother's weight was recorded at 104 pounds. We now spent days crouching under bushes at the edge of the landing strip while the raids continued remorselessly, and all we could do was wait for a lull and hope that one of the planes would mercifully appear.

When at long last our turn came, it was a mad scramble to get on before any Japanese planes returned: children and luggage were bundled inside and the door slammed as the plane roared off down the crude runway. There were no seats and the inside of the plane was like a huge grey cave, a cold, rather dark and rattling cave. I sat on our bags, feeling bewildered at being so suddenly catapulted into the air, and then I saw that the other children had sweets that their mothers had brought for them. I didn't have any sweets, which was very upsetting, but worst of all was the sudden realisation that precious panda was not there anymore. Panda had been left behind in the bushes where we had been hiding for all those long hours and days, waiting for the plane. This was quite the last straw and is another memory that remains with me as one of the worst moments of that time running away from the Japanese.

The American pilots of the Dakotas were extraordinarily brave and skilled men. These were American Air Force Dakotas, not civilian planes, and the pilots were risking their lives flying a bizarre ferry service for women and children rather than troop transport, which was their more usual activity. Whether their bravery was subsequently recognised and they were decorated for this remarkable humanitarian action, I have never heard. Without them we could not have escaped and would have been left to our fate at the hands of the Japanese in Burma.

The Dakota deposited its cargo of bedraggled families at Chittagong, in what was then Bengal, safely across the border. But the Japanese were already, even then, aiming for India as their next target once Burma was secured. Meanwhile, at Chittagong, the arriving families, including ours, had no time to rest as we were loaded onto a steamboat to proceed up the Brahmaputra River to the nearest train station. Without pause in this miserable excursion, the next journey, laboriously by train once more, was to Calcutta, where we were to be held in the stifling confines of the military fort. Nowhere else was large enough to contain the influx of refugees still arriving.

The fort was like a prison (which indeed it might once have been), and Mother, Elaine and I were pushed into a fetid cell-like room where we all sank down, by now filthy and dishevelled and weary beyond imagining. We had not washed for more than a week nor changed our clothes; we had barely eaten during that time as there had been almost nothing to eat, and Elaine had become very quiet and dazed. In this cell at the fort, Mother amazingly produced from her bag – like a conjuror – a fur coat from Peking that she had not been able to bring herself to leave behind. A fur coat might have seemed incongruous in the furnace heat of Calcutta, but Mother spread it out for us so we could all lie down and sleep at last in relative comfort on its furry softness.

Food was provided at the fort, and for children it consisted mainly of porridge, which I remember was peppered with little black insects. I discovered these were weevils, and when Mother insisted they were there for a purpose because they were full of protein, I simply didn't believe her. The weevils gave the porridge a slightly bitter crunchiness that did not seem to fit with the nature of porridge as I understood it. But there were far too many of them to pick out, so they had to be chewed up and swallowed, or go hungry.

Mother very soon decided to get us out of the fort at any cost. So she went to see the Commandant, who was very edgy and disgruntled with all these refugees camping on his patch, and did not want to be responsible for any of them running off and getting lost in the vastness of India. But Mother had a plan. As usual, she had tapped into her missionary network and this time it was the Canadian Missionary Society in Central India that we headed for. It was a journey of three days and nights by train to Indore, and when we arrived it was a great relief to find ourselves welcomed and embraced by Dr and Mrs Taylor, who took us in as part of the family at their very large and well-established household. I remember the marvel of seeing a big white bath with taps for the first time. Water gushing out of both taps at once, pure water and lots of it; hot water from one tap and cold water from the other. In China and Burma we'd had baths in tin tubs with a few inches of water supplied by servants with jugs.

If Calcutta had been hot, Indore was much hotter and it was impossible to go outside after breakfast. So we would go to the park in the very early morning and then spend the rest of the day indoors behind cane shutters. All through the worst heat of the day, servants would throw water on the shutters from outside to cool the interior rooms, which remained dim and gloomy throughout these interminably long, languorous hours. It felt strange and tedious to be confined like this and I used to peer through cracks in the shutters at the fierce light outside, longing for evening when doors and windows could be opened. Then we would go and walk in the garden, which used to be filled with the fragrance of flowers and drifting charcoal smoke as supper was cooked on countless braziers around the city. Our lives slowly settled into a gentle routine with the Taylors, but we waited every day hoping that news of Father might come through from Burma. The Taylors' son Andy was also trapped in Burma, where he had been working as a civilian doctor.

Months went by and then a telegram arrived suddenly from Andy, who had managed somehow to get back to India, and the telegram read: 'Arrived safely India, no news of Craddock'. This was a severe blow and we started to fear we might find Father's name on the lists given out of those reported 'Missing, presumed dead'.

The Taylors insisted we remain hopeful and stay under their care while waiting for more news. It was the season for weddings in that part of India, which meant all-night blaring and crashing of trumpets and cymbals, while processions of elephants thronged the streets and loud celebrations continued unceasingly, with no sleep possible for anyone. Mother, in her stressed state, found this incessant clamour and lack of sleep almost beyond endurance.

At last, after several months of racked nerves, a knock came at her bedroom door one morning and a telegram was handed in. It read: 'Survived marathon to India. Writing. Love ALC.' Mother fell on her knees with emotion and to express her gratitude to God for this momentous deliverance.

Father had many dramatic exploits after staying behind in Burma. Anticipating large numbers of sick and injured at risk of falling into Japanese hands, with the help of a small medical team he commandeered a train (which he drove himself, despite never having driven a train before) in a bold mission to connect with three ships trapped upriver on the Irrawaddy, loaded with casualties. After transferring them to the many carriages of the train, they then ran north ahead of the Japanese until making contact with the Dakota airlift for evacuation. This was successful and these experiences are recorded in a personal account he wrote that is held at the Imperial War Museum (Burma Diary of Col A.L. Craddock, OBE, MBE), and I have copies of this account in booklet form.

Once the Japanese had seized full control of Burma, the only way out for anyone left behind was on foot over the mountains through dense jungle flooded by the monsoon. Father, with his medical team from the hospital train, set off to make their escape by this route to India. There were no roads and cholera infected the rivers. Along narrow tracks deep in mud, underfoot lay the bodies of countless hundreds who had tried to escape this way. Overcome by hunger, disease and exhaustion, they fell: women, children, soldiers, Burmese, British and others; very few survived the long march. It took Father and his men eighteen days of heroic struggle to get through. Their extraordinary survival was due in part to the indomitable Dakotas, now flying over the mountains to drop supplies as close to definable tracks as they could make out. Apparently one such drop was made within sight of Father's group staggering along, weak and famished. They fell upon the crate, which had burst open on impact, and, eagerly searching among the packets, found – toilet rolls! No food at all. But there were other drops at other times, of rice and condensed milk, biscuits and bully beef, which were life-saving.

We waited anxiously at the Taylors' house for the letter telling us where Father was, and how he was. It came in a few days and said he was at Dibrugah in Assam, which was the first outpost of civilisation the group had reached on emerging from the jungle, safe at last in India. Only one member of the team had been lost, dying of cholera after being so overcome with thirst that he drank water which had not been boiled. At Dibrugah, tea planters took them in and nursed them in their collapsed state, all of them being near to death with debilitation and illness. As soon as they were able to travel again, they were sent to the Military Hospital at Lucknow, which was reportedly in an appalling state with very few staff and overflowing with casualties. Father decided he would have a better chance of surviving if he left there and came back to us to be nursed by Mother.

The day came at last that Father was due to arrive at Indore station, and Mother, Elaine and I went to meet him off the train. All of us were wearing new dresses that Mother had made for the occasion. When the train finally appeared and steamed into the platform, my throat got so tight I felt as if I couldn't breathe for the tension and excitement. Then doors started banging open and a great rush of people poured out of the carriages, but there was no sign of Father. We ran up and down the platform looking for him, but he wasn't there. Mother began systematically searching in every carriage, and in one we found a British officer and thought we could ask if he had seen Father.

There was clearly something wrong with this officer as he sat motionless on the seat, seeming unable to move or speak. He looked as gaunt and emaciated as any beggar in the bazaar; his eyes had sunk down in his face and his worn-out uniform was hanging off him as he sat there holding in front of him an enamel mug with a toothbrush in it, no other possessions to be seen. Mother spoke to him and he turned his head. That was the moment of horror and joy when we recognised this wasted apparition and knew it was him. He was too weak to stand up and greet us, or even to speak, but it was him at last.

Mother summoned help to get him off the train and home to the Taylors', where he was put to bed and nursed by her day and night. All his food had to be sieved because he was too weak to eat properly and was suffering from some form of intestinal disease due to the privations endured on the trek out of Burma. The last time we had seen him he was robust and strong, while now he weighed hardly more than eight stone.

The intense heat of Indore at that time of year was harsh even for a healthy person, let alone a convalescent, and it was decided to move him to Kashmir, which would be cooler and more peaceful. A houseboat on the serenely beautiful Dal Lake was rented and here we lived while Father slowly mended. Each evening we would go out on the lake in a boat punted on long poles, gently gliding through the water; it felt like a dream world. I had my own small boat called a *shikara*, which I could take out by myself, using a heart-shaped paddle on the end of a short pole to drive the boat along.

Now I was nearly four, Mother was giving me lessons each morning on the new 'Look and Say' method for teaching children to read. The idea was to recognise words on sight, rather than sounding-out individual letters. This worked like magic and it was a dramatic revelation when I found I could read by myself. Mother too was highly gratified at her success with this latest innovative teaching method. Encouraged, she moved on to arithmetic. This did not work nearly so well, much to our combined frustration!

Although Father had his new career in the army, my parents were still missionaries at heart and family rituals of church and prayers took place routinely as before. Mother was a compulsive knitter and kept herself busy on the houseboat, knitting baby clothes for the new baby now expected, and making knitted dresses for Elaine and me. She had finished one of these in time for Sunday church and I remember being pleased with the pastel colour and soft feeling of the wool, before setting off down the plank that connected our houseboat to the lake shore. There was a string of ponies being led along the shore under the canopy of big trees, and I was watching these instead of looking where I was putting my feet. The next moment I was off the plank and in the water, going down and down into the mud and weeds. My knitted dress held me down as it soaked up water and everything became very dark and threatening. At last I heard Father's voice shouting, 'Put your hand up as far as you can,' which I did, and he grabbed it and fished me out, covered in weeds. The knitted dress was ruined.

As soon as Father's strength returned, he set himself a target to walk up into the mountains with a mule (to carry him back should he falter) on a test of stamina to see if he was ready to return to work. General Wavell had given orders that all army personnel who had survived the escape from Burma must return to active duty without delay.

In a very short time Father was passed fit by the Army Medical Board and was immediately posted to Hoshiarpur in the Punjab to take charge of the Military Hospital there, which was constructed entirely under canvas. Even the operating theatres were in tents. On this appointment he was promoted to Lieutenant-Colonel.

All army families in Hoshiarpur were billeted on local British or expatriate residents. Our missionary network sprang into action once more and a rather formidable spinster of the American Presbyterian Church took us in. She was called Janet Hodson and she ran a school for 250 girls where Muslim, Hindu and Christians lived harmoniously together. We went to live with her in the school compound, where her large house had ample lofty rooms for our growing family.

Our lives settled into the same torpid routine that had prevailed at the Taylors'. Only Father escaped each day and I used to watch him soon after dawn, cycling off to the hospital in his starched khaki uniform, exceedingly long legs rather out of proportion to the size of the bicycle. He would not ride in a staff car, whether for reasons of economy or keeping fit I do not know.

The school compound held many fascinations for me and I soon found that I could escape from the shuttered house during those hot tedious hours of daytime seclusion while adults reclined in various ways. Life could not stand still for the busy compound outside and apart from daily school routines there were gardens to attend to, and a great variety of tasks being carried out by an army of servants, from the lowest sweepers to the chief stewards of household and school. I gravitated to the lowest ranks simply because they were always tolerant and welcoming to me, where the higher officials did not approve of children hanging about.

I would spend a lot of time watching two old oxen who were yoked to poles projecting from a wooden circular device above a well. As they walked round and round all day, water was drawn up from the echoing depths of the well and delivered into primitive but efficient irrigation channels, which supplied the gardens. Quantities of vegetables were grown to feed the school. There was an ancient, wizened man who was the ox *wallah* in charge of these infinitely patient, gentle beasts, who followed them round with a whip that he never used. Someone had told me (unkindly I thought) that the oxen were deliberately blinded so that they would walk round and round in this way unceasingly, never knowing they were not on a journey along a road that would one day come to an end. I thought this was cruel and wanted to ask the ox *wallah* about it, but he never spoke, and all of us in those long days at the well communed in silence.

The sweepers' huts offered alternative diversion, with their scurrying hordes of ragged children, thin cats and tiny scrawny babies. Dark mutterings were made by Janet and Mother on breeding being out of control, which

25

remarks made my excursions into the servants' quarters more interesting as an observation on what was going on there.

Inside the large shuttered house one day there were baby matters of our own going on. Again without the slightest fuss or warning of any kind, my brother Andrew suddenly appeared at lunchtime in Mother's arms. There she was, up and walking around in a housecoat ready for lunch, while there had been no baby in evidence earlier at breakfast time. I was intrigued by the sight of the baby's head, which was all I could see poking out from the shawl he was wrapped in. His head looked just like a coconut, covered in spiky straw-like wisps. Mother was evidently very pleased to have achieved a son.

All day long on the veranda of Janet's house, sat the *dherzi* (tailor) at his treadle machine, making uniforms for the girls and stitching repairs for clothes and bed linen and any kind of sewing job. He provided another observation post for me as I sat there whiling away the hours and days. The soft whirr of the machine was soporific as Andrew dozed in his pram next to the *dherzi*, who became a sort of unofficial ayah and went to tap on the window for Mother if Andrew woke.

On Sundays, best frocks were worn and church was compulsory. Elaine and I had flimsy white muslin dresses, which were worn unfailingly on Sundays, when of course there were no visits to sweepers or oxen, and certainly not to the bazaar. Once, when it became impossible to endure this agony of self-control any longer, I persuaded Elaine to come with me for a bit of fun. Outside the kitchen door there was a large pile of discarded ash from the wood stove and I had an overpowering urge to jump on it and in it. Elaine, who was only two, was less enthusiastic and stood by the door watching as I leapt from the kitchen step onto the peak of the ash mountain. It was the most rapturous feeling as the ash subsided beneath me and I sank on the billowing cloud of my dress down into the ashy softness, like a featherbed. Elaine, shocked, ran in to tell the adults. So it was that the first of a series of stern punishments began, devised by Janet to instil Christian behaviour into me.

I was locked into the grain shed of the school, which was like a small warehouse for keeping sacks of flour and rice, lentils and other dry stores. This was like being sent to prison, and the length of sentence depended on the severity of my error. It was completely dark inside the shed, but I could measure how long I was there by watching the position of a crack of light between the big planked doors that were padlocked from outside with a chain. Sometimes I got forgotten in there. Janet was a strict and often forgetful jailer, but as we were living in her domain we were subject to her rule. Mother, I sensed, was very much under Janet's influence and preoccupied since the baby's arrival.

I started to create my own life in the shed as I was increasingly confined there. Beams of light filtering in from the door crack held a multitude of dust motes, floating and dancing there, which were like the population of a miniature world illuminated, and I amused myself watching their activity. The beams also revealed giant scales with iron weights for measuring out the stores and I could play with these, weighing handfuls from the sacks. Best of all were the living inhabitants of the store with their engaging antics and demonstrable intelligence: the scores of rats that led their daily lives of hectic and comic activity among the sacks and floorboards. At first they were wary of me, but I had no instinctive fear of them as I had never met rats before or heard any bad stories about them. Gradually they became friendly as I opened sacks for them and helped them to carry hoards of grain to secret hiding places. As a result of this I have remained on good terms with rats all my life.

There were more lively times when we went to watch army regiments marching through the streets of Hoshiarpur, led by their bandsmen; all were soldiers on their way to war at the front in Burma. This happened with an air of celebration rather than dread. Crowds stood at the side of the road, cheering and waving, and everyone looked excited. But for some of the soldiers lying in Father's tented hospital there was no feeling of celebration. A calamity much more crippling than their physical wounds had befallen them.

I used to go frequently to the hospital with Father to visit these despairing men. It was an ordeal for me, firstly because I had to pass through gates at the entrance guarded by two massive stone *Chinthi* (mythical beasts) with snarling open mouths full of jagged teeth. I was convinced they would jump down off their stone plinths and pounce on me if I went too close to them, so I had to be carried through the gates by Father with my face

27

pressed against his chest to avoid seeing them. Once inside the hospital compound, I could compose myself again and carry out my formal duty as a hospital visitor. From a very early age I was expected by Father to visit any of his patients he thought needed cheering up. But it was impossible to cheer these dispirited men, for their plight caused them to be dying slowly from heartbreak at having left their families behind in Burma, where their fate at the hands of the Japanese was too awful to contemplate.

Back at the school compound we often had visits from snake charmers and conjurors, travelling musicians and sellers of instant food: chunks of spicy meat cooked on portable braziers, or pyramids of small sugar cakes, dyed gaudy red, orange, yellow or green, carried on tin trays on their heads. One conjuror had a basket of carved wooden turtles, which could be bought individually for a few *pice* (small coins) and a mark was put on each one to show ownership. When he put the turtles in a large metal bowl full of water, they bobbed about on top. But as soon as he tapped one with a stick, it turned into a real live turtle in front of our eyes and swam about madly. We were invited to retrieve any turtle that was ours out of the water, but as soon as one of us touched it, the creature turned back into wood again. I watched and watched this trick, and begged the servants to tell me how it happened, but all they would say was that it was magic. Which, of course, it must have been.

There were times at the school when sacred cows from the bazaar wandered into the garden and grazed the vegetables. Because they were sacred, no one could touch them or shoo them away, while Janet and the gardeners could only watch crossly and helplessly. Every time this happened I was filled with a sense of elation.

When Andrew started to crawl, the kitchen cupboards held an attraction for him and he climbed in whenever he could, to bash around among the pots. Under the sink there was a tin containing potassium permanganate tablets which, when dissolved in water, were used to rinse vegetables and fruit. I had long wondered what these tasted like as the bright purple colour was enticing, but it also might mean they were poisonous. Andrew, one day among the pots, popped a tablet into his mouth with no such reservation. In a moment, dramatically, the tablet fizzed and purple foam came bubbling out of his mouth. A great commotion followed as Mother was called and rushed off with Andrew to the hospital, where he was given an emetic and no dire consequences followed; except for me, as I started to realise that any untoward incident involving one of the younger children was somehow to be laid at my door as the eldest with custodial responsibility, which disconcertingly no one had explained in advance so I could be ready for it.

As the heat in Hoshiarpur became intense, most European residents moved to the hills, and it was decided that our family (without Father) should make our way north to a small place called Manali, in the very remote and wild Kulu valley of the Himalayas. A cottage had been rented for us, but when we arrived after a long, tortuous journey, the cottage turned out to be a very rickety wooden shack standing all by itself in a wilderness of rocks and icy mountain peaks rising up on all sides. Mother stood observing this scene entirely unimpressed, remarking, 'These mountains seem to be in very close communication with our front door!'

The cottage was shockingly primitive, with no modern amenities and no protection against the piercing winds that shrieked down the valley like fiends, doing their best to blow the house down, I thought, and making it creak and sway all day and night. The attics were jumping with rats, which I did not mind at all for themselves, but at night they made a frenzy of noise, scampering about, squeaking and squealing, as parties of them emerged down the decaying walls to run under and over our beds. Mother, quite distracted by this nightly uproar, would rush in with a shoe to batter any rats she could reach, but this was messy and upset me with the blood and violence.

It was a very strange and alien life in the Kulu valley. I felt that there were many ways to die there. When snow fell, we were quite cut off, and the rivers we might have crossed to reach Manali were now great rushing torrents from snow melting higher up. I felt real terror every time we had to walk along the narrow banks or try to cross on projecting rocks: the water seemed alive with raging power to drag us in. Adding to this fear was a new ayah who had been taken on to help with Andrew, and to take Elaine and me for walks. She was a stiff, unbending woman and was either mad or sadistic, because she revelled in tormenting us. She used to take us out to watch sheep being butchered on the hillside, which was a normal practice for villagers buying meat, but for us having to watch was an ordeal. We found it harrowing, but the next terror would be on the way home beside the swirling river: she would hold me and then Elaine out over the rushing water at arm's length, pretending to drop us in. I think Mother started to become a little demented in this terrible place. I found it much more stressful and frightening trying to survive while we were there, than during any of our previous hazardous times. Manali must have been one of the last places on earth suitable for a young mother with three small children to be sent for a summer retreat.

The village itself was impoverished and squalid, with hardly a means to buy even basic essentials. But the one glory of it came with the Tibetan women who arrived as soon as snow cleared from the mountain passes and they could bring goods to trade. They were fine-looking people, cheery and robust, with rosy faces, wearing ornately embroidered head-dresses that had a tapered panel extending down their backs. They spoke a language that was quite unintelligible to me, but the way they spoke it sounded friendly and jolly. Mother and I now spoke Hindi since coming to live in the Punjab. The Mandarin we had once spoken so readily was fading.

At one point during our stay, the valley became transformed with cherry blossom and bees started to appear as a gentle warmth replaced the chilling winds. A naked 'holy man', who had sat cross-legged beside the path leading away from our cottage ever since we arrived, began to stir his limbs and roll his eyes. This resident holy man was another trial for me as we had to pass by him on our way to the village. He sat completely unmoving, but nevertheless was alarming with his grotesque appearance of long, filthy, matted hair and wrinkled body covered all over in stripes painted with white ash. He did not convey to me a picture of benign contemplation, but of brooding unpleasantness. If cleanliness was next to godliness (as we were always being told), this was no illustration of it, I thought.

Our cottage had been rented for six months and when it came to the end of this time, several things began to happen. I had turned five and was more than ready to go to school as I was getting restless and badly in need of useful occupation; but most notable of all developments in the closing months of 1943 was news that the war in Burma had started to make gains. This indicated a new assignment for Father to go back into Burma, joining the re-occupation force, when the time came. Preparations for this meant that he was to be posted to a secret location somewhere – even Mother did not know where. Hoshiarpur was no longer going to be a base for our family, so once again we were looking for a new place to live.

There was a very good American school at a small hill station called Landour, high up in the mountains beyond the larger hill town of Mussoorie, some way from Kulu, thankfully. The school was called Woodstock and had a large enrolment of American children of missionaries and others from the USA living in India, as well as some like myself. It was the happiest and most lively school imaginable, and presented a completely new world for me of exciting things to learn and see and do. There was a very strong musical tradition at Woodstock, with choirs and an orchestra, theatrical productions, clubs and an astonishing variety of activities, both cultural and fun. Mother was in her element with the music, singing and drama, and joined in at every opportunity.

She had found a very decent house for us to live in so that I could go to Woodstock daily. The house was a typical Himalayan village house, perched on a ledge cut from the mountainside, with strips of garden forming narrow terraces above, and majestic views in front across plunging slopes of deodar forest to the distant hazy plains of India far below. The house had a corrugated-iron roof painted green, and a veranda in front with steps going down almost to the edge of the precipice, where there was a rail fence to catch one of us or the baby's pram should it tumble down the steps. There were glorious profusions of dahlias and other flowers growing wild just below the fence and I used to hang over the edge trying to reach and pick these. If I lowered myself carefully, I could get my feet onto a small outcrop of rock sticking out among the flowers where they sprouted from crevices in the rock-face. Once when I did this, I had a great fright to find my feet landing on something soft and squidgy, which was a snake sunning itself along the small ridge of rock. The snake and its quicksilver spasm of escape, trying to wriggle free from under my feet, remains a memory – as Mother said afterwards: a good lesson in what happens when we give way to temptation!

31

Father came on leave quite frequently from his secret location wherever it was, and these were glorious times when we went off on long treks up the mountain, collecting specimens of plants and beetles. We had collecting jars containing methylated spirits for the iridescent beetles of green or blue, which were later dried and mounted on board. All through my life, when Father was around, we would be collecting things to study and sketch. As we explored and climbed, the air lightened and was filled with the scent of rhododendrons growing wild, and the pine smell of deodar forest, which is forever reminiscent for me of those exhilarating mountains and hills.

Once a stray dog followed us from the village, and we thought nothing of it until reaching a ruined house high up in the forest. The dog stopped some way from the house and growled as if there might be a bear or a leopard inside. We approached cautiously to have a look, but there was nothing we could see and the house seemed empty. We went inside and then it was extraordinary; the most curious sensation: although completely bare, the concrete walls felt as if they were closing in on us; we seemed unable to breathe, yet there was nothing to account for it – only a dense aura of something unpleasant in there. When we got outside, it was a feeling of inexplicable relief to be in the open air and breathing easily again. The dog seemed anxious to be off and we followed it all the way back to the village, where Father related our strange experience to find out if anyone knew anything about the house. The villagers looked stunned to hear we had been anywhere near it. They said no one ever approached within fifty yards of the building because there was an evil spirit living there and we were lucky to have escaped without injury, as the spirit was known to be vicious.

In between Father's visits, we could hear his voice by tuning in to the radio when he was making one of his broadcasts, usually too technical in public health terms for me to understand, but it was a thrill and comforting to hear him. I was allowed to stay up for the evening broadcasts, when Mother and I would sit huddled over the shiny brown box which was the radio, listening intently to Father's voice ebbing and flowing in between the crackles of static.

Mother had somehow acquired a piano and delighted herself with practising and rehearsing for concerts at Woodstock. She could also play with ease both the violin and viola, and often in the evenings other musicians would come to our house and play together. I would be lying in bed, listening and loving it. The violin was my favourite instrument, but always made me cry when it was played, because of the poignancy of its sound.

Earthquakes and tremors were frequent and usually seemed to happen when we were in bed. The corrugated roof of the house would start to rattle and heave. Then the dressing table would begin vibrating and objects on it like brushes and pots begin to slide around or slide off. At this point it was customary to jump out of bed and run outside in case the roof came down. I was never alarmed by these episodes and thought it diverting to be standing outside in the garden in nightclothes, watching the house shake and groan. The tin roof had to withstand a lot of battering one way and another, as monkeys from the forest used it as a trampoline several times a day. With the house anchored on its ledge and the hillside rising up behind, they would leap from trees above to land heavily with great crashing noises, the roof visibly bouncing up and down while the monkeys cavorted, screeching at each other.

There were no cars so high up in the hills, where it was possible only to get around on foot. A circular path winding through the village of Landour was called a *chukka*, as in the game of polo describing one round of activity. Walking the *chukka* was a social occasion, meeting and chatting to other residents along the way. There were a few small shops in the village, but no post office or hospital. For these facilities we had to go down the mountain, on foot again, to Mussoorie. Anyone who was unable to walk or preferred not to, could hire a *kandi*. This was a basket-chair, like a sedan, carried on poles by two coolies. Children would be carried in a smaller version like a laundry basket, strapped to the back of a coolie. The basket had a little seat inside, facing away from the back of the coolie, with a tiny window in front. This provided a great view, but could be disconcerting as the path was often near vertical, and the basket swung about as the coolie scrambled up and down. Inside, I sometimes felt like a peanut in a peanut shell, hanging by a thread over the mountainside.

I went to school each day by myself and this was a scramble too, as Woodstock was several hundred feet down the hillside below our house, and the path was narrow and slippery. When it was raining or too wet to be safe, I went in the basket.

One day a *kandi* arrived at our house with two coolies, and Mother, without any explanation, was carried off down the hill to the hospital at Mussoorie. By this time we had a trained nanny in uniform called Gwen, who was left looking after us while Mother was away. Gwen was a very kind, gentle girl whose father had been a Scottish tea planter and her mother was Indian. When her father went back to Scotland, he put Gwen into an orphanage. She never forgave him for this and was determined when the war was over to go and find him, and confront him with her feelings about what he had done.

Gwen was only nineteen when she came to us and was more like an older sister than a nanny, but she was a very responsible and sensible girl and we passed the time contentedly while Mother was in hospital. She was there a long time and it was a considerable surprise when she arrived home again one day in the *kandi*, holding a small parcel wrapped in a knitted scarf. I was curious to see what was inside and it was even more of a surprise when I found in the folds of the scarf, a very small, sleeping baby. This was my sister Rosalind and I was completely enchanted by her from that first moment peering at her tiny face deep inside the layers of scarf. Ros was a perfect baby: calm, beautiful and full of smiles. I did not know that Mother had nearly died having her, and that was why she had spent such a long time in hospital, recovering. But as soon as she was home, she resumed her busy life of varied interests as before. Greatly anticipated was Father's next leave, to introduce him to this charming new person in our family.

It was four months before he came home and by that time we were all in a high state of excitement. His arrival coincided with an unusually large troop of monkeys erupting from the forest onto our roof, leaping about like dervishes, making a monstrous noise, so that the dignified and romantic scene planned for his first sight of Ros did not go entirely as intended. But it was a very ecstatic homecoming, with a feeling of exuberance all round.

My parents' happiness in each other was a joy shared by all of us. They were thirty-four and thirty-five by this time, a talented, vibrant couple who had survived great dangers and supported each other throughout. The tide of war had turned and Japanese power was diminishing. Father was soon to become part of SEAC (South East Asia Command), going back into Burma with the re-occupation force. It would not be long before we were free, going home at last to England and new prospects. The year was 1945 and Ros had been born on 2 May, just three months before the war finally came to an end on 14 August. Father had to stay in Rangoon to restore hospital and medical services under the command of Lord Mountbatten, who was in charge of the re-occupation. Meanwhile service families like us were sent to a transit camp, which was a sort of vast collecting ground for army people in India waiting for troop ships going home. This was the famous or infamous Deolali Camp, where people complained of going mad with heat and boredom, which became known as 'going doolally'. But for children it was like a holiday camp after so many years of wartime restriction and deprivation. The camp had a very large population of children and we used to be taken off in big lorries, all jammed in on metal benches, on outings to a lake where we could swim or paddle about. There was sand at the lake, like a proper beach, and we had buckets and spades just as if we were on holiday. The lake water was as warm as a bath and grainy with mud, but glorious.

The camp was run on military lines, and Reveille sounded each morning to rouse us and get us going for the day. A bugle would call us for breakfast and we all went to our tables in an enormous dining tent. The food was like a feast to my eyes and best of all was a new wonder – Heinz tomato ketchup – from America, which made everything taste sensational. On some days at the camp I used to attach myself to an Indian sign-writer who went round painting the names of people in white letters on their black tin trunks, ready for going off on the train to Bombay when a ship arrived. I enjoyed giving myself the job of sign-writer's assistant as I was good at spelling by now and could help him make sure he got the names right.

After some weeks at Deolali waiting for Father to join us, he arrived at last from Burma just as our turn came to leave and take the train to Bombay, then to see the amazing sight of our ship filled with cheering soldiers all along the decks as we waited to walk up the gangway to join them. The ship was called the SS *Strathnaver* and had three tall black funnels, which looked very splendid, spouting great billowing puffs of smoke as, with several long sonorous hoots of the ship's horn, we steamed away for England.

CHAPTER 3

On board the ship we joined hundreds of soldiers and families who had gathered in India after surviving the war. There were many POWs on board, released from the horrors of Changi and other Japanese prison camps. Everyone on the ship was celebrating being alive and returning home at last, so the atmosphere was wildly festive and children were made a big fuss of, which suited me very well. Among all this jollity was the enticing diversion of ship's cats, employed as ratters but lovingly cared for as pets by sailors in their quarters below decks. Some of the cats had kittens, which meant I spent a lot of time in cramped cabins, keeping company with sailors and cats.

I was seven at this time and Ros was still a baby, often given presents of exotic food like tomatoes and bananas by admiring soldiers. I had never seen a tomato before and when one of these was being mashed up for her, I stood in a sweat of impatience wanting to try it. When she made a disgusted face and spat it out, I was infuriated at such a waste, and even more outraged when I wasn't allowed to eat the rest of it myself. Andrew, who was watching, still hardly more than a baby himself, thought if Ros got the tomato he should get the banana: according to his logic, size of child = size of fruit. He was uncommonly sharp-witted and articulate from an early age but had his own way of pronouncing words, so that Mother became Muzzer or Muz, and Father became Fa. With his gaze fixed on the banana, he said, 'Muz, that banana looks as if it wants me to eat it.' So he got the banana and I wheedled him for a taste of it. My disappointment was immense, finding the texture slimy and gluey; it put me off bananas for life.

Fa was now a Brigadier, and senior officers like him were berthed in luxurious cabins on the top deck, while wives and children slept squashed into troop cabins lower down, several families to a cabin. Muz was much peeved by this, remarking, 'It's very high-handed of them to set your father up in grand style on A deck while the rest of us are consigned to steerage.' But army rules always prevailed. To distract us from the stifling conditions, she kept us enthralled with stories about the wonders of England, in particular the English seaside, which we were about to see for ourselves. Her parents lived in Bournemouth and were to meet us off the ship and take us to stay with them at their house beside the sea. I had a vivid mental image of the English seaside, having seen pictures in books of golden sand and blue, silky waves.

It was then a considerable shock to arrive in Bournemouth under grey skies, finding that 'seaside' was all drab sand and cold steely waves, much too unfriendly for paddling or swimming. This was a big disappointment, but Grandad had a treat planned for us. He took us to the biggest toyshop in Bournemouth for each of us to choose a toy, which could be whatever we wanted. It was an unheard-of indulgence after our years of austerity. The toyshop was enormous and sparkling with treasures like Aladdin's Cave, which in England at this time, immediately after the war, was a dazzling sight. I wandered around, gazing at all these delights in amazement, too mesmerised to decide what to choose. But the adults with us had quickly decided what constituted a suitable toy and I sensed myself being steered towards a scooter, with similar smaller scooters being selected for the others. So we were out of the shop surprisingly quickly, with the scooters loaded into the boot of Grandad's car and the lid closing as fast as the shop door.

I was, in fact, delighted with this choice and immediately took my scooter out on the street in front of the houses to scoot faster and faster up and down the road, which was a great feeling of freedom with very little traffic. The next day was Sunday when, unaccountably, the scooters were taken away. It was explained that Sunday was a day of rest and no scooting was allowed, or anything else entertaining like listening to the radio or running about; even books were banned, all except the Bible. Church services were compulsory and a torture to sit through, with hours of monotonous droning, all dreary as dust, making Christianity seem like dead bones from which all vitality had long since fled. This dread Sunday regime went on for most of my childhood, so that I grew up hating Sundays. Christmases too were made dismal by the same religious misery, so that I developed an aversion to Christmas as well, which has lasted all my life. Sadly, this caused unhappiness for my own children later on, as my inability to enjoy Christmas affected their enjoyment, which I very much regret and wish I had made more of an effort to overcome this lack of spirits.

The euphoria of surviving the war and returning triumphant to England was short-lived, as everyone now had to adjust to post-war hardships of rationing and a shortage of housing, for so much had been bombed or become neglected during years of making do while all available resources were concentrated on the war effort. SEAC, under Lord Mountbatten, had offered Fa overall command of medical services in South-East Asia, and his promotion to Brigadier had been in preparation for this. Fa had served with Lord Mountbatten during the re-occupation of Burma and they were friends. But, however attractive this offer may have seemed, and despite his decision to join up as an army doctor when missionary work was overtaken by the war, he remained committed to CMS and his vocation as a missionary. So he applied for what was called 'de-mob' (demobilisation) and resigned his commission. When he went to London to hand in his papers and uniform, he was given a civilian suit and trilby hat, which were standard de-mob issue. He came home wearing these, which made us all laugh so much that, despite seldom seeing the funny side of things himself, he was forced to join in, realising how comic he must look in the pinched suit which was too small and too short in the legs, and the hat perched on such a tall man made him look like a spiv. So the hat was discarded, but he needed the suit for presenting himself to the CMS London Committee, reporting back for another missionary posting.

The worthy gents of the CMS Committee had sat out the war safely at home, never missing a heartbeat or entertaining any notion of the reality of war for those who had risked their lives and accomplished great deeds far from home. They scorned Fa's heroic record in Burma, instead regarding him as having abandoned his missionary vocation when he joined the Burma Army Medical Corps, and for this reason he was simply dismissed from the Society. This was a crushing blow to all his future hopes and – I have always thought – broke his heart, as he felt cast out, and his faith was so shaken it never again seemed to provide a guiding light for his life.

However, refusing to be daunted, he wasted no time in finding other employment. Sir Russell Brain, who was an eminent consultant neurologist at The London Hospital, was delighted to take on Fa as his registrar, having been impressed with his earlier achievements as a medical student, winning prizes for the excellence of his clinical work. So Fa started commuting to 'The London' (as it was called) every day, while lodgings were found for us in Loughton, Essex.

Having to move into lodgings was a serious disappointment as Fa and Muz still owned White Cottage, their much-loved spacious house in High Barnet, which had been given to them as a wedding present by Grandad. They had lived there for a short happy time after their marriage, and later, after returning from Nigeria, it had been our home until leaving for China. The house had been rented-out to tenants during the war, and on our return we quite expected they would be given notice and we would move back in. However, in the interim, a law had been passed called the Rent Act. This protected tenants' rights so they could not be turned out, and rents were fixed at pre-war levels. Without any prospect of getting the house back or being paid more than a nominal rent, Fa and Muz felt they had no choice but to sell. The tenants had to be given first option, and only agreed to buy at such a low price that the house was effectively given away. So it was that White Cottage, the last of the wedding presents, very sadly was lost.

The lodgings we moved into were ramshackle attic rooms on the third floor of a large dark house, very unsuitable for small children – but we were lucky to get anything. The house was owned by elderly missionary friends called Varley and Gertie Roberts, who had returned from the mission in Zaria, Nigeria, which had been Fa and Muz's first posting. The Roberts lived like a couple of small brown dormice in the lower regions of the house, with a lot of gloomy furniture; but, much to our surprise, squashed in among all this was a glowing modern invention: a television. It was one of the first sets to be owned by anyone, and we were allowed to watch the flickering grey images that, like voices on the radio, mysteriously appeared with no visible source and kept us enthralled.

One day, while Muz was hanging out washing in the garden and I was helping her, we suddenly saw with horror that Ros, who was only a toddler, had climbed out onto the sill of one of the attic windows and was balancing there, three storeys up. Muz shouted to me, 'Quick, run up and catch her.' There were several staircases to climb and I thought if I didn't get there in time I'd be blamed if she fell. Also, if she took fright, she might fall outwards instead of inwards. With a mad sprint I got there in time, and that was one more terror avoided. My life seemed to be full of terrors in that place. Often I would be sent off to do the shopping in Loughton High Street while Muz was busy doing piles of washing by hand in the sink or bath – no washing machines then. I would be pushing the big coach-built pram with Ros in it, my hands gripping the handle so high up I couldn't see properly beyond the bulk of the pram, and this was a problem. Holding onto my skirt on one side would be Elaine, and on the other side Andrew, while in my pocket were the shopping list and purse, which I kept checking to make sure were still there and hadn't dropped out.

Usually all went well, but one day there was a crisis. We had to cross a busy road at a certain point and I always stopped and looked both ways carefully before setting off. The road seemed to be clear and I got halfway across when a car suddenly appeared from nowhere. I tried to run with the pram and the small children to get to the other side as fast as I could – but disaster: Andrew fell over. I grabbed his hand and dragged him along, his little legs getting scraped by the rough tarmac in my panic to avoid the car. We reached the safety of the pavement in a heap and I felt very ashamed at putting us all in danger by what seemed like my incompetence. But the shopping list and purse were safe!

It was quite normal at that time for children of my age to be put in charge of smaller siblings, doing the shopping and other chores; it was expected and was considered an important part of growing up and learning to take responsibility. But I can see now, looking back, that I often felt quite burdened with worry about making mistakes or being incapable.

As the eldest, a lot was expected, and if things went wrong I was the one in trouble. This may be why, after all these years, I still have 'anxiety' dreams, and have had to learn how to control panic attacks that can come on suddenly without being aware of feeling anxious.

This subconscious insecurity may also have been associated with Fa and Muz's state of mind at this time, as they struggled to keep our lives on track with very little money in the primitive confines of the attic flat which had no heating or proper facilities; no kitchen either, only a gas ring in a cupboard. I wanted to help, but was not a very biddable sort of child – unlike Elaine who at five years old was calm and sensible, possessed of natural obedience and helpfulness. I was the opposite, being inquisitive, questing and restless. Muz found this a trial. We clashed, and, because she was so on edge, the slightest step out of line stressed her. Then I would be sent to my room to wait for Fa to come home and prescribe punishment. I think this was convenient for Muz, as it got me out of the way, and she got out of administering punishment herself. During these dark times, sitting on my bed, I would be wrestling with questions and asking God: 'How can I manage to be good for a *whole day*, never being noisy or teasing Elaine or forgetting to do something?' Achieving goodness was an ideal of Christian behaviour piously preached in church and Sunday School, where it seemed that adults held themselves exemplars for children to emulate; but for me, achieving this state of grace seemed an impossibility, which worried me a great deal as I thought about it while waiting for Fa to arrive.

I would wait, sometimes for hours, until I heard Fa's heavy footsteps coming up the several flights of stairs to the attic. So the first thing that confronted him on his weary arrival home would be Muz directing him to my room with a recital of my sins. I could see he hated being put in the role of executioner, but Christian teaching favoured corporal punishment on biblical instructions: 'Spare the rod and spoil the child'. He would sit on my bed, discussing patiently while I squirmed, how many strokes of the belt or stick or hand fitted the crime, and I would try and bargain with him to get the number reduced. It was sometimes hard to speak as fear would catch at my throat, for any form of violence was a horror. But there was no escape as Muz would be waiting to hear my cries as a signal that justice had been done. I remember bracing myself with determination not to make any sound so that I could keep some self-respect as I bent over, bare back and bottom exposed. Once I even sprang up and shouted, 'That's enough', halfway through the lashes, and hated seeming so weak, but it made no difference. I knew that the beating was done to please Muz and, supposedly, God.

This form of calculated humiliation left scars, not physical ones but others, resulting in a loss of regard for Christian orthodoxy demonstrated in a way that, to me, did not seem reasonable or justified. The beatings became less frequent as I learnt to keep out of the way, detaching myself from family situations where I might be provoked to say or do the wrong things. Usually, these wrong things came to light from being observed by Elaine, so increasingly I went off by myself, finding an escape in reading books or another favourite occupation, climbing trees. Taking a book with me, I could read and watch at the same time what was going on around and about, from the high branches, without being seen. Later, when I reached twelve, I refused to be beaten anymore and warned Fa never to hit me again. Elaine was never beaten as far as I knew; being smarter than I was in covering up misdeeds she learnt how to be secretive, while I just went on blundering into trouble. Andrew, who failed to measure up to those exacting standards expected of an only son, suffered the worst punishments; he wasn't naughty, just different, and defenceless.

Ros, from the moment she was born, was the adorable one of the family: blonde, blue-eyed, talented and sweet-natured, she has always remained the same kind, capable Ros all her life. But despite being so gentle and seemingly blameless, even she did not escape being beaten, and on one occasion was thrashed so hard with a bamboo cane that it broke and left splinters in her bottom. Muz was very cross with Fa about this and Ros has never forgotten the double trauma of being beaten, and then having to go through the extra torture of having splinters pulled out.

I was glad to start school in Loughton as soon as a suitable one was found, and Elaine joined me now she was old enough. To get to school we had to walk through a corner of Epping Forest that even then was notorious as a haunt for so-called perverts, but such things were taboo subjects, never mentioned. Certainly no warning was given to avoid talking to strange men, or that we might encounter any danger on our way to school. I remember nothing about the school itself, but my recollections of the forest remain clear to this day. It was a spooky place, full of dim shadows, where we walked on paths of squashed leaves under the high dense spreading branches of beech trees. Despite its darkness, I was never afraid of the forest, or of the strange furtive men who lurked among the trees, sometimes holding open their raincoats when we passed so we could get a full view of their exposed bodies underneath. This did not embarrass me at all, as both Fa and Muz (surprisingly perhaps for ex-missionaries) often walked around at home with no clothes on, so it was quite normal for me to see adults in the nude.

Some of the men used to give us sweets, which we thought was very kind, and we always thanked them politely and walked on. One day, coming back from school, one of the men gave me some sweets and said I could sit on his lap while I ate them. The closeness of his body pressed against mine as I sat there eating my sweets truthfully did not disturb me at all; no automatic instinct kicked in suggesting that this behaviour might be wrong and, luckily for me as I now realise, he didn't go on to molest me or do anything nasty. He seemed content to let me sit there, undisturbed by this intimate contact, calmly chatting to him. Maybe my lack of fear defused the situation, but in any case I soon slipped off his lap and ran to catch up with Elaine, who had gone on ahead. She was a more reserved and less outgoing child than I was, and possibly felt, with some sense of caution, that it was unwise to be too friendly with these men. When we were having supper that evening, Elaine mentioned the incident to Muz, who immediately became very agitated and phoned the police. Two policemen arrived the same evening and I was taken to the police station to give a statement and be examined by the police surgeon. This experience at the hands of the police was, by contrast, the truly violating one; the men in the forest never behaved like that.

Looking back to even earlier experiences in India, it was customary during the long languid afternoons of intense heat, while adults reclined indoors, children went out to play. Servants would be having a short break, eating or snoozing, and their quarters were always a magnet for me. Scrawny children and animals tumbled in and out of huts, where inside it would be cool and dim. Whole families lived in a single room, so there was no privacy and few inhibitions, but plenty of fun and affectionate behaviour. Men sat chatting and smoking, stripped to a loincloth, with a child or cat on their laps being stroked and petted. I wanted to be stroked and petted as well. Whenever a child or cat got bored and slipped off a lap to run outside, I would climb up to take their place. It was a curious but pleasurable sensation to be held close and caressed without any self-consciousness in the sultry torpor of those hazy afternoons. What might have seemed shockingly intimate to European sensibilities, appeared fond and perfectly normal behaviour to me, with no connotations attached. It was only much later, at the hands of the Essex Police, that I saw there was another side to this.

During our time at Loughton, Fa was working all day in London and studying late into the night for his membership exams for the Royal College of Physicians.

His health had never fully recovered from the ravages of war, and now he began to suffer the strain of this punishing regime, as well as living with a young family cooped up in the small attic flat. There was not much peace or relaxation for him. When he came to take the exams, to everyone's dismay he failed, not once but twice. Sir Russell Brain, who had admired Fa's prowess since student days, was completely baffled as to why Fa, who was such a brilliant physician, could possibly fail. This was of particular concern because Sir Russell (later to become Lord Brain) wanted Fa to take over from him when he retired, so that Fa could carry forward the pioneering research and clinical work in this important department of medicine that The London Hospital was noted for.

I think both my parents were affected at this time by post-war fatigue, lack of money, and the many physical and psychological effects of their traumatic experiences during the war with no recuperation period. Everyone just got on with life as best they could, without any state assistance or sympathy. There was no NHS or other state service to help out, and with very little understanding of concepts such as post-traumatic stress, stiff upper lips were the rule.

It was at this time that Fa's lifelong school friend David Anderson came up with a plan. It was his father, Dr Webb Anderson, who had paid for

Fa to go to medical school since his own family was too poor to pay the fees. Dr Anderson had attached a condition to his philanthropy, which was that Fa, in return for being funded through medical school, had to agree to become a missionary doctor after qualifying. This was not too onerous for Fa who was already a committed Christian, but it did set a course for our family which otherwise might have turned out very differently had Fa and Muz stayed in England, instead of being sent off to a war zone and never fully recovering from the effects of this dislocation.

David Anderson's mother (affectionately known as Nonnie) had a house which she rented out in the small Sussex village of Partridge Green, and the plan was for us to escape from the cramped flat in Loughton and move into Nonnie's house, which had lots of space and a big garden so it was ideal for a family. The village school was close by, as well as a railway station, so Fa could commute to London while he decided what to do next, since the normal route to becoming a consultant at the hospital was now closed to him.

Partridge Green in 1947 was an idyllic English village, surrounded by fields and farms, populated with cheerful, strong, hard-working country people. The contrast with busy Loughton was a revelation. Elaine and I were enrolled at the village school where, on my first day, I was given one of the double desks next to a girl called Barbara Tullett, who helped me catch up with the lessons they were doing. While she was showing me what to do, I was at the same time trying to avoid getting hit by the terrifying teacher who stalked around the class with a ruler, whacking anyone who was not getting their sums right. I had not done long division before, but this was no excuse as far as the teacher was concerned, rapping my knuckles furiously with the ruler. Luckily, Barbara let me copy her sums while the teacher was busy hitting someone else, so I escaped further punishment but had no idea how the working-out was done until later, after lessons, Barbara showed me how to do long division.

It was a rough primitive school, the complete opposite of happy civilised Woodstock in Landour. Here in Partridge Green when the bell rang after break time and we went back to our classrooms, sometimes there would be an inert body lying on the grey concrete expanse of the playground, the victim of bullies or a fight. One of the teachers would go and drag the body away without comment. It was such a common sight, no one took any notice, but for me it was shocking to see this casual indifference to an injured or unconscious child. In the spirit of the times just then after the war, there was no place in the world for weaklings.

The winter of 1947 has been written into history books as exceptionally severe, with snow and ice causing the deaths of those who succumbed to the extreme conditions. Pneumonia carried off large numbers of elderly people, not just then but every winter, and was called 'the old man's friend', as it was seen to be a natural form of release from chronic infirmity. With no NHS, the cost of medicine and doctors was often beyond the reach of poorer people, and antibiotics were a very new resource. In the later stages of the war, an anti-bacterial sulphonamide drug called M&B 693 became available, and when I was given this wonder drug for the chronic middle ear infections I'd suffered all my childhood with no treatment or pain relief available, it seemed to me miraculous suddenly to be cured and free of pain.

One day, when I was walking to school during that terrible winter of 1947, I slipped on the icy pavement and fell flat on my face. Picking myself up after lying stunned for some moments, I looked down to see blood spreading a red stain on the ice, and blood on my hands where I'd touched my face. There was no question of turning round and going home for a wash and comforting word – the main concern was being late for school!

Later on that year I was given my first bike. It transformed my life, and from then on I rode to school. Barbara had a bike too and at weekends and holidays we went off on long bike rides to other villages like Steyning and around the countryside, visiting friends. With little traffic on the roads it was safe and gave us a glorious sense of freedom and independence. Barbara was the eldest child of a large family living in a tied cottage on a farm not far from the village. Her father was the farm's head man, and her mother was one of those warm, capable farm women with her front door always open and food on the table. The farm soon became our headquarters for all kinds of games and exploits, with Barbara's brothers and sisters joining in.

One of our favourite games involved an old wagon that at one time had been drawn by horses but was now abandoned at the bottom of a hill beside the farm road. The wagon became our chariot and we used to drag and push it to the top of the hill, then all jump on board as it ran back at great speed. Inevitably it would run off the road and go bumping along rough ground on the verges, jolting some of us off as we tried to hang on, shrieking and screaming. Then we would start all over again and this could go on for hours. In the end with this mistreatment, our chariot fell to pieces one day as we were roaring downhill; the wheels came off and we all fell in a heap in the road. Bumps and scratches and cuts and gashes were to be expected as a normal part of childhood adventures, and we were allowed to do mad things off on our own without adults interfering, as they were much too busy to bother about supervising children's activities. There was also an attitude that getting into scrapes was all part of childhood and growing up. Any piece of us that got scraped badly enough to bleed would have a handkerchief tied round it, most likely a dirty handkerchief, until later we might get a bandage at home if it was bad enough, and a telling off for being careless.

At milking time Mr Tullett would bring the cows in and we would line up in the dairy, each holding a mug from the grimy assortment kept there, to have a squirt of milk directed straight from the cow's teat into our mugs for us to drink: warm and steaming, frothy and creamy, as good as a cappuccino – no concerns then about bypassing the pasteurisation process!

The routine activities of dairy and farmyard were a source of fascination and diversion. We would climb up and peer over the top of the bull's stable door to watch him stamping and snorting, staring at us with menacing eyes. One day when Mr Tullett and his young assistant were about to go into the bull's pen to fetch him out, we ran round to the back of the building where a big pile of manure stood against the outside wall. Climbing to the top gave us access to a space between the top of the wall and the roof, looking down at the bull inside. We had brought a long stick with us, and the plan was to poke the bull up the backside just as he turned towards the stable door when he heard Mr Tullett and his lad entering. All went to plan and as soon as the door was opened, the bull, prodded from behind, charged out with a roar, knocking the men over and galloping off across the yard. We all had hysterics, rolling around in the manure. Later it was the state of our clothes that got us into trouble, while none of the adults could think what had got into the bull to make him charge out like that.

We did go too far one day when we decided to make a den in a mountain of straw bales piled up inside a barn. We burrowed a tunnel through the bales and scraped a big cave-like hole deep inside where we loafed about, hiding from the smaller Tullett children who we didn't want joining us in this secret den. We had a torch in there and it was a perfect warm, dry, cosy hideaway, we thought. But one day the torch battery gave out and we went to get a candle and matches from the Tulletts' cottage. This caused consternation when it was discovered where we were headed, and for once adults did get involved and the barn became forbidden territory, as not only could the whole lot have gone up in flames, but the big hole we had made could cause a collapse of the bales, burying us under tons of straw. Such hazards never entered our heads in the thrill of inventing new games.

Possibly, adults were more on edge than usual as the Tullett family had just increased its size with twins. Barbara and I were delighted with them, but Muz disapproved and I gathered from her mutterings about it that, to her, twins somehow indicated a suspicion of over-indulgence. Several years later, when we were living in Tunbridge Wells with a large garden where a gardener called Perkins was employed (never Mr Perkins, as it seemed that people considered to be of low status did not merit a title), Muz displayed the same baffling disapproval towards this perfectly decent man whose wife had produced not one but two sets of twins. I thought such a rare event must be a special blessing and loved to see Mrs Perkins with the four small girls arriving with a lunch box and tea in a Thermos for her husband. This was the signal for all of us to sit in the greenhouse on chairs with spindly iron legs, having a cup and a chat, which I enjoyed. But I was forbidden by Mother to chat to Perkins in the greenhouse if I was by myself, as if this was somehow improper and I might end up with twins!

My idyll at Partridge Green with the Tulletts came to an abrupt end when Fa suddenly announced that I was being sent to boarding school. No reason was given; children were never consulted about such things. It was not considered necessary to discuss or explain any decision and was simply accepted by everyone that parents knew best. I was to be nine that year and the school was one of the new so-called progressive schools, for boys and girls from age eight to eighteen, run by a group of visionary educationalists. Fa had odd ideas about education, from time to time taking me out of school altogether, to be taught by him at home with set lessons to be done each day on my own while he was at work. This was mostly learning about mountains and rivers, all kinds of natural history and geography, biology and science, as well as famous historical events, reading lots of books, writing summaries of these and drawing illustrations or diagrams to illustrate what I'd learnt. I liked this but got bored at home on my own, with Muz disgruntled at having me under her feet.

The Sussex boarding school certainly was no ordinary school, hidden away in ancient woodland at the end of a very long drive that twisted and turned for what seemed like miles, and then emerged into a wide landscape revealing a lake and fanciful sprawling red-brick mansion beside it. The building and grounds had been purchased by this obscure educational charity to found a school with bright new ideas about how and what children of the modern post-war era should be taught. The guiding principles seemed to be directed at providing an environment where children were encouraged to explore their capabilities, developing confidence and resourcefulness, while living as part of a community where each was expected to contribute in their own way, making their own decisions based on collective responsibility. Above all, embracing a culture of freedom, both of expression and freedom to roam, spending a lot of time outdoors close to nature – in effect, running wild and being happy. I decided very quickly that this would suit me perfectly. There were no rules and staff were called by their first names, presenting themselves as friends and facilitators rather than objects of authority. Older children were expected to help look after the younger ones and gradually all of us came to resemble a strange ragged tribe, loosely organised into *ad hoc* daily activities.

Lessons such as English were taught through the medium of writing and performing plays in a Nissen hut, which had a stage at one end. Maths would involve practical exercises in role-playing as shopkeepers or producing plans for building elaborate dens in the woods, which required exact measurements and specifications. Dens were an important part of life, as we learnt building and survival skills and how to create our own society among the great forest of trees. We all had bikes to get around and bike races up and down the long drive were regular events, so fast and furious that crashes were standard. I still have scars from frequent collisions and falls. Cricket and rounders were played every day, as all types of sport and physical activity were thought essential to our well-being and given great prominence. Swimming in the lake was one of these pastimes, in particular at night, and more especially in moonlight, which was thought of as very health-giving, and produced feelings of such ecstasy I remember these times with shivers of delight. We were encouraged to do daring things, use initiative and show spirit. I didn't need much encouraging and I think this may have led to a premature downfall for me.

I had the idea to persuade other girls in my dormitory to join me one night in an assault on the boys' dorm when they were asleep, with us wearing bed sheets, pretending to be ghosts. When everything was quiet and all the teachers had gone to bed, we climbed out of our dorm windows and crawled across the roof to the boys' windows, which were wide open as it was high summer. Draped in our sheets, we leapt into their dorm, making howling noises and waving our arms around, flapping the white sheets. The boys all woke up terrified and caused such a commotion that it brought several teachers running. The other girls and I all thought it was a great joke and went on flapping around, helpless with laughter. But the teachers appeared not to find it at all amusing, much to our surprise, as usually they were all for brave exploits, in which we thought climbing across a steep roof at night would rate highly. So I was baffled at being taken away and put in a small room next to the sick bay all by myself, with my possessions bundled up in a box. Nothing was said, but a few days later I found myself back at home. Again, no mention was made of the incident at school or my sudden departure and, even more surprising, no one at home seemed in the least concerned about it. After a while, the reason for this puzzling lack of comment was explained as I became aware of a buzz in the household, a new excitement and air of anticipation as trunks and suitcases were pulled out and, all of a sudden, we were packing up for yet another move.

This coincided with the arrival of Nanny Joan, who was to come with us to this new far-away destination of Malta, to look after Andrew and Ros; Elaine and I being thought too old for a nanny. Just as well, as I took an instant dislike to Joan who was starchy and prim with a permanently disapproving face. She particularly disapproved of me, which she declared very soon after arriving, saying she had been warned that I was wild. Had she been told about the roof excursion, I wondered. But no, it wasn't this: it was disapproval of the small business I had started as a way of earning pocket money to buy batteries for my torch. The torch was an essential piece of equipment for me as I used to read books under the bedclothes at night, needing to do this without disturbing Elaine, who slept in the same room. My business idea worked like a charm and no one had so far objected. We had a big garden full of flowers tended by a gardener who liked his flowers to be appreciated and was quite happy for me to pick them and make posies, which I then went round selling door-to-door in the village during school holidays. I didn't make much money, but it was enough to buy batteries and sweets.

When Joan arrived she lost no time in advising Fa and Muz that it was shameful for a doctor's daughter to go round selling things like a common gypsy. But there was no time to lament the end of my flower-selling, as hardly had Joan finished reorganising our household than Fa announced we were leaving it behind, packing up again, this time with our boxes and crates labelled for Liverpool, where we would be boarding the SS *Orbita* on our way to Malta.

CHAPTER 4

Whenever we packed up house to move somewhere else Fa would use the opportunity to throw away most of our possessions. He had a morbid horror of worldly goods due to dire warnings in the Bible about no one being admitted into heaven if they had been encumbered in life by such things as chattels, which to him included children's toys.

'Everything goes,' he roared, as if there was no time to lose. I had somehow managed to save enough money from my flower-selling business to buy a Monopoly set, which was a prime possession, and nothing in this world or the next was going to prise me from it.

'Well, it's not going in any of the boxes and you'll have to carry it all the way to Malta by yourself,' said Fa in the thunderous voice he had lately adopted for getting his own way by intimidation. Joan's criticisms had stung him so that he felt provoked into asserting his authority, which manifested itself in various bellicose ways. Muz stood by, quietly confronting him. 'Paul,' she ventured (Paul was her pet name for him), 'you could allow the children just one toy each.'

'Monopoly is not a toy,' he fumed, 'and that's final.' At this point in my life I discovered an ability to defy him, standing up to him; and, surprisingly, he usually backed down. I wished Muz would try the same tactic and not allow him to bully her into complying with so many of his tyrannical master-of-the-house pronouncements.

After this meagre packing up, we went off by train to board the SS *Orbita* at Liverpool docks, our boxes in front carried by porters, while the rest of us followed in single file up the gangplank, with me clutching the precious Monopoly set tied together with string. Halfway up, something happened and the Monopoly box suddenly came apart. Bank notes and cards flew up in the air, caught by powerful gusts as green houses and red hotels and all the little silver tokens rattled down onto the wooden gangplank, while I scrabbled to retrieve them. How everyone laughed, and Joan declared with satisfaction that this is what happens when children get their own way.

Joan's previous job had been with the children of a famous writer called John Pudney and no opportunity was lost in reminding us of this elevated post, and how she had come down in the world by agreeing to look after such grubby children as us. The Pudney children never played with mud or did silly things; they were always properly dressed, had perfect manners, and loved her as one of their own. Which clearly we had failed to rise to.

'Mr and Mrs Pudney were always very generous to me,' she said, 'while your parents have a streak of meanness.' This was perfectly true. I was painfully aware how stingy they were and put it down to Christian ideals of poverty and self-denial, but I thought Joan's criticism was unfair as, however mean they might appear, they were never spiteful or devious in the way Joan contrived when their backs were turned.

On board the *Orbita* we found ourselves once again sharing a cramped cabin with other families. Muz was disgusted; in particular because one of the other mothers instantly attached herself to us, wanting to be pals, which was never going to happen as this woman was the antithesis of Muz in every way. Radiating what Muz called 'cheap glamour', she was flirtatious and giggly, constantly preening herself in the cabin's one small mirror. On went the Pond's cold cream and bright red lipstick in between breathless bursts of rackety song. Up went the hair in big copper swirls, while she sang and jiggled and flashed her long painted nails at us as we watched from our bunks, fascinated by her upstaging of our small, pale Muz. She did not appear to have a husband and this intrigued us even more, but what she did have was a nasty small boy called Poppet.

Poppet lived on treats and lavish attention from his mother, which caused us to despise him, unfairly perhaps. One day, when adults were upstairs having grown-up lunch while children were confined to cabins for compulsory afternoon rest on bunks, Poppet took his mother's jewellery box from the drawer under her bunk and, leaning out of the porthole, emptied the entire contents overboard. We watched, dumb with horror, as he then pulled out his mother's silk underwear and flashy frocks, each article flung from the porthole with shrieks of glee. A sense of doom descended on us as to what would happen when Poppet's mother returned from lunch; since in her eyes he was an adorable, perfect child, good as gold, never naughty, and we were terrified that we would be blamed.

When the cabin door opened, there was Poppet's mother standing rigid in the doorway as if bolted to the floor, only her mouth silently opening, wider and wider, as Poppet went on stuffing one of her ball gowns through the porthole. We all went stiff, hardly daring to breathe or look at her. After several paralysed moments, she let out a gasp and then started screaming and shaking with frenzy as the rest of us shrank down in our bunks. People ran to see what all the commotion was about and, incredibly, Poppet was seized hold of and spanked so hard and for so long we almost felt sorry for him.

The only fresh water on the ship was saved for drinking, so baths were filled with hot, smelly sea water and children were lined up to take their turn, all of us in the same salty water that stung any sensitive body parts and felt scratchy. Soap refused to produce any lather, so the effect of these baths was to leave us feeling just as itchy and scabby as when we got in. But the enamel baths were huge and we could have a good splash and frolic, which made up for other deficiencies.

Steaming into the Grand Harbour at Malta, we were transported into another world as a vision rolled out in front of us displaying monumental battlements and tall, glorious, ancient buildings, all radiating sunlight, warmth and welcome. I felt elated. Fa's new appointment was as medical superintendent in charge of a newly built hospital called King George the Fifth Hospital right here on the splendid harbour, where patients could look out on all the ships at anchor or sailing in and out. Charities in England and Scotland had raised money for this prestigious project, as part of a post-war effort to restore hope and prosperity to Malta, which had suffered devastation during the prolonged siege by German forces. The George

Cross was awarded to the island in recognition of this collective bravery. Fa was very much looking forward to his new assignment and Muz was happy too. It was a new beginning for us.

Lodgings had been arranged in a rather forbidding but palatial house of noble origin among orange groves in the Boschetto Gardens, which today are open to the public but then were privately owned. The house had been built centuries before as an auberge for the Knights of St John and was now inhabited by a family of elderly spinster sisters presided over by their niece, Ivy. She immediately made it clear that my parents were very welcome but children were not, and would live in separate quarters from adults. These were in one of the upper-floor galleries and were high, cavernous, barrack-style rooms with bare stone walls and iron beds like a dormitory. I was not at all put off by this as I thought the enormous galleries would be a superb playground for running around, making echoing noises and generally having high jinks, until I found out that Joan was not going to be counted as one of the adults and would sleep in the knights' dormitory with us. I expected a grim reaction from her on this news, but she became unusually subdued. I think finding herself in these alien circumstances was such a shock that she felt quite defenceless. She may have begun to see us as allies in this harsh new world of the knights' fortress. To cheer her up I invented a game where Elaine, Andrew, Ros and I pretended to be the Pudney children, sitting primly on our beds with books, so she could go back to being a Pudney nanny in her old comfort zone. She responded by reading to us and becoming unusually kind and soft, so we formed a sort of community of lost souls in that barren household.

We could look out of the narrow windows of our gallery across the inner courtyard of the house to kitchens on the other side, from which at meal times a procession of servants would set off with trays of covered dishes for the dining hall beneath us, where we imagined adults ate in sombre formality. When they had finished, the remains of the meal would be scraped up and brought for us to pick at the scraps. Muz would try to hide food to bring us after failing to persuade Ivy that children needed proper feeding and could not exist on leftovers. Ivy considered that good food was wasted on children who would never know the difference, and nannies were counted as servants, so no special allowance was to be made for Joan either. The regime allowed no variation and Muz became increasingly alarmed as she noticed we were actually starving while being held like prisoners behind the high stone walls, and was doing her best to bring this to Fa's attention, encouraging him to consider an idea that we might try to find a place of our own as well as a school for Elaine and me.

During the peculiar limbo of this time we were allowed out each evening for long walks with Joan and these were full of new excitements and explorations, which provided a solace. My most enduring memory of Boschetto is of the sweet intoxicating smell of orange blossom drifting on the air as we walked through leafy groves to Dingli Cliffs on the other side of the estate.

Dingli was, by contrast, a wasteland of rock and scrubby wild thyme skirting precipitous cliffs hundreds of feet above an expanse of sea so pellucid and shining it thrilled and exhilarated me. Any other consideration was irrelevant compared with this new strangely deserted landscape to explore each day.

I was fascinated by bonfires along the cliff top that would be freshly lit or still burning when we got there. We discovered it was a custom among some of the old Maltese families when someone died, all clothes and bedding and any household item they might have touched would be taken out onto the cliffs to be burnt. I could see all kinds of articles such as trinket boxes and books and pieces of embroidered cloth among the ashes, and wanted to poke around with a stick to retrieve anything that looked interesting or worth saving. But Joan was very strict about this. 'They probably died of TB or polio and all the germs are waiting to jump onto you the moment you touch anything,' she warned.

Often there would be diversions for us in the courtyard back at the house as the spinster sisters, all of whom seemed demented in varying degrees, fought like demons, shrieking and wielding broomsticks while tearing at each other's clothes. Servants would rush out to intervene or douse them with buckets of water, while Ivy's dogs joined in the fray, barking and jumping, mad as maniacs themselves. One day, when a disturbance was going on in the courtyard, we looked down and there was one of the sisters with a long stick, prodding a swarm of bees hanging in a tight ball under projecting eaves outside the kitchen. The other sisters were shouting instructions to her from a safe distance, when all at once the swarm dislodged and fell *thump* right on top of her head, where the tight ball remained stuck like an enormous busby. High up in our safe perch we were convulsed with giggles at this weird sight, while the other sisters fled inside, slamming the door after them. The beehive sister stood there completely stunned and impassive, apart from her lips silently moving with what we imagined were Hail Marys. As we watched intently at what we thought were her last moments before being stung to death – just as the swarm had descended onto her head without disintegrating, all of sudden it rose up intact and, with extraordinary gracefulness, flew off, leaving not one bee behind.

All this time Fa was out of sight, busy organising the new hospital, which was a dream job for him. He was a gifted organiser. Then, just as the rest of us were getting used to the new lightness of our bodies and strange idiosyncrasies of Boschetto, Fa announced that we were moving to a small town called Guardamangia, a short bus ride from the hospital, which would be much more convenient than Boschetto.

Our new home was in Hookam Frere Street, next door to the very grand Villa Guardamangia, where Lord and Lady Mountbatten lived. Fa had served with Dickie (as LM was known) in the war, so they already knew each other and now, meeting again in Malta, Fa had become personal physician to the family. The family included Princess Elizabeth and Prince Philip during the time he was an officer in the Royal Navy, when his ship was based in Malta. Occasionally Elaine and I, from our bedroom window at this new house, caught sight of the royal couple strolling in the formal gardens behind the villa, arm in arm, looking at each other very lovingly, which we found romantic and charming. It is a happy thought that windows overlooking their garden were not thought a security risk and no one bothered about it. A school was found for Elaine and me at Sliema, a short bus ride away, in one of the elegant old houses along the seafront, now pulled down for hotels and high-rise blocks, blighting this once stylish coastal town. The school was called Chiswick House, and the headmistress, Miss Chiswick, was an imposing figure with long red-painted nails like Poppet's mother. In class, as well as at all other times, she wore long skirts and a jaunty cocked hat with nodding feathers. The skirts swished around her feet as we followed her through tiled passageways into the classroom. She had a most unusual teaching style in that most of her lessons involved tales of her love life, which had been varied and eventful. She was eccentric; a word I would not have known then, but I did know that there was something out of the ordinary in the way she reached into a drawer of her desk every few minutes to uncork a bottle, from which she took a glug as her narratives gathered momentum. She explained that these were an important guide for us in writing our own stories for homework.

I had enjoyed writing plays at the free-wheeling Sussex school, so this was easy for me and, drawing on the theme of an island surrounded by sea, I invented a story about a mermaid called Phoebe, who I thought might emulate in a fishy sort of way some of the exploits described by our teacher. I was very pleased with the way it turned out and showed it to Fa, who liked it very much and indulged me with unaccustomed praise. Miss Chiswick, however, was not at all impressed or flattered by a fish-tailed alter ego called Phoebe, and with her red pen she struck out all my laborious lines of writing, adding a sharp comment underneath. When I got home and showed Fa, he was incensed. 'The woman is a philistine,' he fumed, whistling the word through his teeth for emphasis. 'An ignoramus.' The tooth-whistling continued as he searched for a suitable indictment to continue his tirade. One of his many personal mottoes, often quoted, was 'Search everywhere, question everything', which is probably why I developed a sometimes unhealthy curiosity, poking my nose into things best left un-poked. Fa resumed his rant. 'The woman doesn't look, she doesn't see, she's a dismal influence and that's the end of it.' So there we were: she'd been written off and we were changing schools again.

The next one was St Joseph's Convent, inside the ancient citadel of Valetta, where the teachers were Italian nuns living in cloisters attached to the school. This was in one of the enclosed city's narrow streets full of tall, golden stone buildings. Elaine had been pulled out of Chiswick House along with me, and both of us, with Andrew who was now old enough to start school, were enrolled at the convent. Boys and girls were segregated and taught in separate classes at different ends of the school, the boys being taught by priests. We were the only Protestants in this intensely devout Roman Catholic community, but far from feeling like aliens, we were made to feel special and treated with much deference and sensitivity, which was certainly a surprise. The nuns were gentle, sweet-natured souls and all I wanted was to be like them, gliding about on silent feet, holding a rosary. Muz and Fa got into a bit of a fuss about this when I went on to be the possessor of my own rosary and showed them how each bead related to a prayer. But, to their credit, they didn't take it away. What they were much more concerned about was the curriculum, which centred on three subjects for girls: embroidery, catechism and reading aloud. During my two years at the convent I don't think I learnt anything of the slightest academic value, but I was very happy, made many good friends, and picked up some unusual pieces of information.

The nuns told us that when they washed or had a bath they never exposed their bodies, keeping their eyes closed as they removed all the layers of black robes and petticoats, exchanging these for a long white shift, underneath which they washed or bathed, reaching down or up with the soap to get clean. They kept their eyes closed the whole time as an act of chastity, they explained. They said we should try it as a token of purity and love for Our Blessed Lady. When we looked dubious, they giggled and crossed themselves, and I loved them for their innocence.

Following our starvation regime at Boschetto and my parents' frugal attitude to food, none of us had returned to normal proportions and I was so thin that my shoulder blades stuck out through the light cotton of my school dress. Some of the girls used to flick their fingers on my bones in a teasing way, not unkindly, but on one occasion Mother Superior saw this. She stopped immediately and all of us gave her a curtsy, as was the custom. She pointed to my sticking-out shoulder blades and said to the girls, 'Do you know what these are?'

The girls replied in unison: 'Shoulder bones, Mother.'

'No, you are wrong,' said Mother Superior. 'These are angel wings starting to grow. Wendy is blessed with angel wings.' She put out her hand to touch, very lightly, the putative wings, as if giving them a blessing herself, and then, with a tiny smile, she glided on.

After that everyone wanted to touch my 'wings' for good luck, but the nuns said it was forbidden because my body was God's temple, as was everyone else's, requiring the highest form of respect. All of this caused my prestige to rise in a most gratifying, if questionable, way.

Prestige did not supply material essentials, and my need for torch batteries and other things like bus fares to go and see my friends at weekends was as pressing as ever. Going to school in Valetta, where there were lots of shops, provided a new business opportunity and this became an absorbing activity as well as a profitable one. During the lunch hour when we were free to sit outside with sandwiches or go home, instead of eating I went to the shops and bought bags of sweets, filling my satchel with them. All this stock came home with me on the bus and was set out in my bedroom for friends to come and buy – at a mark-up. We had recently moved yet again and there were no shops in our new area, so my bedroom sweet shop was popular and profits were rolling in very nicely. With plenty of money for bus fares I could go off with my friends at weekends, roaming the island, finding new places to swim or explore, or just mooch about.

We were now living in an imposing house called Villa Kingsborough in the select neighbourhood of Ta' Xbiex on the waterfront at Marsamxett harbour. Fa's medical and surgical skills were bringing him a degree of fame, with a following of interesting and influential people, such as Mabel Strickland, whose family owned *The Times of Malta*. She was a very generous, unmarried lady, who often invited us to her house. It was ancient and charming, with a long, cool garden at the back where she and Fa would stroll, absorbed in conversation, while I followed on behind. It was Miss Strickland's suggestion that we should move to Villa Kingsborough, which she thought more suitable for us. Also, quite possibly, it may have been more comfortable for her on visits, entering through the impressive marble hallway of this elegant house, rather than the narrow cramped one at Guardamangia. Despite the Mountbattens' residence next door, it was not a fashionable area, having been badly bombed during the siege.

Muz had Maltese maids and a cook to help out at the new house, which was designed for staff to run as it had numerous bedrooms and reception rooms, with enough space for Joan and a nanny friend of hers to open a nursery school in one of the large rooms. Very convenient for Ros, we all thought, as she was the right age to attend. But Ros longed to escape Joan's clutches and join the rest of us going off to Valetta each day instead of staying at home being squashed by Joan. Even worse, this form of control was now acted out on Ros in front of the other children as a sort of deadly deterrent, showing what would happen to them if they strayed from the rules.

With staff doing the chores at home, Muz was free to take up her Apothecaries qualification (which she had in addition to her nursing) and joined the Dispensary at Fa's hospital, a job she enjoyed so much it gave her a completely new take on life and she began to blossom. With Fa also in good spirits from the satisfaction of his job and outdoor life, sailing and swimming, as well as all the socialising – even going to grand dinners and balls – my parents seemed released from the struggles of the war years and post-war miseries. Their preoccupation with these new excitements meant that I was left very much to pursue my own inclinations, which suited me perfectly. We were all happy and relaxed, and wonderfully suntanned. All except Ros. But it was a different story for her at weekends.

Since Joan started the school, she was given weekends off and went away with her friend Muriel to meet sailors – or so we imagined. I was given the responsibility of looking after Ros, which I was not thrilled about at first, until by accident discovering her commercial potential, when suddenly Ros became hot goods. Weekends were a time for bus rides around the island with friends, and the first time Ros came on the bus with me I was embarrassed about imposing a four-year-old sister on them, but Maltese girls were used to the responsibilities that came with big families and Maltese people in general are kind, tolerant and warm-hearted. That first day on the bus was exceptionally hot and Ros was wearing her usual ragamuffin clothes, as all of us Craddock girls wore cast-offs, relics of missionary boxes and hand-me-downs. Along with her worn-out dress, Ros had on a little white cotton sun hat which she removed and, wriggling off the seat next to me, went tottering down the aisle like a waif, her hair and dress sticking to her skin with sweat. I did feel a pang to see her looking so bedraggled. But the next moment as she was passing rows of seats with the limp hat in her hand, other hands started reaching out and putting coins in her hat with pitying glances. Ros, who had the face of an angel, smiled at them and more coins were fumbled out of purses, until, turning round, she beamed at us sitting at the back of the bus, and returned very pleased with the unexpected bounty. I could see this had unlimited possibilities and weekends became popular for all of us, including Ros.

Occasionally, Fa would take a day off at a weekend and instead of bus rides, I helped Muz pack a picnic and we would go to one of the golden beaches to swim, or I would go sailing in the dinghy Fa had bought and moored below our house. The dinghy was called *Merlin*, with a standard Bermuda rig, easy for me to handle on my own and the day that I could go off solo was a supreme time of freedom and exhilaration.

When the Malta Yacht Club closed for the winter, it was a signal for Fa to take *Merlin* and me out beyond the harbour entrance in a challenge against the wild open sea, which always seemed eager to test our mettle with lots of furious tossing about and attempts at engulfing us. My job was to bale energetically, while at the same time straining to keep hold of the jib, which was trying to be a spinnaker, as Fa yelled instructions into the raging wind and the boat skimmed and bucked, waves slopped in and water rose around my ankles. I did not entirely share Fa's enthusiasm for this form of extreme sport as I became soaked and freezing and sometimes a bit terrified. If the off-shore wind veered too forcefully it would be impossible for us to turn around and tack for the harbour, and instead we would be driven further out to sea (which is why the yacht club sensibly closed at this stormy time of year). But when this happened, Fa just pointed *Merlin* into the wind, yelling louder with the excitement of pitting himself against the fury, and we would wallow like this while the sky grew darker and the wind chillier, until at last it ran out of breath towards evening, and we could trim the sails and tack for home.

However scary these death-defying trips became, I never doubted Fa's judgement, believing him to be super-human, as he had truly seemed to demonstrate during the war. Our family, having emerged with renewed vigour from those ordeals, was now strong, healthy and full of hope during these exuberant, glorious days in Malta. It was a new experience for me to see Muz on a Saturday evening throwing off her usual caution and working clothes, coming to our room to say goodnight, wearing an astonishing ball gown and even more astonishing jewels that Fa had given her; in particular a necklace of moonstones, which glowed and shimmered in such a captivating way it became one of her dearest treasures.

Villa Kingsborough had an imposing marble staircase rising from the chequered marble floor of the enormous hallway. The staircase was wide and rose from the centre of the hall, dividing halfway up in graceful curves to right and left, connecting with a gallery of bedrooms above. The banisters were marble and a foot wide – ideal for sliding down; you just had to try and stay on instead of falling off, as the silky marble made for a very fast, slippery slide. When important guests came to dinner, Elaine and I were allowed to sit on the stairs to watch them arrive, and then, at a signal from Fa, we would go down in our dressing gowns to be introduced. Sometimes I was so overcome with the honour of the moment and the eminence of such grand people, I would forget where I was and drop a curtsy as this was a standard form of courtesy at the convent on encountering Mother Superior or Reverend Father, any prestigious figure now found me automatically curtsying. When this happened, Joan would hiss from the shadows where she lurked ready to whisk us off back to bed, 'Curtsying in your night clothes not only looks ridiculous, but is the height of bad manners.'

Whenever Muz and Fa were preoccupied giving a dinner party or going out to one, Joan took the opportunity to practise tortures on us. One of these was a strict rule that once we were in bed we were not allowed to get out for any reason whatsoever, including going to the lav. This was a seriously cruel ordeal for me and particularly for Ros who suffered what were called weak kidneys, resulting from a severe infection when she was a baby. Elaine seemed better able to contain herself, but I would lie in an agony of bladder spasms, stiff with terror about wetting the bed, which would result in a worse punishment than being caught out of bed. Desperate to avoid an accident, I would lower myself from the bed very carefully, trying not to make a sound, then crawl across the floorboards to the bathroom. But if Joan heard me, knowing my fear of the dark, she would make me stand in the gloomiest part of the landing or in an empty room for hours; until, hearing my parents in the hall, she would allow me back to bed before they came upstairs. If I protested to Muz about this the next day, she would say, 'Don't be silly; making up stories, telling such awful lies about Joan is a sin against God, who is watching you and writing it all down.' If God is watching all this and seeing what Joan is doing, I thought, why isn't he standing up for me? It seemed that God and adults were in league together and children were the only ones who sinned, while grown-ups were exempt.

My best friend Lally was always getting into trouble, in her case for seriously bad sins that included on one occasion stealing money from her mother's purse and blaming it on the maid. When she was found out, Lally was locked in her room for a week on bread and water. I went to throw stones at her window to get her to look out and she appeared like Rapunzel, leaning over the sill with her long dark hair hanging down. I had brought a basket of sweets and snacks and a long piece of string that I tied to a stone and aimed through her open window. The basket was then tied to the end of the string and Lally pulled it up.

The next stage was getting Lally out of her room, and this was easy as there were plenty of things like mooring ropes stored in our garage. Waiting until after lunch the following day, when grown-ups and maids would be horizontal on beds, resting, I took a rope and tied one end to the string which Lally let down. She then tied the rope to a bed leg and slid down like a pro. Her clothes had been taken away to stop her escaping, so I had brought some for her, and as soon as she put these on we ran like hares, dodging the rocks and wild thyme bushes between the houses, till we got to the rowing boats at the harbour, which took people across from Ta' Xbiex to Guardamangia on the other side, for two pennies. It was a slow creaking ride of ten minutes or so, and once there we bounded up the hill looking for the boy gang I used to hang out with when I lived there. I knew where to look. School was out and there was only one place they would be.

The bombed and flattened houses on the other side of Hookam Frere Street gave us a playground of infinite possibilities for mad games, and more sober ones like flying kites. We all had dens there, painstakingly fortified among the ruins, where much time was spent building elaborate edifices or rebuilding them when they got destroyed in fights. I knew the boys would be there. They saw us first, and picked up stones to throw at us, but it was only pretence. I told them about Lally.

'Lally got locked up for stealing.' They were impressed.

'And she escaped, so we've come here where they can't find her.'

The Miller brothers, Robin and Charlie, fidgeted as they weighed up how useful it was going to be, having us tagging on if the police were sent looking for Lally. With boys, I figured it was like dogs: if you stood your ground, not moving or saying anything silly, they always gave in.

'Fabio's got a new den. You can see it if you want to,' one of the others remarked after a while, extra casually.

Some of the dens were small bunkers underground in collapsed cellars where we had to crawl through tunnels of debris to get in. We were not the only ones using the tunnels, as rats and other scurrying animals had their runs down there, leaving smelly droppings and chewed bones along the way. I looked at the uninviting hole that led to Fabio's den and, instead of going in, I turned round, grabbed Lally and ran off, knowing the boys would follow.

Running away was the signal for a game that followed an invariable pattern. The boys ran around inside the ruined houses while we ran around outside the walls that were full of holes, as were the floors of derelict upper rooms. The object of the game was for the boys to aim streams of pee through a hole while we ran past, trying to dodge being hit. The boys would wait until one of us moved to make a dash past a hole and then let go a squirt, all of us shrieking and panting with excitement. Even when the boys ran out of pee, the game continued, as just the sight of a pink penis appearing at a hole sent us into paroxysms. Eventually, breathless and spent, we would fall in a heap, rolling and gasping and giggling like loons.

As soon as we caught our breath, it would be the carpenter's shop next and he would give us a drink of water in return for letting us sweep up his wood shavings, as by now we would be desperate with thirst. The carpenter made coffins for the mortuary of St Luke's Hospital, which was conveniently next door. It was a large hospital, busy with deaths, so the carpenter was never out of work, and while sweeping we kept a look out for hearses arriving.

The hearses were very ornate black-glass coaches, drawn by two black horses with tall black plumes on their heads. As soon as we heard a hearse arriving with a crunching of wheels on the road, we nipped off through the long grass between the buildings to lie hidden, peering through grass stalks to get a clear view of the mortuary to watch what happened next. We would lie there mesmerised as the big doors opened and bodies were revealed, wrapped in white sheets, stacked up like cocoons inside. One of the cocoons would be removed from its slot to be fitted into a coffin and the lid nailed down with satisfying hammering noises. Keeping ourselves unobserved was always tricky as the grass was itchy and Fabio had allergies, so when he started bottling a sneeze we had to keep his face pushed down into the dirt. One afternoon the horses, sensing a minor commotion of squirming bodies in the long grass, became spooked and started prancing about. The coachmen shouted, we lifted our heads, Fabio let out a giant sneeze, the horses reared up like circus performers almost tipping the coffin out of the back, and then, hoofs flashing, they bolted. As the glass coach flew along like a vision of the apocalypse thundering down the street, devout onlookers crossed themselves and called curses on the coachmen running like lunatics trying to catch up, their black tailcoats flapping, and top hats rolling in the road.

We strolled back to where the carpenter was standing outside the shop and found him slapping himself with glee. He had a long-standing feud with the funeral men who, he grumbled, grew rich while paying low prices for his coffins. He didn't only make coffins, but chairs and tables and cupboards and anything people ordered for their houses. One day he was making a large box- shaped object and when we asked what it was, he said it was going to be a surprise. This intrigued us, so we kept returning to see what was going to emerge, often calling in on our way home from school, and then one day we saw that it had become a huge doll's house with a staircase and pitched roof like an English house. Maltese houses had flat roofs.

'Who is it for?' we begged him to tell us.

'A very rich family,' he said with satisfaction. 'For a Christmas present for their children.' He looked at us pointedly. 'No one who you would know.'

And no one who was rich would want raggedy children being invited to go and play with their children's beautiful, expensive doll's house. But while it was still in the carpenter's shop we could look at it and imagine playing with it. Even Lally, who was such a tomboy, was enchanted by the house with its windows that opened and closed and even had glass in them, and a proper staircase with tiny banisters. The carpenter's wife was making curtains, and then the carpenter started making miniature furniture. It was all too much.

One day when we went to the shop, the house had gone. 'The rich gentleman has come and paid for the children's house and it has gone on a van,' said the carpenter with a dismissive wave of his hand. So that was the end of it; we would never see it again or find out who the rich family was. Later, when I told Joan about it, she sniffed loudly at the idea of such indulgence. 'Well, it's not as if you don't have plenty of treats yourselves on Christmas Day,' she said, 'what with the carry-on at the hospital and everyone wanting to make a fuss of the Medical Director's children.'

Fa had started a Christmas Day tradition at the hospital where we joined members of staff in a procession, singing carols around the wards that were draped in paper chains, while the staff dressed up as clowns or Christmas fairies. The climax to all this came at lunchtime when everyone gathered in one of the wards and Fa appeared carrying the Christmas turkey, which he then carved to great applause as plates were passed around. The best thing about this was being excused church and joining in the merriment, having a jolly time. Crowds of visitors arrived, perching on beds, telling jokes and teasing the nurses. Even Joan, with a little encouragement, loosened up and became quite amiable.

On Christmas Day 1949, we woke up to the crackle of wrapping paper as our feet stretched out in bed, finding stockings magically bulging; and later, when we went down for breakfast, there in all its glory, wonder of wonders, was the doll's house! Right there in our dining room, for me and Elaine and Ros! The carpenter never knew that the 'rich man' he spoke about so admiringly was our Fa.

I puzzled myself with this and turned over in my mind: were we rich? We lived in a big house and had a shiny new green Jaguar car with proud headlamps like twin orbs on each front mudguard. Fa had been given five hundred pounds as a thank-you present by Mabel Strickland (doctors were often given presents by grateful patients, but this was exceptionally generous) and bought the car in a rare burst of indulgence, with some more jewellery for Muz. Maybe we were rich, but I still had to earn my own pocket money. And the carpenter could never have suspected that the scruffy children playing on the bomb site near his shop would be from anything but poor families. He might have wondered about Fabio, though. Fabio's mother didn't look poor; in fact, she looked anything but poor and was the most embarrassing mother anyone could have.

When we were lying in the long grass or hanging around the carpenter's shop, what we dreaded most was hearing in the distance the sound of Fabio's mamma in her high heels coming click-clacking down the street, click-clack, click-clack, and worse than that was when she started singing. It was bad enough having a bouncy Italian mother making a spectacle of herself coming down the street, but singing at the same time was too much to bear. Especially as it happened when she got near the carpenter's shop her voice would start swelling like an ice-cream seller:

Fabiolino, Fabiolino,
Dove sei, dove sei? (Where are you?)
Dove si nasconde? (Where are you hiding?)
Vieni qua, vieni a casa. (Come here, come home.)

The carpenter would go all wobbly with emotion when he heard this and, quickly wiping his dusty hands on a dusty cloth, would run out to ooze charm all over the lush mamma and make the most cringing remarks and gestures, as Fabio slouched into sight from around the corner, head down, his face tight with shame.

Lally's escape was punished in an unexpected way, as the next time I saw her after that incident she told me she was being sent off to boarding school in England to learn better behaviour. The school was called Wycombe Abbey and several of my friends followed, once it was reported that the school was doing wonders for Lally.

The upstairs bedrooms at Villa Kingsborough had large ornamental stone balconies and we often slept out on these when it was hot at night. The view of the harbour with the lights of all the ships at anchor, looking like Christmas trees, kept me awake, gazing through gaps in the balustrade as I lay there on my mattress. One night, unable to sleep, I got an idea while testing my balancing skills along the top of the balustrade. I thought it would be a great spectacle if I gathered all my friends one day to watch as I jumped off the balcony, holding an open umbrella like a parachute, with me suspended underneath, floating down gracefully onto the flower bed below. This was years before Mary Poppins had the same idea.

When a day came that both Joan and my parents were out, I managed to persuade a good crowd to come and watch, thrilling me with ever more confidence as I stood theatrically on the balustrade, opening the umbrella and flourishing it about. I took a great leap, as far out as possible to catch a good quantity of air in the canopy of the umbrella, but disaster: the umbrella turned inside out and I fell like a sandbag with an inelegant thud into the flower bed below. There were gasps from the crowd that gathered to peer down at me lying there as I caught my breath, composing myself to scramble as delicately as I could to my feet. I didn't even have a scratch, but the umbrella was ruined and the skirt of my dress had somehow parted company from the bodice, which was going to be difficult to explain later at bath time.

When my husband Charles and I visited the villa fifty years later, we stood beneath the same balcony to judge how high it was off the ground, and thought it to be about twenty feet and the flower bed rather small! The Demajo family, who now own the villa, welcomed us warmly and showed us round so we could marvel at the grandeur of the interiors with the marble hall and staircase, and they later gave a party to introduce us to their friends and family. I had brought photos to show them views of the house in 1949, with the harbour full of warships of the Royal Navy: destroyers and frigates, submarines with their depot ship HMS *Forth*, a hospital ship, HMS *Maine*, minesweepers and cable layers, all very busy coming and going on exercises. There were also the smaller merchant ships at anchor; these were sailing ships, trading up and down the Mediterranean, carrying cargoes of watches and perfumes, with families living permanently on board, their washing lines hung between masts while children and dogs played on deck. I envied them the nomadic life. Fa was often called to these little ships when someone had fallen sick and he would come back and report on their exotic lives.

Since Fa had taught me how to sail *Merlin* and I could take it out on my own, I often sailed around the harbour, doing the rounds of ships where sailors waved and threw sweets down to me from the high decks. Bigger ships like the aircraft carriers HMS *Glory* and *Triumph* lay at anchor in the Grand Harbour at Valetta as our harbour of Marsamxett was too small for them. The navy used to give elaborate children's parties on board the carriers, where we were driven around the huge flat decks in tiny electric cars and went below to great feasts of party food and drinks. On American Navy carriers we were given exciting new Coca Cola, which wasn't fizzy then, and was reputed to contain cocaine as a secret ingredient. Without question it was like nothing I had ever tasted before and was different in some distinct but indefinable way from the Coke of today.

Muz had started me on piano lessons during the war years in India when, despite lacking basic essentials most of the time, we were never without a piano. When we arrived in Malta, I was already working my way through the music grade system and Muz decided I should have a professional teacher to take me on through the exams. My new teacher was a small, shrivelled woman called Miss Pim, who lived in a traditional Maltese terraced house on a narrow street, where all the houses had identical iron balconies and wooden shutters. She had an aversion to sunlight, keeping her shutters closed at all times; these were also covered inside with the remnants of wartime blackout, so the interior of her house was dark as night, even at midday. The only place where a crack of light was allowed to enter was in her kitchen, and the first thing she did each time I arrived for my lesson was to sit me down beside this beam, where she had a snack ready. This was a prickly pear sitting in an egg cup, the prickles snipped off and the top sliced open, with a teaspoon ready for me to scoop up the goo inside. It was wonderfully refreshing and novel. This set me up for the lesson, which had its own novel elements.

Due to Miss Pim being paranoid about light, either natural or artificial, sheet music was indecipherable in the gloom of her parlour, so she had devised an ingenious method of teaching. She would sit down at the piano and play me the set pieces for my exam, then get me to pick out the notes by ear and touch, after which I could learn to play them by heart at home. I thought this was more fun than conventional music lessons, and Miss Pim's piano was more fun than anyone else's too. At the start of each lesson when she sat down to play, the first few chords would disturb nests of mice that lived in the depths of the piano's interior. Erupting from the open top, they shot out, scurrying to disperse themselves among the furniture. Miss Pim either didn't notice, didn't mind, or was so used to it, none of it registered and no remarks were ever made about this or any other irregularities.

Each year I took the next grade of piano exam, and one year these were held in Valetta in an old palace that had an enormous ballroom on an upper floor, where the exams took place over several weeks. Examiners came out from England and everyone was in awe of them. I felt overcome before even meeting mine as I arrived at the palace and climbed its majestic echoing staircase, like a staircase to heaven. This opened onto a vast room at the top with an excessively high ceiling, occupying the whole of that floor. This was the old ballroom and it was completely empty except for a grand piano at one end with a small desk and chair for the examiner. He came forward to shake hands and, to my surprise, was jovial and disarming, not at all like other examiners. When he indicated he was ready, I sat down and started playing my set pieces, which were all well rehearsed. I was feeling reasonably confident after getting over my initial nerves on entering the great looming edifice of the palace, so it was a shock when suddenly he rapped on the piano lid and told me to stop. I didn't think I had made any serious mistakes.

'I don't want to hear that,' he said sharply. 'I don't want to hear your exam pieces. Anyone can play that chuffing stuff.'

I was speechless. What was Miss Pim going to say? How would I explain that I'd failed without even getting through the repertoire?

The examiner strolled over to the window while I sat mute, and after staring out for several long agonising moments, he turned round and said, not unkindly, 'Play me your favourite pieces, anything you want, anything that comes into your head, and go on playing until I tell you to stop.'

I thought I almost caught Miss Pim smiling over the top of the piano lid. She often played her favourite pieces for me, and I played mine for her in the darkened room with no music propped up in front. For the examiner I played everything I knew, and pieces I'd made up, and pieces of Muz's compositions I'd learnt from her; and all the while the examiner stood staring out of the window, so I thought he had forgotten to stop me and the next exam candidate would walk in and find me cheating. At last he turned round, and all he said was, 'Thank you. That is all.'

Miss Pim laughed and smiled and made us a cup of tea when I told her later, and when the results came out I'd got a Distinction.

Sundays in Malta became happier days as Fa and Muz held open house at teatime, when friends and nurses from the hospital dropped in, and Muz, who was an accomplished pianist, entertained them with her playing. Everyone loved this as she could play by ear any tune that was requested. One Sunday, two new nurses called Babs and Doreen dropped in for tea, introducing themselves all round and at once making an impression. Babs was glowingly blonde, while Doreen was dark and slightly more reserved, but both of them, as twenty-seven-year-old nursing sisters, startled everyone with their unexpectedly giggly, skittish behaviour. It was unusual for girls at that time to go on behaving like teenagers well into their twenties, as the impetus of war had caused most girls (and boys) to grow up fast. Another nurse, Enid Palmer, at nineteen, had been working under battle conditions on the front line in Burma, and when she came to join us in Malta she found peace of mind in the music Muz played. By contrast, Babs and Doreen, instead of enjoying the music, spoilt it by playing the fool, which did not find favour with Fa or Muz, as quite rightly they expected teatime guests to behave respectfully – apart from which it was Sunday after all. This did not deter the new girls who kept on coming back, not just on Sundays but at other times, dropping in and making themselves at home, even inviting themselves to our picnics and having their photos taken with Fa, one on each arm.

I did notice a slight shift take place after a few weeks of ingratiating themselves in this way: Doreen stopped coming. We thought she had found a boyfriend and gone off to pursue other interests, but it may have been that Babs wanted her out of the way, so there would be no competition, as it started to appear at this stage that she was setting her sights on our Fa.

At thirty-nine, he was at the height of his powers, physically and in terms of career and social status. In addition, he had great personal charm and charisma. I could see this in the way people responded to him, especially women, sometimes adoringly, and despite his high principles, Fa was not impervious. But I didn't think much about it at the time as there were lots of admirers buzzing around him and someone like Babs was much too silly and frivolous to last long in his orbit, I thought.

Both my parents were very absorbed in their lives, busy and happy, each with their own interests and careers; particularly Muz at the hospital dispensary, where she was highly regarded as a meticulous and capable practitioner. Possibly a year or so had passed since Babs' arrival when I began to sense that Muz was not her usual confident self and seemed slightly unsettled and anxious. Fa, however, was in rip-roaring spirits, perhaps even more so as the hospital was prospering and becoming well known for the excellence of its medical, surgical, maternity and outpatient departments.

At that time, before the invention of polio vaccine, serious epidemics were common; not just polio but other potentially fatal illnesses like scarlet fever. A whole ward at the hospital was sectioned off for scarlet fever cases during one of these epidemics. I caught the fever myself and was put in the ward, sealed off to avoid contaminating others. It was a ferocious illness – people died and I thought I might too, as no on from outside was allowed to come and see me. I imagined I'd been sent there to die and felt as if I was being eaten up by the red spots and fever. After what seemed like a month but may have been just a week, the fever subsided and I was allowed to get out of bed, but my body had shrunk and I felt like a ghost. All I wanted was for Fa to come and rescue me and take me home, which eventually he did and my bed was put out on the balcony, so I could lie there looking at the ships, while strength slowly seeped back into my legs and I found I could walk and run around again.

Things had changed at home while I had been away, or possibly my absence gave me new eyes and antennae. Muz was not herself. She didn't say anything and it was only years later that I found out what had been undermining her usual equanimity. Babs, either for fun or as a subtle way of demoralising her, had engineered a series of incidents that looked trivial, but Muz felt were aimed to discredit her; such as accusing her of making mistakes in the dispensing of medicines at the dispensary, so that she felt obliged to resign from her job, despite the chief dispenser assuring her there was no truth in Babs' assertions. These incidents were brushed off by Fa, which left Muz feeling she had no one to turn to. Except that suspicions were aroused among other staff at the hospital noticing how Babs manoeuvred herself into positions where she could work alongside Fa, and that she was flirting openly with him while pretending that Muz was her best friend; and even that all three of them were best friends. I know this because staff who were there at the time talked to me about it later, and the matron, Joyce Ryde, said Babs was brazenly, 'setting her cap at Dr Craddock'.

When the wheels of a household are turning reassuringly each day with familiar routines and rituals, any slips or stumbles are usually absorbed and smoothed out by the rhythms of domestic normality, so our lives continued through 1949 with no major events – only small ones, like Granny Craddock coming for her annual visit. She was our one surviving grandparent and was a curiosity from a different age and culture as she spoke with a northern accent, and shocked us with stories of her deprived childhood in a dark alien place called Dudley, where it seemed the sun never shone and there was no brightness in anyone's life. Children like her from poor families left school when they were eleven, to start working lives often unrelieved until they were too old to carry on.

But Hannah Louisa, our Gran (known as Hanna-the-Granna or Hand-Grenade, which were Andrew's names for her), had other ideas and had climbed a couple of rungs up the ladder to marry Ernest Craddock, who was a craftsman with a skilled job in London, making surgical instruments. They had four sons: Francis, Alfred (our Fa), Gilbert and Ronald. They lived in the same street as Muz's family in Stoke Newington and went to the same church, so the families knew each other and the children grew up together. Sometime later, both families moved out of London to a new life in 'the countryside', which was High Barnet. When Francis got married, his wife Kay wanted to have one of the modern houses being built along the river at Leatherhead for her new home. They didn't have enough money to afford anything so expensive, but Ernest had died the year before of heart failure caused by Grave's disease (over-active thyroid), leaving Gran in their very nice big house at High Barnet, where her youngest son Ron, aged nineteen, was still living at home. Gran and Ron consoled themselves after the grief of losing Ernest by looking after each other, which was a very happy arrangement. This didn't last long when Francis persuaded Gran to sell her house and put the money into the Leatherhead house so he and Kay could buy it, promising that, in return, Gran could move in with them and they would look after her for the rest of her life. Ron, meanwhile, was, 'Pushed off into rather inferior lodgings', as he described it later. The convenient arrangement for Gran to live with Francis and Kay didn't last long either, as it became a burden for them having her there all the time, so she was sent round to stay with other married sons each in turn, being passed around like a parcel. I felt sorry for her and tried to make her feel better when she came to have her turn with us, by listening to her stories and telling her mine, but not the naughty bits!

By the time Louise was born in 1964, Gran was in a Methodist Home and the matron gave a celebration for Gran's new status as a great-grandmother. She was thrilled that Louise's name reflected her own second name and the matron helped her send a telegram of congratulations, which was followed by a letter written in Gran's careful script with loving sentiments. Happy that her first great-grandchild had arrived safely, Gran died soon after with the baby's photo beside her.

Not long after Gran's last visit, everything changed. Fa announced that I had been booked into a girls' boarding school in Sussex where I would be starting in the next term, and he was taking all of us back to England, driving overland in the Jaguar. We would be looking for a house 'back home', he explained, where Muz and the family could stay while I was settling into my new school. Meanwhile, he would be returning to Malta to live in the resident medical officer's flat at the hospital. This was all very sudden and puzzling, but the prospect of an adventure driving overland to England was too exciting to allow any doubts.

After the usual manic clear-out of everything we owned, which tragically this time included the beautiful new doll's house and, of course, Muz's piano, all of us were packed into the Jaguar for the start of this epic journey: Muz in the front seat with her hatbox tied to a headlamp outside where she could keep an eye on it, and Joan squashed in with us four beanstalk children on the back seat. With hardly time to say goodbye to anyone, the car was trundled onto a ferry and we steamed off once again, this time to Syracuse in Sicily, on the first leg of our tour of southern Europe en route to England.

CHAPTER 5

A rriving at Syracuse, the minor oddysey of our European tour began as we folded ourselves back into the green leather seats of the Jaguar once it was unloaded onto the docks, and set off for the hotel Villa San Pancrazio in Taormina. This was a small intimate hotel with pastel views high above a little bay, its gardens drowsy with scents of moonflower and oleander. Meals were taken sitting outside on the patio in April sunshine, attended by elderly waiters in white jackets. We swam in the bay and walked down steep winding paths to the small town that was still patching itself up after the war. Everyone was kind and smiling under the gaze of Mount Etna, which dominated the view, smoke rising from its snowy peak. I thought life could never get better, with the whole family together on a holiday that for the very first time included all of us. Even Joan tolerated the miasma of the back seat with good humour, forcing a few smiles along the way – not because she was enjoying the trip, but because she was going home and would be leaving us the moment her feet touched England.

Fa had not included any leisurely exploration of Sicily in the programme he had planned, so we had no time to linger in this southernmost region of our tour and very soon set off for the Straits of Messina where, after another ferry crossing, we started the long climb up the toe and lower leg of Italy. The road followed a route through Calabria, east of the barren-looking Apennine mountains. Calabria was still a desperately impoverished region: even now, five years after the war had ended, its devastating effects were conspicuously evident in the lack of basic amenities to support the lives of its inhabitants, let alone catering for travellers. In rural areas, children in rags looking starved would run out into the road begging us to stop and buy goat's milk, which was the only thing they could sell to earn a few coins.

We had brought a primus stove with us and Muz would set it up by the side of the road to boil a kettle for tea and cook spaghetti. The primus became a centrepiece of our lives as all meals were coaxed in some form out of a single saucepan balanced on top of this rickety paraffin cooker, keeping us fed during frequent breaks on the long, hot drives. Whenever we stopped at a village to buy bread or supplies, the sight of such a luxurious car with its foreign occupants drew swarms of curious people peering in at the windows, exclaiming to each other in torrents of unintelligible language.

At one of these villages Muz became alarmed as the car was engulfed, and before she had time to do anything about it, her cherished hatbox was seized off the headlamp and the thief ran away through the crowd. What made it worse was that inside the hatbox was her jewellery case containing the moonstone necklace and many other valuable and sentimental pieces. She had objected from the start of our journey to the foolishness of tying her one piece of hand luggage to the headlamp, and never forgave Fa for refusing to allow her to keep it inside at her feet, where it would have been safe. She grieved for her lost jewels all the rest of her life, and it came to seem almost as if this loss signalled the first chime of a clock striking midnight on the happy life she had been enjoying with her family. For, at last, having recovered from the war, all of us were healthy, lively and looking set for good things, with no thought that fate could intervene.

Fa was always an enthusiast for new ideas, experiences and discoveries, with an unquenchable appetite for seeking whatever was out there to find out about, while generally living life at a high level of energy and exhilaration. It was in this spirit that we arrived at Pompeii, which was completely deserted of visitors or any living soul, except an old man who looked after the museum of grotesque figures that had been captured and fossilised in the very act of flight or death throes, when the ash cloud from Vesuvius buried them. Parts of the city of Pompeii had been excavated, revealing the ruins of a highly organised municipal society, with skilfully crafted buildings and paved streets laid out in perfect symmetry. The contrast of extremes between the demonstrable orderliness of city life and the savage chaos of its sudden end, have stayed with me as indelible impressions.

Our next big moment for historical revelation came at the end of a day's drive when we arrived triumphantly in Rome, which Fa had glorified to us as the peak of thrills. He had booked us into a rather grand hotel, where we could at last have baths and proper meals after so much slumming. The four of us famished children, joined by Joan, gazed longingly into the big white cave of the dining room. But Fa and Muz could not be parted from the primus and insisted on setting it up in their bedroom, where they continued to cook stews and rice or pasta concoctions, delighted that this would save having to pay for hotel food. This was a serious disappointment for the rest of us, and on top of that we were embarrassed by this squalid behaviour, so I was gratified when the cooking smells brought one of the hotel managers knocking on the door to investigate.

He was shocked to find the room full of steam, with all of us squatting on the floor like vagrants gathered around the primus. Waving his arms about in a very Italian way, protesting theatrically, he insisted we must leave at once as it was not allowed for clients to cook in their rooms and, worse than that, it was insulting to the high quality of the hotel cuisine.

Fa was forced to relent, and after that we ate in style in the hotel dining room, all of us sitting at a big round table with a stiff white cloth and napkins, waiters bending over us attending to every request. Menu choices, however, were subject to Fa insisting we always had the cheapest item, but after living on primus scrapings, every dish, however cheap, was food from heaven. To the end of his life Fa kept up this miserly attitude to food, so that later, whenever the rest of us went out to a restaurant together, we would say in unison, 'Don't do a Craddock and look down the right side of the menu first to see what's the cheapest!' Fa's penny-pinching became legendary in our family, and stories about the excruciating embarrassments caused by it can still reduce us to hysterics the moment any mention sparks off a memory.

Our dash through Sicily and Calabria had been planned that way by Fa to avoid wasting any time, in anticipation of a leisurely stay once in Rome to absorb its glories. These, now we had arrived, sent him into a high state of animation and euphoria. Every morning after an early breakfast, we set off on foot, led by Fa striding ahead like Moses with the guide books. One of Fa's great passions was teaching and enthusing others with his favourite subjects. These included history in all its forms, but above all Greek and Roman history, since Fa admired the conquests and culture of those far-reaching civilisations and wanted us to appreciate their important influences on world history. Using the ruined columns of the Forum as a stage, he waxed on about memorable debates and personalities famous in their time, and at other ancient sites he translated Latin inscriptions on tombs and monuments, very pleased to be impressing us with his language skills. More theatrical moments came as we stood in the great glaring dusty arena of the Colosseum, with Fa conjuring up for us the drama and heat and blood, while lions and the crowd roared, and death was celebrated as a public spectacle.

A contrast was the even larger public space of St Peter's Square, like an apron spread in front of the great domed edifice of the Basilica, built to impress God and Christian pilgrims who converged from all over the world. The interior of the vast building was richly ornamented, having as its centrepiece directly beneath the dome, a bronze canopy, ninety feet high, supported on spiral columns of the same dark bronze entwined with gold vine leaves, reaching high into the vault above. We felt like ants, craning our necks to peer upwards. In front of the altar, excavations were taking place, intended to uncover the tomb of St Peter that was reputed to be there, following an instruction of Christ that his church was to be built upon 'the rock of St Peter'. At the great door of the building was a statue of the saint, raised up and seated, with his feet at a convenient height for the faithful to kiss. His toes had been partially worn away by centuries of reverent lips pressing themselves to the cool marble. I wanted to join the queue waiting patiently to apply their lips, as it appealed to me in a reverential sort of way, but Joan pulled me back. 'We don't do that sort of thing,' she said.

Despite the grandeur of St Peter's presiding over its colonnaded square, of all Rome's sights and sensations the most memorable for me was the ancient Appian Way. This flawless example of Roman engineering had escaped being ravaged through conflict or neglect and, perfectly preserved, was immensely satisfying in the harmony of its scale, striking out as if constructed as a path to eternity, straight as a lance, paved to the horizon, lined by iconic trees. In my imagination it was easy to visualise the millennia of sandalled feet marching or walking in the shade of those trees along this most splendid route out of Rome, and, if followed to its end, arriving at Italy's east coast.

On then to Florence, keeping ourselves occupied with a game we invented and played during all these long tedious drives. Large hoardings would appear at the side of the road advertising all kinds of services or merchandise and each of us chose one of these for our own symbol. Mine was the Michelin Man made out of bulging rubber tyres, looking very jolly. Every time 'our' advertisement appeared, we added another mark to our score. Too bad if anyone wasn't looking as their sign came up, the rest of us would let it go by and then tell whoever it was that they'd missed it.

As I had found the Appian Way to be the most arresting sight of all those in Rome, so it was the River Arno in Florence that held for me a most irresistible appeal. Its great wide heaviness of grey water, like molten lead flowing without a ripple, was extraordinary as it passed through the ancient arched bridge of the Ponte Vecchio, crowded with shops and houses, inexorable in its progress to the Tyrrhenian Sea.

We stayed at a small *pensione* where, thankfully, as at the hotel in Rome, the primus was forbidden, and we strolled out to eat at cafés whenever there was a pause in between guided tours led by Fa exclaiming at the genius of Michelangelo and the famous treasure houses of painting and sculpture. In the long galleries, art students sat at easels copying paintings and selling the copies to visitors. Small copies could be commissioned and would be produced by the next day in ornamental frames, delicately carved and painted. Muz bought a small round miniature of Roberto Feruzzi's 'Madonna and Child' that subsequently went everywhere with her and became one of her treasures.

Fa became progressively more exuberant as he strode along at the head of our small straggly group, pointing out the notable features of each famous sculpture or building. Our little procession must have looked incongruous to the Florentines as we trailed behind this very tall, loud man, who from time to time greeted passers-by in what he believed to be fluent

Italian, which from their startled expressions might have seemed to them as baffling as Mandarin. After having mastered Mandarin while living in China, Fa remained convinced throughout his life that he had a natural gift for languages, and used to embarrass us cringingly whenever he found an unsuspecting audience in some foreign non-English-speaking place.

When we came to Michelangelo's famous sculpture of David, Fa, in his lecture to us on its merits, emphasised the anatomical perfection of each detail: the veins on the back of David's hands precisely defined, as were some of his other parts. The rest of us shuffled about, unsure how polite it was to stare in public at David's nakedness, displaying genitals that looked suspiciously discreet. This feature seemed out of scale with the towering size of the statue and the pose curiously nonchalant. More interesting for me, on the opposite side of the piazza, was Cellini's bronze Perseus, holding high in his left hand the severed head of the snake-haired gorgon Medusa. This was a much smaller and more dramatic statue than the monumental David. The dark metallic sheen of Perseus added to his mystique as he stood victorious in the winged sandals and helmet borrowed from Mercury. These classic myths were stories I had read over and over from childhood and never grew tired of them.

Onwards from Florence, up and up the very long leg of Italy, we stopped in Milan to gaze on the ethereal pinnacles of Milan cathedral, but were not allowed inside as we had forgotten to take hats. Women needed to have their heads and arms covered as a sign of respect when visiting Roman Catholic institutions. It had been the same in Malta.

One of Fa's most excitable moments came when we reached the top of Italy and arrived at the foot of the great massif marking the border with Switzerland. He was a railway enthusiast and the car was to be loaded on a train to go through the Simplon Tunnel. This was one of the longest railway tunnels in the world, cutting through the base of the Alps, linking the two countries. There was something wonderfully novel about going into the tunnel in Italy and emerging in Switzerland. Fa was in a ferment of anticipation for this experience. Out came his camera, the latest Rolleiflex, to record the moment the car was secured with cables onto a flat-bed rail truck, while the rest of us were looking for seats in a passenger carriage.

Photography was another passion of Fa's and the Rolleiflex went everywhere with him, hanging from a strap around his neck, ready to capture any rare or remarkable scene that might suddenly pop up. He had a dark room in our house in Malta where I had acted as his assistant, developing and printing films. Some of the photos he took at that time are still in good condition now, sixty years later.

It was a long dark journey through the tunnel, but as the train came out at last into the daylight of Switzerland, we were transported to a Christmas card landscape of silent white snow and fir trees, with rustic chalet houses just like those in the *Heidi* books. Everywhere was shiny clean, no rubbish to be seen, no dirty marks in the snow, no trashy sights along the way. With the car unloaded, we drove to a small hotel on the shore of Lake Geneva, and this continued the fairytale as we found ourselves welcomed into the warm panelled interior, smelling of pine wood and good cooking, while later we were tucked up in feather beds for the night. The experience of a real feather bed is one of extreme sensuousness; being enveloped in goose-down quilts – one on top and one underneath – was a luxury none of us could have imagined. Adding to this indulgence, I was given my own room in a turret where I could look out on the smooth blue glittering expanse of the lake, long and lustrous, with icy peaks rising majestically on the far shore, a sight so heavenly no one could fail to be awed by it. Early the next morning, while looking dreamily at this scene from my turret window, lower down in the nursery Ros was opening her eyes in astonishment at finding herself lying in an old-fashioned wooden cradle, with no memory of being put in it the night before. She was probably too exhausted to notice.

Fa was impatient to explore the mountains, which reminded him of similar snow-covered peaks he had climbed in the Himalayan ranges, describing with rapture those high-altitude experiences. He couldn't wait to start leaping up these Swiss mountains, but they were not a project for amateur enthusiasts; added to which, he had a family tagging on. So the compromise was to urge the big heavy Jaguar up a steep, winding mountain road to see how high we could get. The car had a superb engine and in low gear purred and hummed as we climbed higher and higher, stopping frequently to gaze at the ever-expanding views, while Fa took photos and

Muz hauled out the old primus to make tea. We were doing very well until we reached a point where the road started to get icy, and the sky suddenly went very dark. Without warning, the car became enveloped in a dense cloud of heavy grey snowflakes that were pelting down, and the temperature dropped several degrees.

'We've hit a blizzard,' said Fa, not in the least perturbed as he drove on, more slowly now. 'I think we might have to allow discretion at this stage and turn back.'

As he said this, the car began groaning and slowing down. It got slower and slower until it stopped altogether for a few moments, and then, almost apologetically, started sliding backwards downhill. Joan gripped the back of Muz's seat and went deathly pale. Muz stared straight ahead and when Andrew piped up, 'Where are we going now?' she replied sharply, 'Don't distract your father while he's driving.'

He wasn't driving. He was trying to hold onto the steering wheel, which was going this way and that all by itself. We were going faster, sliding backwards, and when I looked out of the rear window, all I could see was the sky as we shot off the road and became airborne. There was a feeling of time being suspended while moments passed, until at last with barely a sound except a slight hissing and a sort of muffled sigh from the chassis, we landed, without so much as a crunch, in a billowing snowdrift. We all sat, frozen like statues, waiting to see what would happen next. Joan went on gripping the back of Muz's seat, making little choking noises, but the rest of us stayed silent, our faces too stiff with fright for speech or sniffles.

Fa, who had sat motionless for a brief moment assessing the situation, opened his door and got out. 'Right,' he said, '*nil desperandum*, everyone out, and start digging.'

We used saucepans and anything we could find to excavate the car; the snow was like candyfloss, so it wasn't too much of a labour. But it was very cold and, as usual, we were wearing only flimsy rag-bag clothing. Fa, however, had gone into campaign mode, commanding a small batch of troops constructing a dugout. 'Great stuff!' he boomed happily. 'This is what life is all about.'

There was some concern about the condition of the car after this escapade but Fa was impatient to press on, cutting short any further sorties in Switzerland. Now, heading west across France, I was disappointed we were not going to divert to Paris, which had been on the programme, as well as Orléans to learn about Joan of Arc. Fa was in a hurry, intent on driving, ignoring interesting side roads while France sped past. He seemed to have lost his spark and we all felt flat.

When we arrived at the Normandy coast, he attempted to rally interest in stories of heroism on the beaches, with the flotilla of little boats snatching hundreds of soldiers of the stranded Expeditionary Force from under the noses of advancing German forces at Dunkerque. We stood in cold grey drizzle on the bleak sand, trying to warm to the theme, but all we wanted now was to get on the ferry to England and find a new home.

Joan was dropped off with her suitcase at the train station in Dover, her face lighting up as she waved goodbye. Later she found a much more suitable family to work for and spent the rest of her life with them.

They had a small estate in the south of England, where Joan joined them when their first child was expected, and then stayed on to look after the next one. When she retired, she was given a cottage on the estate, so it all worked out very well for her – and I was glad, as I don't think Fa and Muz were sensitive to her needs, and her sharp edges, I thought, may have been in reaction to this.

Back in England it was a case of once again plugging into the old missionary network to find accommodation. This time it was the very spacious and not at all meagre middle floor of a large house called Rookley, on the outskirts of Tunbridge Wells. A family with relatives who had been China missionaries lived on the top floor with a son my age called John, and other relatives with children lived on the ground floor. The garden was enormous and divided into three sections, one for each family, with a communal area used as a cricket pitch where the families made up teams with friends, and we had cricket matches every weekend in the summer. The downstairs family had a very large organising mother who baked lavishly, with great spreads for cricket lunches and teas. There was lemonade for children and no shirkers were allowed: either we were in a team playing, or we were handing round refreshments.

On one of our first mornings at Rookley, when we were having breakfast, there was a sudden loud whoosh outside the window as a fireball fell from the sky, exploding so close to the window that burning fragments splattered onto the glass. As the fireball hit the ground there was another loud bang, and when we looked down all we could see was a black smouldering object on a patch of charred grass. Andrew was convinced it was a meteorite and was impatient to go down and investigate, but breakfast had to be finished first. This did not go smoothly as the next disturbance was the sound of an ambulance arriving, and when we looked out, there was downstairs dad Jim being loaded into it. Surely he could not have been hit by the fireball, so what had happened?

We all went down to find out and by then John's dad Peter, from upstairs, had joined everyone out in the drive as the ambulance went off. A story emerged as Peter, looking embarrassed and shuffling about, told us what had happened. He had been frying sausages and wandered off to get something. When he returned the kitchen was full of smoke, the pan was on fire and flames had reached the ceiling, so he grabbed the pan and threw it out of the window. As the window was above ours, what we had seen was the fiery pan hurtling past with sausages exploding out of it. Below us in the downstairs bathroom, Jim was shaving as the fireball landed and burst into an inferno outside his window, giving him such a fright he cut himself with the razor so seriously that his wife had to dial 999.

There was always something going on at Rookley, with very little missionary inhibition on display. John and I discovered a mutual interest in stamp collecting and spent hours assembling albums and swaps, or playing Mahjong with his parents who had a fine set of ivory and bamboo tiles brought home from China. All the Rookley flats were crammed full of Chinese porcelain and artefacts collected by generations of missionary relatives. Our flat had several giant urns, standing about rather grandly like sentries on either side of doorways, ornately decorated with dragons, fish or flowers. They looked expensive and precious, but no one took any notice of them. Rookley had become a sort of depository for all these treasures and they were viewed as part of the furniture in each flat. The upstairs and downstairs families were not at all like my parents' usual missionary friends. John's parents were very relaxed about life in general, enjoying good things and a good laugh; they were warm-hearted, generous and deliciously unstuffy.

There was an attic the size of a bungalow above their flat that was full of discarded furniture and old chests smelling of camphor. Inside these, when John and I were able to open the heavy lids, were layers and layers of carefully packed and perfectly preserved ancient clothes and shoes. These had been hand-sewn from rich fabrics, velvets, satins and brocade: court dresses; capes; men's tunics and jackets; stockings; shoes with silver buckles, stout heels and pointed toes; wigs and hats and fans. One chest was full of stiff glowing silks, exquisitely embroidered, that looked as if they might have been worn at court by Chinese Mandarins. We used to dress up in these and swagger about, tripping on the long hems, shoes flapping on our feet, reciting fragments of Mandarin, pretending to be very important. John was quite different from the bomb-site boys in Malta. He had been to prep school and was controlled and courteous, polished and clever, with not a trace of vanity. It was a new experience to be treated with the respect he showed me.

I was looking forward to starting at my boarding school, as soon as the long list of complicated uniform had been bought and packed. All compulsory items had to be ordered from Harrods and Daniel Neal in London, which had been a shock for Muz who was scandalised at the prices. 'Two pounds for a hat; what kind of hat can that possibly be? And two different styles of Sunday dresses – no one needs more than one best dress.' She went on, 'Half a dozen Viyella blouses and the same number of square-neck poplin blouses. How can any child need so many blouses, and what for?'

Fa was consulted on how savings could be made, as if our family were paupers while driving around post-war England in the big shiny Jag. Substitutions for items on the list like black gym shoes were easily found.

'Wendy has a pair of white plimsolls already, that ought to be enough,' he said.

'What about the black ones for gym, which it says on the list?' I asked warily.

Muz put in, 'You can wear your white plimsolls for gym as well as games. No one needs two pairs of plimsolls. I've never heard of such things as black ones.'

'I don't think they will want outdoor games shoes coming indoors for gym, probably,' I suggested.

'Lots of parents won't be able to afford two pairs. You won't be the only one, you'll see.'

When it came to it, inevitably, I was the only one. Everyone else had neat black gym shoes with elasticated tops and soft soles for the flexibility required when jumping over the vaulting horse and doing floor exercises.

It was not just the shoes: other economies were invented, causing me to be ridiculed from day one, while Muz and Fa congratulated themselves on the money saved. Worst of all was the ignominy of my dressing gown. All the other girls had fluffy Ladybird dressing gowns bought from Daniel Neal. Unfortunately for me, other styles were allowed and Muz seized on this cost-saving opportunity. She excelled this time, as she managed to produce from one of the Malta boxes a pair of old dining-room curtains that she considered ideal for the purpose. They were heavy linen, now faded and worn, printed with a pattern of giant purple tulips. Muz had been very attached to these curtains, which she had picked up second-hand for our first home in Malta, and now they had come with us in case they might be useful. She was delighted with her brainwave, and out came the Singer with scissors and pinking shears, so that in no time I had something long, misshapen, heavy and hideous enough to have been copied from a Hogarth print.

Home-made knickers were usually her standard line, as even she disapproved of second-hand knickers. 'Easily run up,' she used to say, heaving out the Singer with its wooden handle that we were allowed to turn for her. We enjoyed doing this, watching the needle rattling up and down with a line of stitches appearing faster than you could blink. What was not so enjoyable was the end product, as Muz did not believe in gussets. This refinement would use up extra material and was a more complicated sewing procedure. So the knickers were pinched in the crutch area, making them eye-wateringly tight. This was relieved, I discovered, by undoing a few inches of stitching in a vital part, leaving a gap that was draughty but practical.

While this solved the problem of the torturing knickers, it was a different matter when it came to shorts worn for games and athletics at school, as well as, most excruciating of all, school sports day. Muz made shorts using the same knicker pattern for all of us, including Andrew, for sports days that Ros and I still remember with a shudder. I had inherited Fa's grasshopper legs and was a good hurdler and long jumper, but the home-made shorts acted as a vice on any vigorous lower-limb extension, and looked very strange gathered up in the middle. We limped around, gazing enviously at other children with normal shorts. This was bad enough for us three girls, but for Andrew it was a disaster as we watched him, shy and nervous at the best of times, walking painfully with bandy legs, trying to ease the misery of the groin-pinching, ball-strangling shorts.

Despite these misgivings, as my school trunk was packed with snappy new items in school colours of lavender blue, I was excited about starting school again. This time with proper teachers instead of nuns and, best of all, the school had a swimming pool. I was a strong swimmer after daily swims in the harbour at Marsamxett with Fa. I had a bronze badge for life-saving and I could swim confidently underwater, often having to untangle ropes that had snagged under the hull of *Merlin*, all slimy and slippery. It was a tricky job down in the dark water, holding my breath, Fa on the quay shouting, 'Get a move on, for goodness sake, we haven't got all day to fiddle about.'

Collecting the requirements for school took so long that the summer term had already started when we drove up to the junior house. Eleven was the age for entry into the first form and I would be twelve later that year in 1950. I was impressed by the imposing buildings and surroundings of the school, which stood in a hundred acres of wooded grounds in a very rural part of Sussex and looked ravishing.

Popular books of the time about girls' boarding schools in England were all about jolly times, having midnight feasts, rollicking games of hockey, nature rambles with a gang of good friends and fun in the chemistry lab with Bunsen burners. No hint had come from Fa and Muz that the school was run on principles of extreme religious conformity, enforced by what I discovered was a tight core of zealots who pounced on any girl who didn't instantly fit in. My parents, while on the one hand firmly committed to their own interpretation of Christian values, also regularly behaved with no regard for conformity, in many cases rejecting any notion of compliance.

Fa could certainly have been described as an unruly free spirit, frequently taking outrageous liberties and being quite shameless about it.

Just as I had met Barbara Tullett within minutes of arriving at Partridge Green village school, becoming lifelong friends with her, my first day at this new school provided another lifelong friend, Verity. Without her I could not have survived the alien desert of bleak dormitories, meals taken in silence and baths just once a week. Every tiny detail of life was subject to inflexible rules and inspections as I found myself trying to navigate a way through this hostile territory. I had never encountered seriously nasty girls of my own age before, but here in this Christian school there seemed to be a posse of them, led by a tall, sharp-faced girl who practised subtle humiliations such as forcing juniors like me to stand in a line stripped to our knickers in the dormitory, while she inspected our buds of breasts to see whose was the smallest. Whoever was unfortunate enough to be the least developed was then subjected to scorn for being backward. This bullying girl, from a revered evangelical family, was very much the housemistress's pet and enforcer, so had licence to use and abuse her powers.

Fa and Muz had been very pleased to find a Protestant Christian school, assuming it would provide a nurturing environment; but for me it felt like a penitentiary, in which I was incarcerated, and decided my best course was to be like Brer Rabbit, lying low and saying nothing. Apart from Verity, I had allies in two Siamese girls who were floundering like me, mystified by rules of behaviour far removed from anything we had known before. They were Buddhist and kept this secret for fear of pressure to convert, telling me, 'We could never become Christians like these girls here, they are so cruel.' Forty years later, meeting at a school reunion the girl who had practised such miseries on us, I was curious to see if she had softened, and greeted her with a smile, which she returned with the same cold eyes that had drilled fear into me all those years before.

Meanwhile life at Rookley trundled on, with Elaine, Andrew and Ros starting at a day school, where they all thrived. Fa had returned to Malta and Muz was left coping and driving the Jaguar, which she viewed nervously as a big beast that might at any moment break free of her grip on the steering wheel and run amok among the traffic. When I went home for the holidays I noticed how forlorn she had become; having lost weight, she seemed unaccountably adrift and preoccupied, but rallied herself for the busy season of Rookley cricket, garden parties and musical events in Tunbridge Wells.

Fa's absence was not seen as anything out of the ordinary. It was quite usual for husbands to work abroad while families stayed in England for the sake of children's education, or children were left in boarding schools with both parents abroad. Missionary children at my school often didn't see their parents for several years at a time, depending on the standard length of tour for overseas missions.

It was during the autumn term, after I had gone back to school, that a major alert was flagged up at home. Joyce Ryde, the matron at King George the Fifth Hospital, wrote to Muz saying she must return to Malta at once if she wanted to save her marriage, as Fa and Babs were involved with each other and this was causing a scandal that Muz needed to go and deal with. Muz was galvanised by this message and, with help from neighbours, farmed out the three younger children and got on a plane to Malta, dreading what she might face on arrival.

When Muz arrived at Fa's flat in the hospital, exhausted and weak with anxiety, she found Babs installed there in high spirits, presiding over a welcome party. All Muz wanted was to rest and be left alone with Fa, but Babs took command, determined to use the occasion to give an appearance that they were all the best of friends, with Muz over there for a holiday that all three of them had planned together.

Fa, inexplicably, seemed powerless to resist this chicanery, allowing himself to be swept along and, shockingly for Muz, giving every indication of being hopelessly infatuated with Babs. It was all too much and Muz, who was already debilitated with worry, became ill with nervous exhaustion and a fever that came on suddenly, provoked no doubt by her frail physical state. She went to bed, refusing to see anyone. This didn't stop Babs, who had free run of the flat and breezed into the bedroom at all times of the day, chattering on about how lovely it was to have a friendship embracing all three of them. Under this barrage, Muz began to think she was losing her mind and maybe Fa and Babs were the sane ones. She made an effort to get herself together and reassemble her thoughts to find a way through the maze of emotions.

Seeing Muz slightly revived, Fa suggested taking a picnic and going for a sail in *Merlin*. It would refresh them both and give them time to clear their minds. Muz was not a good sailor – being a non-swimmer she had a fear of the sea and small boats. But the chance to escape out into the fresh air with Fa persuaded her, and they set off for Marsamxett harbour where *Merlin* was moored. Fa was very solicitous, helping Muz into the dinghy, and she began to feel a weight easing from her mind as he prepared to cast off, with a light breeze lifting her spirits.

Something was holding him back as he paused with the mooring rope in his hand, and when Muz looked up she saw that a car had stopped on the quay, and the next moment to her intense dismay, there was Babs, breathlessly jumping out and waving to them.

'Just in time!' she shouted as she ran across. 'Just in time. I got held up, but I knew you wouldn't go without me.'

Muz was incredulous and so dumb with shock she couldn't speak. She was also scared because the boat was too small for three people and, as Babs tumbled in, it rocked from side to side precariously. Babs and Fa laughed at the wobbles and took what she assumed were their customary places in the boat as the sails filled and they surged forward. Muz found her voice and said, 'I hope we're not going out of the harbour.' The Malta Yacht Club had already closed for the winter, which she knew was for good reason. The Mediterranean could be fickle at the best of times, but in winter was unsafe for small boats.

'No point footling about inside,' said Fa brightly. 'We'll just poke our noses out to get a bit more wind.'

Muz felt sick with dread and premonition. The boat was already low in the water with three of them on board, and as they wallowed out of the harbour entrance the wind caught them with a sudden powerful gust, heeling the boat over so waves slopped in and water rose around their feet. Fa put Babs in charge of the sails while he steered, and Muz was put to baling, which got more frantic as water poured in. She was leaning out to throw yet another scoop over the side when Fa shouted, 'Ready about,' as the boat changed tack. The boom swung across and hit Muz hard, pitching her forward, and she felt herself being swept overboard as a wave smacked into the side of the boat, momentarily engulfing her. In that second, seized with fear and fury, she determined not to let herself be drowned and somehow, with hands and fingers stiff from cold, she clawed herself back in and collapsed into the bow, soaked and stunned.

To the end of her life she maintained the sailing trip had been planned to 'dispatch' her, as she put it, making it look like an accident, but it is impossible that Babs and Fa could plan anything so extreme and demonstrates the extent of Muz' fevered emotional state that she would think this. Fa was remorseful afterwards, wanting to make amends, while Babs tried to laugh it off, but Muz would have none of it and as soon as she felt well enough she flew back to England.

Life continued at Rookley as if nothing had happened and holidays were full of social events, while in term time I was concentrating on trying to survive at school. The new year of 1951 arrived with Rookley's famous paper chase, known as the Rookley Hunt, when large numbers of people were invited to join this annual sport. It started with hot punch distributed to everyone out in the driveway, while the 'foxes' set off, laying a paper trail. The rest of us were the hounds. We were held back, milling about for half an hour to give the foxes a fair start until, on a whistle blast and fortified with punch, we raced off, following the trail for miles through woods and over hills and fields, even taking to rowing boats one year to cross a lake. Hours later, the first two hounds arriving back at Rookley after completing the course got prizes and, as they were the first ones to return, they had the advantage of diving into mounds of hot sausage rolls and mince pies served with steaming mugs of soup, while the last hounds were left with crumbs and scraps.

Later in the year, when I came home for the summer holidays, there was a new buzz in the household with news that Fa was arriving back any moment. The full story of what happened in Malta after Muz left so miserably those several months before was never disclosed, but it seems likely that the scandal resulted in both Fa and Babs deciding to leave, or being asked to leave the hospital, although the official version is that Fa's contract had come to an end. The Babs affair having come to an end as well, we assumed.

The excitement of seeing Fa again made us all dizzy and a bit crazy. After such a long absence, everyone wanted to sit on his knee to be hugged and kissed and reassured that he really was home for good. Being kissed by him was not an entire pleasure for me, as his moustache was prickly and his lips grainy and cool like a dog's nose, which I disliked as I got older and more critical. Others might have thrilled to the sensation, but not me. However, I allowed him to kiss me as I knew the sentiment was genuine and he really did love me and was not shy about showing it.

Fa's homecoming was the best surprise we could have had in that difficult year, but hardly had we adjusted our minds to having him back with us than there was an even bigger surprise. He announced that he had a new job, starting shortly, and the new job was in Kenya. There would be no time for me to return to school, he said, almost apologetically, unaware of the intense relief I felt at being spared another term at the dreaded school.

Possessions were gathered up and flung out in the usual indiscriminate way, but I held onto my stamp albums and no one objected this time. The Jaguar was sold, and one very dark early morning in October a taxi arrived to take us to Tunbridge Wells station for the train to London.

We were to catch a morning flight from London Airport, setting off for Nairobi on the latest airliner. This was a Lockheed Constellation with a streamlined fuselage, four propellers and three distinctive tail fins – but no pressurisation, the effects of which soon became apparent as we headed off, flying south-east towards Africa.

CHAPTER 6

The Constellation flight to Nairobi was not the glamorous experience expected on first sight of this new airliner, all silvery and gleaming as we climbed up the steps. As my only previous flights had been a night-time dash over mountains from China to Burma, then Burma to India escaping the Japanese, neither experiences were particularly encouraging advertisements for flying trips, so I was looking forward to this new peacetime one.

The Dakotas had not been pressurised and neither was the Constellation, so on each occasion I was in trouble with my own internal ear-related air-pressure system failing to adjust as the aircraft gained height; it felt as if my eardrums were bursting, which was an extreme form of agony. In addition, perhaps related to the ear problem, I became airsick as well. I remembered feeling like this on the Dakotas but thought, surely, in this latest modern Super Constellation, such miseries could not happen again. None of the others succumbed. I envied them and started agitating that it might indicate some kind of personal weakness that I was failing to overcome, so it was a relief when we descended to refuel at Tel Aviv, where we were able to get out and walk around. To us, as a Christian family, this brief landing had its own significance as we set foot in the Holy Land where Jesus himself had lived and walked. The shapes and colours of hills and dry landscape had changed little, we imagined, through all these centuries, so we were seeing them much as Jesus would have done nearly two thousand years before, and this was deeply affecting for all of us.

After Tel Aviv we flew south towards Cairo, setting course as the great waterway of the Nile opened up like a smudged green living map several thousand feet below – which seemed very convenient as we followed it all the way to Khartoum. The absence of pressurisation meant that our flight was restricted to an altitude providing enough oxygen to keep us bright-eyed and conscious, while having the added benefit of being low enough to enjoy superb views of the river and surrounding desert spreading out into the immensity of Africa. Such detailed views from the air with identifiable land features clearly visible are denied to modern air passengers flying in the jet stream; a great loss for them as they will never know what they are missing.

Andrew was euphoric about flying for the first time; it was a particular thrill for him, due to his interest in all things celestial. While showing little interest in school subjects, he immersed himself in books about planets and galaxies, the moon, sun and stars, quoting stats and facts on these to anyone who would listen. Now, sitting in his seat high up in the sky, he was staring intently out of the window for anything that could be spotted beyond the clouds, including UFOs, which were one of his passions. Public interest in UFOs had been sparked by random sightings and books were being written in an authoritative tone about these and alien landings. It was a type of science fiction but with a frisson of possibility that stirred the imagination of children like us, eager for a sight of any extra-terrestrial activity.

Andrew turned round urgently to where I was sitting rigid with nausea. 'Wendy, listen. Please listen. Quick, go over to the other side and see if there are any UFOs coming up over there. Go on.'

I was clutching my sick bag, scared to move in case it brought on another wave of queasiness. Fa was sitting behind us, deaf to any interruption, reading his *British Medical Journal*, while Muz carried on calmly with her knitting. She took this everywhere with her in a large linen bag embroidered with gaudy flowers, its wooden handles looped over her arm; the bag was an everyday part of her life. Next to her, Elaine was reading a *Heidi* book to Ros, and no one was in a mood to be looking out for UFOs, so Andrew was left as chief spotter, excitedly squeaking updates.

It was a long flight with several stops for refuelling, and when we finally landed at Nairobi, we emerged into a different world as the hot burnt colours of this immense graphic landscape with its great mountains and scorched plains came into focus. There was a smell of dust and wood-smoke, baked earth and dry grass, scents that, combined in a bottle, I would have sniffed every day of my life from then on; like smelling salts, instantly reviving any flagging spirits.

Instead of the usual missionary reception waiting for us at foreign destinations, this time we were met by what seemed to me a very exotic couple who were clearly not missionaries. They were called Tilly and Maurice Williamson. Tilly was dark and statuesque, with glowing skin and waves of raven hair that tumbled to her shoulders. Maurice was dark too, but more reserved and formal in his manner. They had been sent to meet us by Fa's new partner, Dick Johnson, an Australian surgeon who had set up practice eighty miles north of Nairobi in the small Rift Valley town of Nakuru, after war service as an army doctor. He had advertised in the *British Medical Journal* for a partner and Fa, sensing adventure far away in Africa, had applied for the post and been accepted.

Maurice was a dentist, with a dental surgery alongside the medical practice that Fa was joining. This was convenient for patients, who were able to get their teeth and other body problems fixed at the same time, in the one suite of rooms that occupied a whole floor above Karimbux grocery store on the main street. These consulting rooms were presided over by Betty Blackler, a qualified nurse and capable manager of both the office and nursing side of the practice.

Maurice and Tilly, we discovered, were Jewish and were survivors from a concentration camp. Their lives had been spared as Maurice's dental skills were deemed useful by the Nazis. They had two daughters, Ruth and Naomi, who survived the camp with them, and all four of them had emigrated to Kenya as soon as the war was over.

As we became accustomed to life in Nakuru and began to make new friends, we met several other concentration camp survivors who had settled there. One of them was a young woman I remember in particular as her story was so horrifying. I met her when she and I were helping to serve teas at a church social. It was a hot day, but she was wearing long sleeves, unusual in that temperature, especially as we were confined to a small kitchen, boiling kettles and filling tea pots. After a while she remarked how steamy it was and, rolling up her sleeves, I noticed a long number tattooed on her forearm. She saw me looking at it and explained that it was her camp number; then, without any embarrassment, she went on to tell me what had happened to her.

She had been sixteen when she was deported to one of the Nazi death camps where, on account of her age and being pretty, instead of being sent to the gas chambers she was sent to a medical experimentation unit. For the five years that she was a prisoner there, she was part of a group of young girls subjected to abortion experiments. The girls would be made pregnant by German soldiers – in the process, presumably, providing a useful service for them – then at various stages of their pregnancies different methods of surgical or medical abortion would be tried out on them, in the interests of German medical science.

She said she was one of the lucky ones as she was still alive when British forces rescued the camp inmates. Many girls had died of injuries or septic abortion in the course of the experiments. She had come to Nakuru with other camp survivors and had recently married, but was worried she would never be able to have children after what had been done to her. Fa was her doctor she told me, and had been very reassuring in his support and advice which, she said, gave her new confidence and hope. I heard later that she had succeeded in having a normal pregnancy and a healthy baby, which was a happy outcome after enduring such horrors.

This was before the new Jewish state of Israel became established after the war, and many displaced Jewish people then went to live in what they regarded as their historic homeland. Before the creation of Israel, while that region was still Palestine, there had been a suggestion from the British government to provide a substantial area of fertile land in the highlands of Kenya for Jewish settlement. The land was inspected and considered by a delegation of Jewish leaders, but was rejected, as it could never fulfil their aspirations for returning to what they saw as their own promised land, promised to them by God.

The Great Rift Valley can be seen from space, stretching all the way from Egypt to central Africa, marking its route through Kenya with a series of lakes and volcanoes that define this massive geographical fault, carving a wide furrow from north to south. The small agricultural town of Nakuru lies in a serene pocket of the valley at the foot of a high and sprawling dormant volcano called Menengai, its crater the second largest in the world. Beyond the town, Menengai's lower slopes flatten out to a wide basin holding the supremely beautiful Lake Nakuru. Shallow and shining like a mirror, it is populated by millions of flamingos crowding the fringes, so these look pink from a distance while the blue water reflects images of purple mountains rising up behind. This was our new home.

Tilly and Maurice had found a house for us to rent on the outskirts of the town, where residential plots had spacious grounds of five or ten acres. The house was a bungalow in the style of most colonial houses at that time, built of grey stone with a green corrugated-iron roof and a long veranda in front with rooms leading off, so doors could be left open to catch any breeze in hot weather.

There were no concerns about security, but open doors were inviting for snakes and other wildlife to come inside where it was shady and cool. As time went on, I found that snakes under the bed could be encouraged to leave with a broom, brushing them warily towards the door, squinting through my eyelashes in case the black ones turned out to be spitting cobras. I did meet one of these long black snakes later on when it was lying along a windowsill basking in evening sunshine as I went to close the window. It was so motionless I hadn't spotted it, and in a flash it reared up with its hood spread threateningly, tiny black eyes glittering, but instead of spitting or striking, it streaked out of the window into the flowerbed below.

The driveway to our house had been planted long ago with an avenue of pepper trees, their delicate leaves like ferns with long lacy fronds forming a canopy overhead through which sunlight glinted, making patterns on the dirt road underneath. In front of the house was a large open field of lumpy, dry grass referred to as a lawn, diligently mowed by one of the gardeners with a push-mower for hours under the baking sun, making very little difference to its appearance except where patches of bare earth were churned up by the rusty blades. At the back of the house was an even bigger field, divided by chicken wire into runs with old hen houses the size of small sheds, immediately commandeered by Elaine and me for dens where later we would hang out with friends and spy on each other.

Staff had been taken on by Tilly and Maurice to prepare the house and garden for us, and were lined up in their uniforms ready to be introduced when we arrived. There was Alfredo the houseboy, in his long white *kanzu*, an Arab-style gown high at the neck and low at the feet (which were bare), a red fez with a black tassel on his head and, for special occasions, a green cummerbund. Head of household was the cook, Otieno, who wore an enormous khaki apron and a gap-toothed smile as he led the way to the kitchen, eager to show us a couple of steaming loaves just out of the oven, ready to put on the table for lunch with a stew and vegetables. The kitchen was not in any way like an English kitchen and looked disturbingly primitive. Its main feature was a cooker called a Dover stove that squatted at one end like a small, black cast-iron rhino huffing to itself as spouts of smoke rose from the firebox, adding to the general smokiness and grime of the interior. I could see Muz looking dubious. There was a hot water supply to the sink, draining into a bucket underneath. We were registering all this without saying a word, while hungrily sniffing the bread and stew smells. Meanwhile, Alfredo was unloading the car and taking suitcases into bedrooms, when I realised these must be inspected so that Elaine and I could grab ours before Andrew and Ros got there.

All African domestic workers, whether employed indoors or outdoors, were called 'boys' if male, regardless of age. Fa and Muz were addressed as 'Bwana' and 'Memsahib', as were all adult Europeans, and deference was expected at all times. Very few African labourers or manual workers spoke any English and most were illiterate. Their lowly state in the eyes of settlers seemed to justify their being treated with a lack of courtesy that appeared to me deplorable and frequently abusive, but these workers remained unfailingly tolerant and cheerful in the face of this disrespect, accepting their place in the social order and being grateful for paid employment that generally included housing and rations.

The main street of Nakuru was lined with shops all hugger-mugger, mostly owned by Indians, who were very efficient businessmen, keeping stocks high and overheads low by employing their families. Always courteous, they were a mainstay of commerce in urban and rural communities. They also kept the railways running efficiently, with expertise learnt in India. Many railway employees were drawn from the Sikh community who were also skilled artisans working as mechanics and joiners. Fa quickly built up a following among these communities, who spoke languages that were familiar to him during our time in India. He had a very high regard for Indian people, admiring their cultures and character.

All schools, hospitals, sports clubs and even some churches were segregated into separate facilities for Africans, Indians and Europeans, which was considered normal and sensible by the colonial administrators of the time. There was a small cottage hospital in Nakuru for Europeans and a big general hospital for other races, always busy and crowded, but it made no difference to Fa, who was happy to work wherever he was needed.

All four of us children were enrolled at Nakuru School, which had several hundred boarders drawn from around the country, while we were lucky to live close enough to go daily. The teaching was of a high order with many teachers recruited from England, but the health and welfare of pupils was a very secondary consideration. When Fa later became school doctor, he was shocked at conditions in the sick bay and standards of care generally. It was one of those schools where surviving the harsh environment might have been thought a main concern for pupils, with lessons less of a priority. Every morning, on arrival, we stood lined up for inspection against the wall outside our classrooms, with a clean handkerchief held in outstretched hands. Teachers came along the line inspecting our nails, hands and handkerchiefs, to make sure all were clean. Anyone who did not pass the inspection was sent to wait outside the headmaster's office.

The headmaster had a size 12 tennis shoe called a 'tackie' displayed on his desk like an executioner's axe, and at any time of the day there would be miscreants lined up outside his office waiting to be beaten with the tackie. The office was next to my classroom so I would have to pass these shrinking victims, some of them quite small children, many of them weeping and terrified, as I walked to class trying not to hear shrieks coming from inside the office. I was thirteen by now and had learnt how to avoid such humiliations myself. But there was a different kind of humiliation waiting as I was to take the KPE (Kenya Preliminary Exam) in my first term and the curriculum at my Sussex school had not included all the subjects required for this. One of these was Latin and I asked to be excused the paper as I knew no Latin at all, apart from Fa's often-quoted mottoes. The authorities were willing to allow me an exemption, but Fa in his high-handed way refused to let me off, insisting that I must attempt it.

'Latin is a noble language, following laws of logic,' he pontificated. 'All you need to do is learn the basics and the rest will be obvious.'

It wasn't obvious at all when I sat in the examination hall with the blank paper in front of me, as none of the questions bore any relation to the 'basics' glibly referred to by Fa. I wondered about writing an essay in English on the absurdity of the situation I found myself in, just to pass the time, but decided if the Latin experts marking the papers had the same intransigent mentality as Fa, this would be pointless. Adults always won somehow.

KPE was the entrance exam for secondary school in Nairobi, which I needed to go to without delay as I was already old for my class. Due to Fa's insistence on me taking the Latin paper (with consequent zero marks), my overall score, despite being high in other subjects, caused me to fail KPE, so I had to stay on at Nakuru for another year.

Andrew was completely adrift at this school, which had no tolerance of children like him, who consequently sank to the bottom of the class, unable to cope with the demands and stresses of that uncouth regime. He was sensitive, artistic and highly observant, with a phenomenal memory for facts and figures relating to obscure areas of science, which, unfortunately for him, had little relevance to normal school subjects or normal, regular conversation. He seemed to view life from a different perspective to most other people and would come out with startling statements that were perfectly valid and plausible, but were usually dismissed as stupidity. His intelligence and aptitude in niche areas of knowledge were thought weird and valueless because they did not fit the norm for children of his age.

Autism was known about then but thought of as a mental defect, with that generalised label applied to children like Andrew. Fa, who was such a clever and sympathetic clinician whenever a young patient was brought to him with educational problems, seemed completely unable to extend the same understanding and assistance to his son, and, worst of all, made it clear that he regarded Andrew as a failure and a parasite on the family. He actually used the word 'parasite' as a name for Andrew, which shocked Muz and the rest of us, as it was intolerably cruel and also untrue. All

Andrew wanted was to please his father, and he continued to make heroic efforts to do so. Enid Grant, one of the nurses who had been in Malta with us and was now in Kenya, where her parents lived, remarked at this time on Andrew's forlorn state, saying: 'Andrew is not mentally defective. All he needs for a successful, happy life is to be listened to, and loved.'

Fa's solution was to send Andrew off to Kenton prep school in Nairobi that would 'make or break him'. The outcome was entirely predictable, and he was sent home within days, having refused even to get out of bed in the mornings, being scared witless by what to him was an indecipherable environment. The next solution was to send him to a farm in a remote forested area called Bahati, some way from Nakuru. There, the farmer's wife Mrs Green, who was an ex-teacher, looked after him during term time, as very gently and patiently she started to teach him and bring out his confidence. He thrived in the calm orderliness of her household, with good food and kindness, but it was lonely for him on that isolated farm with no other children, and he missed Ros, who was his friend and playmate.

Meanwhile, at home, Fa was very much enjoying his new job and partnership with Dick Johnson. They were ideal partners, each a specialist in his own field. Neither of them had any interest in money or prestige: they were only interested in making people well. Patients came from far and wide to the Nakuru consulting rooms and the practice grew so fast that an assistant had to be recruited from England within the year. This was Arthur (Bunny) Griffiths, who was an obstetrician and gynaecologist, relieving Fa of maternity work involving night calls and time-consuming pre-natal and post-natal checks. Bunny was a young and excellent clinician with new skills that were extremely useful. He had been trained in procedures such as Ventouse delivery, using a suction cap applied to the baby's head instead of forceps, which was safer and less traumatic for both mothers and babies.

Bunny's brilliance, however, was overshadowed by a problem. We soon discovered that he could not be relied on to be sober all of the time. This was an unexpected blow, and the search began for a teetotal obstetrician to help out. Dr Geoffrey Bird, who was a member of the Moral Re-Armament movement that had strict puritanical rules forbidding alcohol, became the new assistant and turned out to be a very capable practitioner. Entirely reliable, he went on to be much in demand. Unfortunately, this caused another kind of problem, as his popularity led to him setting up his own practice in competition with Fa and Dick, taking most of their maternity patients with him. This went against normal ethics and was a surprising move for someone with such high principles. The rival practice caused much loss to Fa and Dick, as well as causing strained relationships, since Bunny was sometimes too unsteady to attend to his patients, they went to Dr Bird instead.

A decade or so later it was Dr Bird who saved the life of Louise – and probably me as well – when he was called in by Fa to take charge of her birth which had developed complications, while Bunny, who was my doctor, had gone off to have another drink and failed to return.

The Nakuru doctors' practice extended over a huge area, and at weekends Fa would set off to do house calls as far away as eighty miles in any direction, staying overnight with patients who were always glad to give him hospitality in return for a personal visit. Often these visits would be to patients who could not afford the petrol to drive all the way to Nakuru, let alone doctor's fees, and they would not be charged anything. Fa was grateful for the experience of visiting these remote farms with the adventurous journeys involved, often on roads that were no more than tracks deep in mud, or part washed away, with rickety bridges spanning raging torrents; the more challenging the better from his point of view.

Our car was a basic Morris Minor and this provided various mechanical challenges in addition to the fiendish road conditions, needing only one big puddle to splash up into the engine for it to cough and die, which it frequently did. Morris Minors were ubiquitous in Kenya, very stout-hearted but limited in performance and internal space. When our whole family went out together in the car, it was an itchy squeeze being pushed up against each other in the back, and we all had to get out to reduce the load whenever there was a steep hill – often having to push the car up as well.

I used to be taken along as Fa's assistant on his farm visits, to open gates, help dig the car out when it got stuck, guide him over makeshift bridges or just keep him company on the long drives. He also liked me to act as a sort of therapy for elderly patients, chatting to them and cheering them up if they were lonely, as many were who lived alone on remote farms. Some of these old settlers existed in considerable poverty, striving to keep up standards, with dinner served at eight by arthritic servants in threadbare uniforms, family silver polished up for the occasion and laid imposingly with starched napkins and the best food that could be found. All this was spread out for us while we sat under rotting thatch on antique chairs humming with white ants eating away at the legs, mud floors at our feet and mists of insects batting at the candle flames or falling in the soup. Electricity had not extended to these outer fringes and lighting would come from Tilley lamps hissing with a soft glow, which now produce instant nostalgia for me whenever I hear that soothing sound again. This happens rarely since camping-gas lamps have replaced the familiar Tilleys with those evening rituals of wick trimming and topping up the glass reservoir with paraffin.

Many young families struggled on small, uneconomic farms far from main roads or amenities. The image of Kenya as a haven for hedonists was a popular distortion served up to feed those with an appetite for scandal and intrigue, as those English aristocrats who lived indulgent lives occupied a negligible section of society. Most people lived frugally and worked hard to coax an income from their farms or businesses. The European population of Kenya at this time was about 100,000, spread out through the country on farms or in colonial administrative positions such as the Kenya Police, District Officers, District or Provincial Commissioners, with the Governor at the top living in style in Government House in Nairobi.

Among the African population of about six million, representing twenty-six different tribes or sub-groups, very few were sufficiently well educated to hold professional or office jobs, so that most, if not employed in manual or menial labour, were living traditional lives in tribal areas. It was a generally held opinion among those in government – and most of the white community – that everyone was happy with this *status quo*, and political dissent was dismissed as insubordination and quickly suppressed. It was easy to feel unconcerned and carefree with a relaxed lifestyle in the congenial climate of the Kenya highlands, with sunshine every day and all the joys of an outdoor life. But even at this stage, while we were calmly settling into our new life and Muz was making curtains again (just as she had been doing ten years before on the eve of Pearl Harbour), hidden away deep in the forests, Dedan Kimathi was preparing his ferocious gangs of fighters for the terror of Mau Mau.

This struck shockingly and cruelly without any warning on an otherwise normal day in 1952, when Fa and Dick Johnson were called urgently to the hospital to perform life-saving surgery on a woman doctor who had been savagely attacked by a gang on her Kinangop farm. This was Dr Dorothy Meiklejohn, who was the first of many such victims ambushed in their own homes, often by Kikuyu members of their staff who had taken the Mau Mau oath. Fa would return exhausted at the end of these operating sessions, his clothes and skin saturated with the smell of ether that was the anaesthetic they used then. It was the beginning of the rebellion that slowly brought an end to colonial rule. Various security measures were announced for Nakuru, but the main thrust of the bush war remained confined to high-altitude forested areas to the north, far away from us, so the normal routines of life in our household continued much as before – at least for a while.

During this lull, on one of Fa's weekend visits to patients we went to see Dick and Miranda Parbury at Kitale, a long drive on dirt roads and tracks. When we arrived at the farmhouse, Fa was given the only spare room, while a camp bed was made up for me in the office, which was a mud hut. Before going to bed, Dick explained to me that snakes and other creatures liked to retreat at night to the warm thatch overhead, baked by the sun all day, and I must not be alarmed to hear rustlings as they burrowed into the straw roof above my bed. I had a torch and when I heard the first rustling I was in a dilemma whether to switch on and see if it was a snake, how big it was and what kind, or just lie there, hoping it would not fall out of the thatch on top of me. Bits of old straw and disturbed insects came drifting down as more scuffling activity went on overhead, and I understood now why Africans cover themselves completely with a blanket over their heads at night when they are sleeping in their huts.

Nearer to home was a farm called Long Acres on the Njoro road, where I used to go for early-morning rides with the farmer's children, Martin and Merriel. The family were patients of Fa and were the most charming, hospitable people, not well off but generous and warm-hearted. This was the Molony family, and tragically their mother Evelyn was dying of cancer. This affected Fa very deeply as he had been the one to make the diagnosis and break it to the family; with no surgery or treatment available that could save her. I remember going to see her in Nakuru Hospital, thinking how beautiful she was, like a Rossetti figure, with long chestnut hair braided in a thick plait. It was hard to take in how such a vibrant, vital person could be struck down in the prime of life, leaving a family who needed and depended on her. Desmond, her husband, was a gentle, reserved man, while Evelyn, one felt, was the matrix that held the family together. The early morning rides were a form of solace for me, and Martin and Merriel. I would arrive at 6.30, when the small Somali ponies were already saddled up, and we would ride off across the bush in the crisp sparkling air with dew shimmering like crystal on every leaf and blade of grass; going fast up Ngata hill and alongside the railway line for a mile or two, then crossing back and following the Njoro river as it flowed through the farm. We'd be back in time for breakfast, which was always maize-meal porridge and bright yellow scrambled eggs, with lots of toast that had been browned on a fork held by the cook against the open fire of the Dover stove, so it was smoky and crunchy, sometimes with a light dusting of ash – unforgettable.

How startled I would have been then to think that in twelve years' time I would find myself living on the next farm downriver from Long Acres; its land spreading all the way to the Nakuru municipal boundary. The river flowed down through these farms to join the lake, where hippos had wallowing pools at the river mouth, sometimes trekking upriver to graze on crops along the banks. This was not popular and hippo hunts became a part of farm life. It was illegal to shoot them, but we had great sport shooing them off with thunder flashes filched from army surplus supplies.

One of the farms further upriver towards Njoro was Nellie Grant's, where she lived in a weather-worn, shingled house smothered in creepers, its windows peering through cloudy panes shrouded by the dense growth. Nellie was one of Fa's patients often visited by him at weekends, and I would go along anticipating her legendary teas when fine china was produced with cakes and sandwiches. Nellie was Elspeth Huxley's mother and one of the original pioneers who had come out from England, leaving behind gracious lives of comfort in large country houses for the challenge of new lives in a wild land, carving out recalcitrant farms from raw bush and forest.

On the banks of the river, where it flowed through Nellie's farm, were small caves of prehistoric antiquity that she was eager to explore; her thirst for finding out about things was insatiable. Seized with curiosity, she wanted to delve further into the caves' dank interiors to see if anything had been left behind that might indicate human occupation during stages of evolution when ancient tribes lived close to water. She wanted to look for any archaeological fragments that might be of interest, but the caves were too narrow and small for her to enter. She had many enthusiasms and extraordinary energy for someone her age (she must have been more than seventy), and was always engaged in some new project. The caves had tunnels that led to other caves still waiting to be explored and Nellie, observing how thin I was, hit on a plan to send me down the tunnels, like a ferret, to retrieve anything interesting that might be there. We set off one afternoon with torches, some lengths of coarse sisal rope, and a bag to put any discoveries into.

The previous inhabitants of the caves must have been pygmies, as I had to fold myself up with some difficulty and reluctance to be able to get into the cave Nellie indicated. Locating the narrow tunnel at its rear, with the torch and bag held out in front, I flattened myself to squeeze inside, feeling like Alice but without the White Rabbit as a guide. Nellie's voice came eerily from somewhere behind me. 'Keep still a moment. Don't worry. I'm tying bits of rope to your feet to pull you out if you get stuck.'

Unsure how reassuring this was, I inched forward gingerly on my elbows. The earth walls of the tunnel were strangely cool and smooth and I could see traces of animal hair caught in small cracks, while whiffs of mammal smell hung in the static air. It was a primal smell of the sort that might suggest a leopard's den somewhere in the depths of the tunnel. I would be in a bit of a fix, I thought, if confronted by a leopard hurtling towards me in the torch beam. At least there were no slithering signs of snakes I noted nervously with my face at ground level, but lack of air in that confined space became the most obvious problem as my breath started coming in short gasps. No fragments such as Nellie had described were visible, or likely to turn up as far as I could see. I decided to start edging backwards and then noticed what looked like some small pieces of rubble pressed against the wall on one side. Without pausing to see what they were, I scraped them roughly into the bag and backtracked as fast as I could, enormously relieved when my head at last popped back into the cave and I could breathe more easily again.

Nellie was very pleased with the scraps of rubble, which she was going to wash and inspect with a magnifying glass, convinced they were a useful find needing further tunnel explorations to develop her theories about human habitation of the caves, and I think she was disappointed at my lack of enthusiasm for more burrowing sessions. I never did return to the caves after this, not because of cowardice, but because everything in my life started changing that year.

Nineteen fifty-two was a bad year for Kenya and a bad year for me in several different ways. I had become a teenager with a rising sense of frustration at Fa's overbearing tendencies and sudden whims. The meekness of the rest of the family, who complied without protest, irritated me beyond measure, as did the infuriating devotion of his patients who worshipped him like some kind of golden oracle, knowing nothing of what a tyrant he could be at home. I began to think my parents were decidedly weird and how could I be related to them when I was so different? Maybe I was adopted, and I started to imagine that my real parents were nice normal people who were looking for me and would arrive one day in a big car full of dogs and smiling faces, coming up the drive in a swirl of dust to claim me and take me home.

Day-dreaming on all the permutations of this happy thought helped to soften the upset of Fa's latest announcement: that we were moving again. There was no explanation for this sudden upheaval, except that the new house, which Fa insisted was much more suitable for us, was next to the railway line as it started a long climb out of Nakuru. Fa was passionate about trains, and nothing would suit him better than the prospect of watching and listening to them clanking past the back garden at all times of day and night.

The new house was a dismal interpretation of 1950s architecture, as plain and drab as a shoe box, only uglier, with a bright orange tiled roof. 'Mangalore tiles,' declared Fa with satisfaction, 'imported all the way

111

from Mangalore in India.' The hideous colour perversely impressed him while glaring with sickly orange-ness at the rest of us.

We had loved our old house with the field at the back full of hen houses, many of which were now fitted out with broken furniture and old rugs, where we hid out with friends at weekends or after school. We didn't want to leave. But Fa was already going round like an exterminator, clearing out cupboards and drawers, throwing away anything he could find that would make the removal boxes lighter and cheaper.

We petitioned Muz to save the small flock of chickens living in the back field among our club houses, hoping to ensure they came with us as they were pets and we loved them dearly. The pride of the flock was a magnificent Rhode Island cockerel we had named Julius. A regal bird, he fluffed and rattled his Titian feathers as he stalked among the hens, indisputably cock of the roost, marshalling his troop and, if he got a chance, us as well. Muz reassured us that Fa would agree as the hens were an asset, providing eggs and chicks, and the new house had a big garden with plenty of room for them.

Moving day loomed as we spent our last weekend in the old house. Fa was uncommonly genial, inviting neighbours to join us for lunch to make it an occasion as he was very excited about the move. Whether it was the novelty of a modern house filled with the fumes of new paint, or the railway running close beside it with trains permanently chugging past, it was unlike him to display such indulgent hospitality since normally he showed little interest in entertaining at home. When he was invited to other people's houses he would suddenly perk up, eating their food and charming them with compliments, indulging them with his lively personality and conversation.

On this Sunday full of affability nothing could have prepared us or caused more consternation than Alfredo arriving with a roasting dish on which, when we looked closer, we saw with horror, reposed our beloved Julius. Fa looked round the table beaming, while none of us could speak a word or eat a mouthful except for the neighbours, who had no inkling. Whether it was revenge on Julius, who was provoked to crow in an arrogant manner whenever Fa appeared, which Fa may have regarded as subversive, or complete insensitivity to our feelings, who could know. Whichever it was, we got our own back on him in due course by scripting and enacting a long-running soap opera in which all four of us had speaking parts, never missing an opportunity to launch an episode in Fa's hearing. Each episode was a recital of Julius's heroic character and exploits, which drove Fa to distraction. We had only to open our mouths intoning the opening line, which never varied: 'Jooo- lius . . . Jooo-lius . . . where art thou, Jooo-lius . . . '

Apart from everything else that was happening in 1952, I was having to repeat a year at Nakuru school, which added to my rebellious mood as it was all Fa's fault. Most of my friends had gone to senior schools in Nairobi, and the new area we moved to was isolated as no one else wanted to live bang up against trains. This meant we had no near neighbours, having left behind our homely bungalow that had families both sides, with children our ages who had been good friends and playmates.

We did have one neighbour, a feisty widow called Nellie Downing, who was too deaf to notice any trains and, in any case, had lived in her ramshackle bungalow too long to mind. Her husband had been a saddler by trade and, as a young man, had left his home in Yorkshire to emigrate to Kenya in the early days, opening one of the few shops owned by English people in Nakuru at a time when horses were important providers of transport. Everyone needed saddles, harness and tack of all kinds. After a few years spent getting his shop established, Mr Downing went back to Yorkshire to propose marriage to Nellie who had been his sweetheart before he left. They became engaged, but Nellie had promised her elderly parents that she would stay to look after them until they died, so the marriage would have to be postponed until this happened, and Mr Downing generously agreed. This type of arrangement was not unusual, as younger daughters were expected to put off getting married and having children themselves in order to care for their parents at home for as long as might be required. No institutions existed for older people at that time and there was no state help, so families looked after their own.

Nellie's parents, however, went on to live long lives and by the time she was free at last to marry, she was over fifty, so it was too late to have children and too late to enjoy many years of married life. But the marriage was a happy one, and when Mr Downing himself died, some years later, he left her comfortably off with the shop running profitably. Nellie used to entertain me with stories of her life over many lunches together, when she cooked steak and onions with chips for the two of us. This was wonderfully indulgent for me as we never had onions at home due to Fa's lingering gut weakness since the war. Chips were not favoured at home either. 'Too extravagant and rich, glugging up all that fat,' said Muz.

Nellie had an African grey parrot called Joseph who talked incessantly in a loud cracked falsetto, peppered with hysterical shrieks and cackles, while Nellie burbled away to him in companionable Yorkshire dialect, the two of them sounding like a dotty old couple, neither understanding a word the other was saying. While this was going on, Nellie would be feeding Joseph pieces of grenadilla fruit and tapping him on the beak affectionately.

One afternoon when a train was labouring up the hill behind our house, pistons clanking as it slowed to walking pace on the steep incline, one of the passenger doors flew open and several wild-looking men jumped out and ran into our garden, pursued by policemen. Shots were fired and we watched from the house in some alarm, thinking they might be Mau Mau, which indeed they were. All of them were soon rounded up, except for one, who ran to Nellie's house. Joseph, who was Nellie's alarm system, knew exactly what to do in this situation and set up ferocious barking noises in different tones, sounding like a pack of fierce dogs guarding the house. Hearing Joseph's alarm call, Nellie put her own emergency system into action. Grabbing her shotgun from beside her bed and locking herself in the bathroom, she fired several blasts out of the window to show that she meant business. The escaped Mau Mau prisoner it later turned out had not been intending to stop at her house, and being a fast runner was already on his way bolting across maize fields down to the lake, where it was reputed a Mau Mau gang was hiding out. The only people getting their ears blasted by Nellie's gun were the policemen.

This escape, and rumours of a hideout at the lake, prompted the Nakuru Police to insist that all families living in outlying suburbs, must move into town every evening at 6 o'clock to sleep at a community protection point. Ours was the Lake Road Flats, where Dick Johnson lived, and we decamped each evening to stay at his flat. Muz cooked supper for all of us and Dick loved these family times. We loved Dick too, so it was an ideal arrangement, especially as he had a piano, and Muz and he played duets after supper to entertain us. Muz became quite animated, we noticed, in Dick's company, as he flirted with her and complimented her on her looks, her cooking and her piano playing. This was unaccustomed attention for her and she began to blossom as she had done in Malta when she was feeling happy and her confidence was not being dented by setbacks outside her control. I noticed that she responded very positively to praise and laughter. Laughing and being a bit silly and girlish transformed her.

She used to tell us sometimes about her life as a child, growing up in the warm cocoon-like intimacy of her extended family in their small terraced house in London, where her grandmother lived with them. Her father, Robert John, entertained them with stories and singing around the piano, all of them enjoying themselves with a lot of larking about.

'When I met your father at the age of seventeen, at church,' Muz said, 'he was a very serious-minded boy, very Christian and pious, going round with a Bible under his arm. No larking around or having laughs with him.' She went on, 'He was not my type at all and I told him so when he asked if I would go out with him. But Gran, his mother, came to see me afterwards and said he was heartbroken at my rejection and couldn't eat or sleep. She said she kept telling him there were plenty more fish in the sea, but he just went on getting more and more depressed, so please would I take pity on him and accept his invitation.' Muz felt guilty and was sorry for him, thinking she should try a bit harder to get to know him and might start liking him after all. Their friendship did grow, as we know, leading to marriage after a seven-year engagement while waiting for Fa to finish his medical training. On reflection, Muz's initial gut reaction may have been prescient, as the austerity in Fa's character increasingly stifled the sparkle in hers, so the very thing that had drawn him to her became gradually extinguished. Ironically, it was then Babs' sparkle that drew him to her and away from Muz. It was during the war, when their survival depended on each other, that they came closest together, and again during the brief happy times in Malta.

For me, the saving grace of 1952 came with a new friendship when the whole family was invited to spend a long weekend with patients of Fa who had a farm at Londiani, fifty miles north-west of Nakuru. The farm was called Avondale, a surprisingly English name for an African farm, and it looked very English, with post and rail fences surrounding lush paddocks and lakes. This was not one of the usual impoverished, struggling farms we often visited. Stephen and Joan Hemsted, the owners, were efficient, experienced farmers, and the farm was highly productive as well as gloriously beautiful, with its rivers and forests among pastures grazed by pedigree Ayrshire cows. The farmhouse was long and low, built of cedar wood, and inside Joan had copied décor and furnishings from *Homes & Gardens* magazine, which gave the interiors a brightness and feeling of elegance very different from our own scrappy rooms at home. Joan's father, Marc Lawrence, lived with them. He had been a cavalry officer in the Indian Army and kept several horses, including one exceptionally handsome and well-mannered animal called Arak, who was an impressive 17 hands. Very soon I was up in the saddle on Arak, riding with Marc, who gave me expert instruction on riding technique, and we became close friends despite the age difference. After this, many weekends and other times were spent at the farm, whenever I had a chance to visit.

Africans working on the farm used to bring orphaned animals to Joan, who had a tender heart for any helpless creature, unable to resist taking them in. One of these was a baby colobus monkey they called Horace, who was no bigger than a kitten when he was brought in starving and pathetic, the mother having been killed by local hunters. Among Joan's numerous dogs there was one with puppies and Joan persuaded this nursing mother to adopt Horace, who ever afterwards attached himself to this patient animal, clinging to her underside or riding on her back like a small comical jockey.

Later, when he became too mischievous to remain in the house as a pet, Joan found a new home for him at London Zoo, where I visited him when I too became an exile in England.

Joan and Stephen had a small son, Edmund, and I think it may have been an illness of his that first led them to seek advice from Fa. They were anxious about him, as their first child had been born with what they called 'problems' and was in England with a foster family. This child was a daughter and whether it was due to her absence or whatever other reason, I began to feel absorbed into their family as a sort of surrogate daughter. The warmth and welcome of their household gave me a feeling of stability that was missing in my own home, and ten years later it was Stephen who gave me away at my wedding, while Joan was the one who helped me put on my wedding dress at their farm where I was staying, popping tranquilliser pills into my mouth, so that I went through the whole day in a trance. My own parents did not come to my wedding. They were living back in England by then and fares were much too expensive, they explained.

CHAPTER 7

After repeating a whole year at Nakuru school with nothing better to do than absorb enough Latin to pass KPE, I finally cleared this exasperating hurdle at the end of 1952 and went off to join my friends at the Kenya Girls' High School in Nairobi. They were now a year ahead, which bugged me, but that extra year had propelled me to the top of the class at Nakuru, and now in Nairobi I was still riding high at the top. It gave me a quite undeserved status but was very gratifying after all the aggravations that had caused this situation. KGH School was known by all as 'The Heifer Boma' (*Boma* being Swahili for enclosure), and the Prince of Wales Boys' School next door was 'The Cabbage Patch' (where the heifers grazed in normal times presumably). Due to worsening security problems with Mau Mau, which was especially bad in rural districts close to Nairobi, the school was surrounded with barbed wire coiled into impenetrable fortifications. Limuru Girls' School had moved into town to join us behind the wire patrolled by guards, so there was no grazing in the cabbage patch. KGH was big enough on its own with six hundred girls living in large semi-detached houses, fifty in each house, so when the Limuru girls arrived we became a vast campus that I found uncomfortably impersonal with no sense of communal identity. It really did feel like a huge herd of heifers milling around in a *boma*.

We had a remarkable head girl called Annette Wilkinson who had been born with only one arm, but there was nothing she couldn't do and she was a dynamo of energy and inspiration. During one term, we were in a sewing group together, making cushion covers, and Annette was machining at top speed, holding the material with her stump while turning the handle with her one hand, which I thought extraordinarily clever. She went on to marry Andrew Emms, who was an estate manager for African Highlands Tea at Kericho, and they had four children, two of whom were twins. Nothing stopped her doing whatever she wanted.

The highlight of 1953 was the Queen's coronation in London and KGH with Limuru girls held a pageant as the centrepiece of a whole day of celebrations, with all of us dressed in Elizabethan costume. I was a shepherdess and noticed for the first time that my shape was changing and suddenly I had a waist instead of being straight up and down like a boy. It made me feel that my life was changing shape as well, as I began to realise that in moving on to senior school my horizons had widened and I was entering a different world, even becoming quite sporty, and making lots of new friends. Everything was looking good, except for a recent development that was a bit disconcerting. I had started waking up at night finding myself standing barefoot in the darkness, in strange rooms in different parts of the building, with no idea where I was; all alone and panicking – was this a dream or a nightmare, or had I died in my sleep and this was some kind of transition stage? After properly waking up, I had to get back to the dorm. This necessitated looking for familiar landmarks, discovering each time that I had come down a couple of flights of stairs and along several corridors, opening and closing doors on the way, usually ending up in a locker room.

I felt ashamed of these night-time wanderings, realising I must have been sleep-walking, but didn't tell anyone as I didn't expect any sympathy. Several years later, Ros, by then living in London, slept-walked out of her flat on the busy Cromwell Road and walked all the way to an airline terminus in her nightdress with a mac on top. She woke up inside the terminus among crowds of people, where she was having an argument with a woman who thought she was mad. This was the first of a series of sleep-walking episodes. She thought these might have been caused by the constant all-night traffic disturbing her, as the excursions ended as abruptly as they had started when she moved to a quieter place. My own episodes ended after a few months, so I concluded they were due to the anxiety of adjusting to a new place and regime.

When the holidays came and I got a lift home to Nakuru, I was quite peeved to find all the others happily getting on with life without me, and all kinds of things happening that I hadn't been told about. The dining room had been cleared of furniture to make room for trestle tables set up along all four walls, with a flap inside the door that lifted up for access. This new arrangement accommodated an elaborate electric train set that Fa had bought for himself, not content with the real thing chuffing past the back of the house all the time. He tried to make out that the train set was for Andrew, but as none of us was allowed to touch it without Fa being present, this excuse fooled no one.

Operating the trains was a complex business involving printed timetables strictly followed, with correct signalling procedures, while working the points manually to avoid crashes. When all went smoothly it was mildly entertaining watching the little engines and carriages clattering in and out of tunnels, climbing hills through forests of miniature trees made out of bits of sponge painted in shades of green and brown, stopping at stations, timed to the minute. It seemed to me that the only excitement to be had from the train game was to engineer pile-ups and have races. But the trains were fragile, intricate scale models made by Hornby – not toys, Fa explained sternly – and operating this system was a serious business that needed to be seen as educational and instructive rather than a childish pastime. All of us, including Andrew, thought it very odd for an adult to be engrossed with an activity so excessively boring, while Muz lamented the loss of a dining room where we could all sit down comfortably together. Fa graciously allowed our big dining table to go into his study, which was so full of books it felt like eating in a library, but we gradually came to admit it was quite cosy and less formal than the much larger dining room.

Fa's idiosyncrasies were not all selfish or daft, and his disregard for conventional modes of thinking or behaving had many positive aspects. One of his themes, surprisingly, was homosexuality. This subject was taboo in polite society and homosexuals were often despised and treated as pariahs, so most took pains to hide their sexuality and often suffered intense emotional anguish and shame as they were unable to express their needs or even talk about such sensitive issues. Fa had great sympathy for those who felt conflicted or were in distress, and when it became known that he was sympathetic, many went to him with their problems. He felt the clinical environment of a consulting room was unhelpful in assisting the more seriously disturbed of these individuals, and often brought them home to be nurtured and counselled by him. Spending time in what possibly to them seemed a normal happy family situation, it was hoped they might recover some equanimity while feeling more relaxed and being cared for. We became quite used to finding strange men at the table when we went down for breakfast. I remember one who was too strained to say anything and seemed utterly broken. It was Andrew, with his direct way of speaking, who said of him: 'That man is ship-wrecked.'

Fa discussed these situations with us and put to us that where there is sexual attraction between adults of the same sex, whether intrinsic or acquired – why should they be denied a loving relationship like anyone else? He never missed an opportunity to make us stretch our minds with new concepts, or question old ones.

Nothing was off limits and he used to bring home microscope slides stained with varieties of bacteria, blood or parasites to show us. We always had a microscope at home so Fa could work undisturbed on his research projects and, as well as this, there would be test tubes on his desk containing ticks and other arthropods which he collected while writing his paper on Rickettsial diseases. This paper attracted interest from other countries where similar diseases occurred, such as Rocky Mountain Spotted Fever in the USA and Lyme disease, caused by ticks infected with *Rickettsiae*. Fa wanted us to be involved and enthused, and we were.

Muz was less so when Fa brought home more gruesome specimens such as, on one occasion, a very premature miscarried foetus. He wanted to show us how perfect all its features were even at that early stage, to demonstrate the miracle of human reproduction. What Muz really objected to was Fa washing the tiny miracle at the kitchen sink while she was getting lunch ready.

Every Friday lunchtime Fa brought home Muz's housekeeping money in bank notes to last the week. If it didn't last, she had to ask him for more and this was an embarrassment for her. There were times when we would be on FHB (family hold back) if she was short and food needed to be rationed, making sure that Fa, as breadwinner, had enough to keep up his energies while the rest of us ate less.

Due to Fa's altruistic tendencies where patients were concerned, sometimes on a Friday when Muz asked him for the housekeeping money he would look pained. We all knew what that meant. One of his more impoverished patients would have been to see him in the morning with a plaintive story of hardship, resulting in Fa handing over the entire envelope of money just drawn from the bank.

'Why didn't you just give them a bit of the money, enough to buy petrol or pay for their shopping, instead of the whole lot?' Muz would say indignantly.

'I couldn't give less than what I had,' was the usual reply. 'Their need is greater than ours.' A big sigh would go up from the rest of us. One of the chickens would have to get the chop.

It seemed a good time for me to start another small business. After leaving Otieno behind at the old house, I had taken over most of the cooking when I was at home. I liked trying out new recipes and Muz was an indifferent cook. My plan was to make iced sponge cakes of different flavours, with a list of regular orders for these, to be picked up from the surgery every Friday morning ready for the weekend as everyone liked to have cakes for Saturday and Sunday tea. It worked well and was modestly profitable.

The doctors' practice had outgrown the space above Karimbux grocery store and moved to new rooms in Lake Road, where a laboratory was added with a technician recruited from England so tests could be done on site. This was a big asset for Fa in his research work and collaboration with other research teams in Nairobi and Makerere University in Kampala. A colleague of Fa's in Nairobi, Dr Michael Wood, had founded with two others a Flying Doctor Service with a research arm called AMREF (African Medical Research & Education Foundation). It was a time of energetic strides forward in medical care and knowledge, which thrived despite current political uncertainties.

This climate of innovation and energy was communicating itself to Muz, who was branching out in her own way with her considerable gifts as a musician. It had always been a dream of hers to own a Blüthner grand piano and now with a larger house there was enough space, and she was able to buy one with money that had come from her father. It was installed in the sitting room and she immediately made up for lost time by practising and playing at every opportunity, inviting other musicians to come with string or wind instruments to form trios or quartets. A professional opera singer called Winifred started coming to practise her repertoire, with Muz accompanying her. Winifred had an imposing physique and wore enormous kaftans decorated all over with strident designs that bounced up and down as she sang. Our Stuart Crystal glasses bounced in unison in their glass cabinet, as the rest of us, watching from the doorway, choked off giggles, waiting fascinated to see if Winifred's piercing mezzo might actually cause them to shatter. Muz, on occasion overhearing our stifled spasms, would bang out a thunderous chord and jump up, shouting, 'You know perfectly well that Winifred and I have a concert we are preparing for. Thank the Lord none of you will be in the audience disgracing us.'

Since the Blüthner arrived and Muz had perfected a repertoire fine enough for concerts at the National Theatre in Nairobi, she and Winifred regularly went off to join other musicians presenting an evening of musical entertainment. These concerts became popular and demand for her music led to Muz having her very own Voice of Kenya radio series called *Musical Cameo* that went out on Saturday evenings, having been previously recorded in the studio. She practised her pieces at home for hours to get them perfect and I would time them for her with a stopwatch. Each piece, with her introduction, had to be timed to the second to fit precisely into its half-hour programme slot. Muz started to be famous in her own right instead of just being Dr Craddock's wife. Now that she had her music, with the particular joy that it brought her, what Muz longed for next was a dog. She loved dogs, always having had one or several which were part of her family when she was growing up. Fa was not in favour of animals, either inside or outside the house, seeing them as a nuisance and full of parasites, but we kept pestering him. A dog would keep us safe, we argued; while Mau Mau were still prowling around or liable to jump off trains into our garden, a dog would scare them off. In the end he agreed, and Muz lost no time when a friend offered us two black Labrador brothers, fully grown and trained as guard dogs. She arranged for them to be delivered to our house quickly before Fa could change his mind.

A few days later a car drove up to drop off the dogs and we all ran out in excitement to get a first glimpse, but there was no sign of them. The driver got out and when we said, 'Where are the dogs?' he laughed and went round to the boot, opening it so we could see the poor animals stuffed inside. We were dismayed as the space was much too small and stifling for two large dogs, but this was often the way animals were carried in cars, rather than have them jumping about on the seats inside. Not everyone had a pick-up or a van. The dogs however seemed none the worse and leapt out, instantly friendly in the sloppy way of Labradors, beating our legs with their tails and making themselves at home. They were called Jasper and Taffy, muscular animals bounding with energy for guarding us. They did this so efficiently that none of the shy antelopes that used to come down from Menengai to graze in our garden came any more, and the merry vegetable sellers who brought baskets full of fresh produce damp with dew to our back door each morning, never came again either.

In addition to all the routine work of the doctors' practice, Fa was kept busy with a series of polio epidemics that continued to be a world-wide problem, while a great deal of effort was going into research to find a vaccine. The main victims of polio seemed to be children, young men, and young pregnant women. With no effective treatment yet discovered, complete recovery was rare and in many cases led to varying degrees of paralysis or death. Among those who died one year, very sadly, was Desmond Molony's new wife Venice, who was pregnant. It seemed unbearably tragic that he should lose Venice so soon after finding happiness with her, having pulled himself through the grief of losing Evelyn. It was another very difficult time for all of us, as we tried to make sense of what seemed an utterly inexplicable, arbitrary act of fate. Fa was always desolate when patients he cared very much about died, despite his best efforts to save them.

Many discoveries and inventions we take for granted now were unknown at that time, with death from other infectious diseases such as TB and smallpox being accepted as inevitable in many cases, as were deaths from heart defects and other deformities and illnesses now routinely corrected with surgery or drugs. But we seemed to manage quite well without future inventions such as Sellotape, plastic in all its forms, ball-point pens or computers. No one had ever seen or heard of a plastic bag. We used paper bags, and parcels were tied up with string and sealed with red sealing- wax that came in small rectangular bars the size of a stick of KitKat. The end of the bar had to be held in a candle flame so that it melted and dripped onto the knotted part of the parcel string (to prevent it coming untied) or, in the case of letters, on the back flap of the envelope. It was then stamped instantly with a seal, if one was available, as the wax hardened very quickly. The melting wax had a hot aromatic smell now completely absent from modern life, and the common sight of a small, shiny crimson bar in its box with a stump of candle on a desk, complete with fountain pens, ink bottles and silver propelling pencils, has completely disappeared. Fa had his own personal seal, which had been made for him in China, carved from pale green jade with his initials in Chinese characters inscribed on the flat end, a tiny mythical lion carved on the other. We often played with this small, smooth, intriguing object when he allowed us to play with things on his desk. We loved being allowed to stamp the seal into a fat blob of sizzling wax on the back flaps of envelopes when Fa was sealing them.

We never had family holidays or visits to game parks, and never went on safari – too touristy, in Fa's view (or, more likely, too expensive) – and the first time I went to the Kenya coast with its exquisite white beaches was when I was twenty. But we often packed a picnic at weekends if Fa was not doing house calls, and would go off on the long hot drive to Baringo to swim in the lake. Lake Nakuru was too alkaline and too shallow for swimming. There were crocodiles in Lake Baringo, but we were never bothered by them; local Tugen tribesmen said there were enough fish in the lake so that crocodiles didn't have to eat people. Despite this, I did find it disconcerting if one surfaced alongside when I was swimming, staring at me with unblinking yellow eyes at water level while I was out of my depth, feeling uneasy. 'Don't splash around and frighten it,' Fa would call out, more concerned about the croc's sensitivities than mine.

As an alternative we might take a picnic to the Bahati forest, a classic rain forest of tall luxuriant trees with undergrowth full of butterflies and birds. Walking along game paths deep inside, we would be looking out for a sunny glade where we could spread the picnic and sit listening to all the mysterious forest sounds: bird calls and sharp barks, maybe a leopard's cough, as colobus monkeys peered down from safe perches high in the canopy. At ground level, displaced insects would scurry over and around our picnic cloth if it was in their territory. One thing we looked out for was any sign of *siafu* ants, as they were cunning and could creep up unnoticed in their shiny brown marching columns, getting up a sleeve or trouser leg; then at a signal, a whole army of vicious pincers would bite simultaneously. Once bitten, the experience was seared into memory for ever.

Most popular of all the weekend excursions were those when we went fly-fishing for trout on one of the many fast-flowing surpassingly beautiful rivers that tumbled down from high, forested mountains, stocked with brown or rainbow trout. We could be confident we would never go home without a good catch. Once, when casting from a bank with overhanging trees, Fa felt himself being watched, and looking up, saw a leopard lying along a branch overhead. Fa and the leopard gazed steadily at each other for some moments with neither making a move until Fa decided, as he was the intruder, it was for him to defer and move on.

Since arriving in Nakuru, Sundays were much less dreary as church was excused if we had one of these excursions planned. If we were at home, church was compulsory, but we didn't mind because St Christopher's Church had a new young vicar who was big-hearted and open-minded, with a refreshing view of Christianity as all-embracing, joyful and lively. This was Gordon Mayo who, together with his wife Sheila, was organising the building of a large church hall, financed by the community – even Fa contributed money to it – where various activities could take place. These were theatre, music and discussion groups, Scottish dancing, badminton and a youth club. Every night of the week there was something going on and the hall radiated energy. The only requirement for joining in the many activities was attendance at church at least one Sunday a month, which wasn't difficult, and people of all ages who had never been to church before, started coming.

At home we continued to have family prayers led by Fa each evening, which I began to find increasingly irksome as we got older, while Elaine, who was very devout, liked doing readings and prayers. But instead of

127

speaking normally, she used to put on a wheedling voice for praying and Bible reading as if God was mentally slow and needed to be spoken to with careful, cajoling words. This made me cringe and squirm with discomfort and, much as I struggled to contain myself trying to hold in the groans and rude sounds that kept rising inside, one evening it was too much and the resulting eruption so unedifying and vulgar that Fa slammed his Bible down on the table and shouted, 'That's enough, that's the end of it. Wendy is excommunicated.'

It seemed to me that there were many contradictions in adult behaviour as I observed Fa's enigmatic attitudes, trying to make sense of these and how Muz's sensitivities were affected by them. She had become preoccupied again just when I wanted to talk to her about things I needed, like clothes that fitted my changing shape, more suitable for a teenager, instead of wearing other children's cast-offs, which were getting too tight. Maybe even a bra – for the sake of modesty as well as comfort. Muz fumbled about in one of her drawers and produced some old bras of hers that had lost their shape and the elastic had lost its stretchiness.

'These will do,' she said. Then the dread words: 'I'll put some stitching in the cups to make them fit you.'

'But the straps are much too long,' I pointed out.

'Well, those can be shortened. It will only take a jiffy.' Once the stitching had been done, I tried on one of the deformed bras which, despite the straps being shortened, drooped with two grey pouches halfway to my waist, missing the point altogether. Muz looked slightly disappointed with the result of her efforts: 'It's not quite right . . . but it's the best I can do,' she said. 'Anyway, it saves buying new ones.'

I must have looked sufficiently dispirited at that moment for her to feel slightly abashed as, switching to a conciliatory mother-and-daughter tone, she said confidingly, 'Maybe now you are older I can talk to you about things that possibly you should know about.'

This was a bit unnerving, but I waited for her to go on. 'I feel you should know that your father and Babs are corresponding with each other, secretly, behind my back.' Babs' name hadn't been mentioned or thought about since we'd left England, so this was completely unexpected and certainly a shock. I needed a few moments to think about it.

'Well, she's not coming out here to bother us, so it doesn't matter about the letters. She and Fa can just be pen-friends,' I said, trying to sound convincing, as much for myself as for Muz. But we both knew this was a body blow for the family, and the move to Kenya had not, after all, put enough space between them to end their relationship. Instead it seemed to have provided only a temporary reprieve.

It was about this time that Elaine suddenly became very ill with a brain infection and, once polio was discounted, a diagnosis of viral encephalitis was thought the most likely cause of her symptoms, which included paralysis of her legs and lower body. She was admitted to hospital as an emergency and stayed there for several weeks until she had recovered sufficiently to stand and walk a few steps on her own. Then she was able to come home and lie on the sofa in the sitting room while her strength slowly returned.

I was at school when this happened and later, when I came home for the holidays, it was frightening to see her looking so debilitated, just a wisp of her former self, and dragging one leg. She was due to join me at KGH the next term but it seemed unlikely she would have recovered enough for this to be possible. It was just at this point that Fa made an astonishing announcement.

Without any warning or prior discussion, he said that I was leaving KGH and would not be going back next term. He had decided that Elaine and I needed to go to school in England, to the Sussex school. It would be safer 'back home in England, away from Mau Mau', he insisted. We all sat in stunned silence, absorbing this sudden new plan.

Andrew was the first to say something. 'If the big girls are going to England to be safe, what about me and Ros?' There didn't seem to be any answer to this and we were left contemplating what it meant for all of us, as Muz calmly went on with her knitting. 'It's your father's decision,' she said. 'He knows best.'

So it was settled, and in no time suitcases were being hauled out to begin packing. 'You will need one good dress each for going away in,' Muz said to Elaine and me. 'I've given your measurements to Mrs Da Souza who lives down the road, married to that nice Goan mechanic in the railways. She does dressmaking and can run something up. I've given her a picture out of a magazine to copy. It's going to be a surprise, quite modern and fun.' Elaine and I looked at each other. We knew exactly what that meant. Something hideous.

In a few days we went to collect the dresses from the Da Souza's two-room brick house on a railway siding along the tracks. Mrs Da Souza looked sad and careworn. She would be glad of the cash for the dresses. She took them from a pile beside her machine and shook them out for us to look at. They were identical except for the colour – mine was bright yellow and Elaine's bright pink. They were sleeveless and high at the neck, with extra-wide frilly collars of the same material sticking straight out all round like a clown's ruff, and bobbly buttons down the front as cute as giant Smarties. Good grief. Heaven help us, I thought.

Seeing my look of dismay, Muz said brightly, 'They'll look much better when they're on.' We got them on, tugging at the ruffs and the bodices that were much too tight, straining at the ridiculous buttons. 'I think you both look very fetching,' Muz said. 'Everyone will know you are sisters. You could even pass for twins.'

We were not to go by plane to England, but by boat from Mombasa to Tilbury on the *Warwick Castle*. A chaperone had been engaged by letter to escort us on the voyage and we were to meet her on the boat train when we got on at Nakuru station. We had never met this lady before and were curious to see what she was like. All we knew was that she was an elderly spinster from up-country called Miss Cragg, who a friend had mentioned was travelling on the same boat, so Fa wrote to ask if she would accompany us as a favour and she agreed.

All the family came to see us off to make sure we were safely on the boat train, delivered into the care of Miss Cragg. It was a terrible wrench having to leave, saying goodbye with tight faces, trying to keep emotions under control. My chest felt tight too, my heart bursting with held-in sadness, like wearing an emotional strait-jacket, but that may have been partly due to the constricting clown dress that Muz wanted me to wear to impress Miss Cragg. Elaine was excused her dress as she pleaded to wear one of her old favourites as a comfort. She was still dragging one leg and was pitifully thin and pale, by no means fully recovered from the brain infection that had so nearly carried her off. How any parent could bear to send her away in that condition was beyond understanding. Fa tried to make this all right by telling us we should always remember that God was looking after us *in loco parentis*.

If Miss Cragg was supposed to be temporarily taking on the same role, it can never have been properly explained to her, as no sooner had we been introduced on the station platform and dutifully followed her onto the train than she promptly vanished and was never seen again, either then or later on the boat.

So we were on our own for whatever happened next. No one had told us, and we didn't know then, that it would be nearly two years before we would see any of the family again.

CHAPTER 8

The disappearance of Miss Cragg may have been more of a worry for Elaine than for me, as I didn't want to be chaperoned anyway, but Elaine had never been away from home and was not in a good state to fend for herself. Here she was at twelve years old, a shy and diffident girl in frail health with a gammy leg, suddenly being sent on an eight-thousand-mile trip, taking her away from the security and love of her family while she was still needing support and care. Luckily, unlike me, she had a placid nature and was stoic and uncomplaining, possibly feeling that as long as I was there as the older sister I would take charge and look after things.

While we were on the boat train with dozens of other *Warwick Castle* passengers it was like being on a grand outing, rattling down to the coast on a train journey that was legendary for its drama and romance. Everyone had the luxury of a sleeper carriage, with the added indulgence of silver service in a dining car stiff with starched tablecloths and waiters, while the great, vast, tawny African landscape rolled past like a wide-screen film. South of Nairobi, as the series of humpback hills merged into the limitless scorched plains of Tsavo National Park, there were herds of gazelle and zebra, with occasional sightings of something larger and more conspicuous among the sparse scrub and baobab trees. It was both thrilling and heart-breaking as we watched and said goodbye to all this. We went through other carriages looking for Miss Cragg, explaining that she was our guardian, but there was no sign of her. A family with daughters the same ages as Elaine and me invited us to join them, so we did have companions for the trip after all. Once I had screwed up my clown dress and thrown it out of the window, I was set for whatever happened next.

After two previous sea voyages, ships were familiar territory and I knew exactly where to go and what to do. The first things to locate were sailors' cabins where ship's cats lived and then make friends with both sailors and cats, so I could come and go without being troubled by anyone else. This was easy, but I had not foreseen there might be a snag this time. I was now fourteen and my presence below decks in sailors' cabins attracted some disapproval from higher ranks, who reported this to the purser. He very diplomatically, and not unkindly, told me that he was providing an escort to accompany me for visiting the cats. The escort turned out to be one of the sailors I already knew, so nothing changed!

Elaine had been absorbed into the other family, happily making friends with the daughter her age who was as undemanding as Elaine herself. The daughter my age had a figure ripening like a plum attracting wasps, except in this case it was lank, droopy men who perked up on sight of her, sniffing around like tail-wagging dogs. This was not the kind of attention I wanted to share, preferring cats. Besides, I did not have contours developing into blossoming mounds like the ripe daughter, despite being the same age. I did become aware of a slight frisson breezing my skin like goose pimples if I caught the eye or sudden male smell of a sailor or young male passenger passing by, recognising this as a new sensation, but it was no more than a moment's distraction.

As the ship edged northwards up the east coast of Africa, rounding the Horn, there was a gradual change in the air that became heavy and sticky as we entered the Red Sea. The mood on board slumped and even the cats didn't want to play anymore. Everyone was looking forward to visits on shore at ports along the way and it was a relief when Port Said was reached. We could all get off for some exercising of legs and purses as we made straight for Simon Arzt, the famous Egyptian emporium on the waterfront. This funky department store had eye-dazzling displays of every imaginable article, beyond anything seen in Nairobi. I had a little money saved from my cake business and wanted passionately to buy something decorative or ornamental, as the only possessions I had brought with me were plain necessities. Elaine had a favourite doll she could not bear to leave behind, but apart from that only a few clothes and books, so each of us entered Simon Artz like treasure hunters searching for something special to take away. All kinds of leather goods packed the shelves and drew my attention as much for their enticing smell as the rich, dyed colours.

Among these I found a small grey donkey, its body made from some kind of soft velvet and its bridle the finest red leather. The contrast of the red and grey colours and textures was irresistible, so I had to have it, even though it took more of my money than I'd wanted to part with. Elaine more modestly and sensibly bought a little purse, which was to be a present for the guardian auntie we were due to go and live with when we got to England.

As we sailed through the narrow passage of Suez and out into the Mediterranean, leaving Egypt behind, then Malta and Gibraltar, the hot dry air of the African coast grew thinner and cooler and turned frigid as we started plunging through steely waves in the English Channel, where the sun stopped shining altogether.

There is always a feeling of expectation when the end of a journey comes in sight, and when we sailed into Tilbury docks we expected to feel excited and full of anticipation for a new adventure. But instead, it was a sinking feeling of anti-climax for Elaine and me as we watched our friends being met by relatives with hugs and kisses, climbing into taxis to go on holiday or going home. We had no one looking out for us and no home to go to, so we lifted our suitcases and walked, in short white socks and bare legs, feeling the chill, to find a station that would take us to the suburban town where our new guardians lived.

Finding the way on unfamiliar trains, clutching our shabby suitcases as if they represented a last link with home, several hours later after a bewildering number of shuttles, we trudged to an address Fa had written on a piece of paper for us. Our guardians, who we were to call Auntie and Uncle, had sons our ages who we were looking forward to meeting, and hoped they didn't have train sets or cranky ideas. We stood outside in the street, stiffening ourselves to knock at the uninviting door of this drab suburban house in a street of identical houses, all squashed together in a long line on a noisy main road. The door was opened and four suspicious, unsmiling faces looked out, before letting us in and telling us we were late for tea. It was five o'clock and Tea, we discovered, in this household was something peculiarly English called 'High Tea', which consisted of tinned pilchards or an egg on toast, with a slice of cake and cups of tea. This odd meal took the place of supper or dinner, and before going to bed there would be Ovaltine or Horlicks with a biscuit. High Tea was taken in the front room, yards from busy traffic rumbling past the windows, all of us sitting bolt upright on hard chairs in an atmosphere as frigid as an igloo. The boys scowled at us, and when Auntie and Uncle were not looking, they did jerky armpit-scratching monkey imitations to remind us where we had come from. There was no train set anywhere to be seen and we almost wished there might be one, just to break the tedium. After the excruciating meal came to an end, Uncle wiped his mouth, cleared his throat, and said in a voice heavy with foreboding, 'How much money have you brought with you?'

Elaine and I sat dumb with incomprehension. We only had what was left of the pocket money we'd set out with, which was not much after paying for incidentals on the ship, and train fares. We had expected Fa would arrange something for our upkeep. As it became clear this was not the case, I felt a sense of panic rising, almost choking up the food I had just eaten, which had not been paid for.

'We'll have to send a telegram to Father,' I suggested, when I had recovered enough to think what could be done. 'But we have got some of our pocket money left.'

There was no international telephone service for ordinary households, and telegrams were the only means of communication for anything urgent. Later, when Elaine and I went to unpack in our icy cold room (central heating was still years away), we realised it was typical of Fa to try and scrounge free board and lodging off this unassuming family, who were in fact much less well off than he was. This kind of meanness was an embarrassment we'd suffered all our lives. The next worry was school uniform and other requirements for school. We had thought that we would go with Auntie on the train to London, visiting Harrods and Daniel Neal to equip ourselves; but now it seemed there was a problem if there was no money for shopping.

A solution was arrived at that pleased Auntie and Uncle. We were to be sent on the train to school straight away before term started and the school matron would order uniform and other things, making sure we had everything we needed, sending the bill to Fa, and looking after us with other colonial girls who stayed at school for the holidays when they had nowhere else to go.

Sisters were always put together in the same house, in our case the duffers' house, but the upside was that it had the best accommodation in the whole school, occupying an entire top floor of the Victorian mansion that formed the main part of the school buildings. There was a tower room just big enough for two beds, with washstands, lockers and a cupboard, reached by a spiral staircase, and everyone had a turn sleeping up there. This was a fanciful fairytale tower with windows of leaded diamond panes, looking out over the hundred-acre school grounds where there were wooded hills and wild glades full of deer and rabbits. Every Saturday we were let out to ramble all day, with strict instructions not to cross the railway line that marked the far boundary. There was a tunnel covering fifty yards of line at this point and it became a dare to go through it as it was dark and slimy, full of stale fumes and rotting smells, and if a train shot through while one of us was inside, a test of steady nerves.

In the woods near the tunnel I used to meet the ferret men when they came to poach rabbits on school land. I had first met them by chance one Saturday when I came across them netting a rabbit hole and was so interested in what they were doing they let me go along, to help carry dead rabbits. The rabbits' back legs would be tied together with string that I held onto, while blood from their corpses dripped down into my wellingtons. Leather bags bulging with wriggling ferrets were carried by the men. These animated bags excited and fascinated me, and I waited impatiently for the ferrets to be let out on a rabbit hole. I liked the bright eyes and slinkiness of the ferrets and wanted to hold one, but the men warned me they were not pets but working animals with a fearsome bite. The ferrets seemed to relish their job, and needed no urging to disappear down a hole and flush any rabbits that would then dash out to be caught in the nets and dispatched. A good day's rabbiting was a perfect way to spend Saturdays, but I was careful no one knew about it. Rabbiting was not part of the curriculum at this school, and men from the rough side of the tracks, or in any other guise, were banned unless they wore clerical dog collars.

I was disappointed at first not to be put in the same house as my old friend Verity, who was still at the school but now in a higher form, so we didn't see each other very often. Her house was for high-flyers and now, with my tenth change of school, I was behind again and had to catch up on a new range of studies leading to O Levels. Elaine and I were both so stricken with homesickness it was affecting our work and we were often caught daydreaming through lessons, thinking about life at home, wondering what the others were doing, and feeling miserable about missing it all. Elaine's way of coping with her loneliness was to retreat ever further into the safety-net of religion, which was encouraged by the puritanical regime of the school. It worked for her, but she went so far that she used to be found on her knees praying until late into the night, becoming so withdrawn that even the most rigid of Christian extremists among the staff began to worry about her.

I went the opposite way, disregarding the half-hour of 'quiet time' at seven o'clock every morning when a bell rang to stop all washing and dressing activities, which were supposed to have been completed by the stroke of seven. Each bed space had a chest of drawers and washstand with a jug and bowl for what was called 'strip-washing'. Curtains were drawn around this personal space, like hospital cubicles, for modesty, and to allow seclusion for prayer and Bible reading. This extra time meant I could extend my getting-up routine behind the curtains as long as I was silent and didn't disturb those who were busy communicating with God. Or I could just lie on my bed and read the latest novel. This had to be hidden under loose floorboards, along with my packets of chocolate digestive biscuits, shared with the mice living down there, who luckily had very small appetites.

When half term came we stayed at school with the other girls whose parents lived abroad. The missionary girls never went home and didn't see their parents for years at a time. I felt sorry for them, not fully realising that my own situation was just as bad as theirs. I somehow thought our parents would reappear one day, or Fa would have one of his whims and we'd be whisked off back to Kenya or somewhere else. Our only contact with home was the Sunday letter we wrote each week, and the blue aerogramme forms which came back in Muz's wavy writing or, occasionally, Fa's thin, careful script, giving news which made us feel more homesick than ever.

While Elaine's way of coping was to swathe herself in a comforting blanket of Christian faith and ritual, my salvation came with immersion in the musical traditions and events at which this school excelled. I was working my way through piano exams again, and singing at music festivals with the school choir, which thrilled me as we went from success to success. Our music mistress was a thin, animated woman like an electrified elf, who bounced on tiptoes, training and conducting the choir to a very high standard. Up and down the country we won competitions and cups at festivals, even beating the Orpington Girls' Choir that normally basked in the national spotlight. When we were invited to record an album of songs at Decca studios, there was a dilemma, as this kind of exposure clashed with Christian notions of humility and meekness, so the invitation was turned down, much to the disappointment of many of us who aspired more to being stars than being humble.

Once a week the whole school assembled in the great hall for singing practice, as every girl was expected to sing as well as she could, and the sound of these massed voices filling the high vault of the hall was phenomenal, especially when harmonising in two or three parts. Twelve voices were picked for special harmonies, which were sung at evensong on Sundays, and these twelve girls formed the central nucleus of each larger choir group. When I was picked to be one of the twelve, the sense of jubilation gave a great boost to my morale, and in music I was able to sublimate to some extent my longings for home.

Since it had been assumed by Fa that Elaine and I would spend holidays with our guardians, without requiring any financial provision, we dreaded going there as freeloaders. We felt very awkward having to endure the frosty attitude of that household to such a thoughtless imposition on their resources. They were not well off, with two large boys eating quantities of food that stretched our eyes as we watched whole cakes and loaves of bread with jam being swallowed in a few bites. Uncle had a lifetime job in London, commuting each day, while Auntie went on a bus once a week to Sutton to do her shopping, and by train to London each spring to buy herself a new outfit; their horizons extending no further than these modest routines. They did not own a car and the boys went to state schools. The contrast between their lifestyle and that of our family in Kenya was stark, and no opportunity was lost by Uncle in pressing the point that Fa was happy to pay fees for a 'posh' private school for us, while expecting them to look after us for free during the holidays. It was a good point and one to which we had no answer, as we thought surely adults should be sorting this out between themselves, not making us feel guilty about it.

The only solution we could think of was to stay at school for the holidays, but the school required payment for this, so a sort of impasse developed and we were shuttled about, sometimes going home with friends whose kind parents took pity on us. The idea of going back to Kenya, even once, was never considered or suggested. When I eventually went back after leaving school, Betty Blackler, Fa's practice manager, told me that Fa was making so much money he could easily have flown us out for holidays. He was spending money on fares for himself, she said. This puzzled me. If he was taking trips himself, why didn't he come to see us?

He did come once and that was more than a year after we had left Kenya. It was during a school holiday when we happened to be staying with our guardians and Fa came to tea. I was so overcome with emotion at seeing him again, imagining he would be feeling the same, I quite thought he would be staying the night and we would have lots of time with him. Tea, as usual, took place with all of us sitting formally at the table, allowing no chance for relaxed conversation, while Elaine and I were bursting with things to tell him and talk about as soon as we could escape to be alone with him. But, inexplicably, no sooner was tea finished than he jumped up and went to get his coat, briefly kissing us goodbye and driving off down the road. Looking back, I can see he was agitated all through tea, his mind elsewhere, not wanting to engage with us. At the time I thought it was simply an effect of our long separation, but on reflection all these years later, it seems likely that he was beside himself with impatience to get to wherever Babs was.

After he left in such an abrupt way, I felt completely bereft and desolate, fearing that a last hope of ever seeing our own family again or getting back to normal family life was gone. Elaine was very quiet and would never express any feeling. She was always calm and contained whatever happened, but I was not like that. I had to keep hold of myself and pretend that everything was all right, but inside I was falling apart with the utter bleakness of our situation now that even Fa had abandoned us and didn't seem to care anymore, while Muz was invisible. Would we ever get back to Kenya and be a family again? I think Uncle must have succeeded in extracting a cheque from Fa as the mood of the household lifted slightly, just as I was pinching myself to stop shameful tears appearing.

A couple of days later I had a blackout quite suddenly, never having had anything of the sort before. Auntie called the doctor, but he couldn't find anything wrong. Then I had more blackouts and was sent to Redhill Hospital for tests, before being transferred to the neurological unit at The London, which was Fa's old hospital. He had been contacted and had asked that I be put under the care of his old boss Sir Russell Brain. It was suspected that I had some kind of tumour or brain disease. I liked the joke that a man called Brain should be a brain specialist. The ever-uncomplaining Elaine had to go back to school on her own without me, and then I too was on my own, spending nine weeks in a mental ward, having every kind of medical and psychiatric test. Medical students were sent to inspect me as I was viewed as a challenging case, while all the time I went on having the blackouts. This baffled the doctors, including Sir Russell, who was supposed to be a leading expert on all types of brain malfunction. Epilepsy was ruled out and no other diagnosis seemed to be suggesting itself. Meanwhile, Fa had gone back to Kenya promising to write.

Despite everything, I was having a very interesting and absorbing time that was a great deal more agreeable than being at school. The ward was full of mad people whom I found fascinating, despite being quite frightened sometimes. I suspected that everyone thought I was mad too, but I knew I wasn't, which gave me a certain advantage as I was completely in control of my senses, apart from when I blacked out. Some of the patients in the ward had terminal brain tumours and were either comatose or raving, while others had undergone brain surgery and were in a fragile state, requiring to be protected from those manic patients who roamed around in a menacing manner. I made myself useful, helping in a minor way with small tasks for bedbound patients, even in the case of one of the ravers, soothing her, as she responded to me, thinking I was her daughter.

There was no one else of my age in the ward and the porters used to tease me. 'Sweet sixteen and never been kissed,' they sang, which was true and made me blush so violently I could feel the roots of my hair prickling as the cockney banter went on, full of innuendo, which was not unkindly meant but wildly embarrassing for someone as unworldly as I was.

Life on the ward followed prescriptive routines that were undemanding but surreal and I began to wonder, after several weeks without any diagnosis being made, whether I would be sent to a mental hospital as it seemed to be assumed in the absence of medical evidence that I must be a psychiatric case. Sessions with a psychiatrist asking me intimate questions felt ominous, as I sensed that the psychiatrist was steering me towards the answers he wanted.

The breakthrough came, as many breakthroughs do, in an unexpected way. There was a young doctor on the medical team who often chatted to me in a friendly way on his rounds. One day, he took me into a side room and sat me down facing him. Taking my hands in his, he said, 'I think I know what's going on here, and I need you to tell me if I'm right.'

There was a pause as I took this in, and hoped he was not in league with the psychiatrist. He continued, 'I think you are suffering from deep unhappiness caused by circumstances in your life outside your control, and the blackouts are saying you can't put up with it anymore.' He went on: 'I think you are missing your parents and your home and that's where you need to be.'

The kind way he said this made it difficult for me to speak, as sympathy was not something I was used to encountering, and my thoughts were doing several somersaults around the implications of what he was saying. After a while sitting quietly trying to unlock my voice, which seemed to have got stuck, I suddenly felt all the tension inside drain away. 'Yes,' I whispered. 'Yes.'

He went on holding both my hands and said, 'You'll have to go back to school for a while, but things will change very soon, and everything will be all right.'

'How do you know?' I asked suspiciously, and he laughed.

'I can see round corners,' he said. 'Doctors have to be able to see round corners.' That was very enigmatic, I thought, but I didn't doubt him after the insight he had just demonstrated.

I was not allowed to go back to school on the train, and a car came to drive me all the way to Sussex, dropping me off at the school gates with my few things in a bag marked 'Hospital Property'. Everyone was in class, the whole building was silent, and somehow it didn't look so threatening any more as I let myself in through a back door and went to find Matron to check in.

'Glad to be back, dear?' she asked, as if I'd been away on an outing, and nothing more was said by her or anyone else, either then or later. I thought maybe the housemistress or headmistress might want to see me and have a little talk – if nothing else, just to discuss how I was going to make up lost time for exams – but they behaved as if nothing had happened, the clockwork mechanisms of the school allowing no interruption. In the absence of any mention or communication about my illness, I was worried that if I had more blackouts no one would understand and I would be seen as disgracing myself, since at this school nothing mattered so much as decorum. Christian girls simply did not have bodily malfunctions, or if anything of the sort threatened, it must never be seen by others. Before leaving hospital I had been given some little white pills and told if I took one each day I would not have any more episodes, so I was putting my faith in these and waiting to see if the doctor's prediction about seeing round corners was going to come true.

It did, and it didn't take long. A letter from Fa arrived, saying that, because of my illness, Muz was coming back to England so that Elaine and I could be day girls. She would be finding a house near the school where all of us, including Andrew and Ros, could live, but he was going to stay in Kenya due to his work commitments. It was incredible news, especially as Muz was arriving at any moment. I think the doctor at the hospital must have written a powerfully persuasive letter to Fa to account for such a swift turnaround.

Elaine and I were allowed to go to the station to meet Muz off the train and we were so tense with excitement, neither of us could sleep the night before or eat any breakfast that morning. When the train came in, several people got off but no one who looked like Muz was among them. We were bracing ourselves for disappointment when a tiny woman, barely visible in an enormous fur coat, came uncertainly towards us. Even when I could see her face, I didn't recognise her as being Muz. It was a shock as she seemed like a stranger, and we stood there feeling awkward, looking at each other, not knowing what to do or say. Hugging was not something that came naturally at that moment, but we made an effort and the brown fur pressed to my face made me feel as if I were being gripped by a strange woolly animal. Muz was wearing leather gloves that she did not take off, and this felt strange too as I took her hand to walk into the village for tea, and look in the estate agent's window for houses to rent. Andrew and Ros were not with her, having been farmed out somewhere while she came to spy out prospects for a new home for us all.

Later on, when Ros and Andrew arrived, the change in them both was startling after two years' separation. Andrew had always been the skinniest of the four of us, but now he looked bone thin and so tall, his legs were like toothpicks. I couldn't resist teasing him about it, but he didn't mind because he liked me and knew it was meant affectionately. Just being a family again with all the old joking-around was what mattered most to him and Ros. At this point, with the teasing about his legs, Andrew acquired the nickname 'Spindle-legs', which became shortened to 'Spindle' and it stuck. Ros had grown too and was old enough to start at the same Sussex school as a day girl.

Muz liked old houses with character and history, and without Fa there to push her into something modern and horrible, she took a short lease on the oldest house she could find, which was a timber-framed wobbly farmhouse on a hop farm, about five miles from the school. We loved the house, which was huge and rambling, with secret nooks and passageways. All the upstairs rooms had bare plank floors that tilted in different directions, the joists eaten away by woodworm and general decay, so furniture tended to slide about, but we didn't mind. The windows were more of a problem, their frames having shrunk, so there were gaps stopped up with rags. This didn't prevent icicles hanging from the lintels inside as well as the eaves outside. That first winter was ferocious and we kept log fires burning in the big fireplaces downstairs to warm the house. Muz remained undeterred by all the setbacks of harsh weather such as driving through snowdrifts to get us to school, and as soon as driving conditions improved she took herself off to the nearest big town to find a grand piano and get it installed in the farmhouse sitting room, so she was then distracted from all manner of obstacles by her music.

The farm stood timeless in its own green valley, unchanged for a hundred years. No machinery was used, cows were milked by hand and buckets brought into the dairy, which was an extension of our kitchen, leading into a warren of pantries and sculleries, all facing north to stay cool in summer. Some of the milk was poured into large, circular, flat pans to stand overnight, and then the cream was skimmed off each morning. Other milk pans would be heated to a temperature measured by thermometer and left to stand so that the cream, as it cooled, rose up in golden crusts to the top; these were then scooped off and sold as clotted cream. Butter was churned by hand in a wooden barrel on a stand, and we all took turns with the handle. When the butter formed into a big lump swimming in buttermilk, it was taken out of the barrel and squeezed in a muslin cloth with a little salt added. Then it was patted out with wooden paddles and slapped into small wooden moulds. All this unlimited dairy produce transformed our usual spartan Craddock diet.

Farm activities gave our lives new stimulus, as hired hands were taken on to help at hop-picking and wheat harvest times. This was great news for me as I could start earning my own money again. It was arm-aching, laborious work, stacking the wheat sheaves in rows that were called stooks in such a way that air could circulate through, drying the straw and heads of corn. The sheaves were heavy and scratchy and we got rashes on our arms from carrying them. Children of all ages came to do this work alongside adults and when it was hop-picking time we were joined by train-loads of Londoners who came down to pick, living in caravans and having a jolly time, all of us in the evenings gathered around camp fires, eating sausages in our fingers, the men drinking beer out of jugs.

Farm labourers were the least well-paid of any workers and on this farm they lived in primitive cottages that looked like the ones I'd seen in pictures of plantation slave quarters. Scrawny children played outside or stood crowded in doorways, pale with pinched faces. I asked Muz about this.

'Why do they look pinched?'

'It's the mark of poverty,' she said. 'Crammed together indoors, breathing stale air, always hungry, never getting enough sleep all in one bed, and if you look closely you'll see the wife is always pregnant.' Despite sounding disapproving with this latter observation, Muz was concerned and kind, often visiting the exhausted mothers with gifts and providing a helping hand if any of them were ill or in difficulties.

Ros has memories of the farm similar to mine that she sent me after reading my account:

Overy's Farm. Hot summers, all through harvest time with hop-picking and then a bitterly cold winter, Wendy very ill with measles and the phone getting struck by lightning, the doctor having to walk through the snow. Jack Frost patterns on the inside of bedroom windows. An exciting little doorway off the stairs leading to an attic full of treasures. The farmyard barn full of hay bales and hidden nests of kittens, the last of the cows Milky Moo and Daisy being hand-milked in there. Gentle, slow, wide-backed horses we were allowed to ride – Dolly and Captain. Stooks of wheat in the fields and haystacks we slid out of. Yellow sticks of brimstone burning with mysterious blue flames in an oast house with the toasty smell of hops drying overhead. A stream in the valley where Andrew and I sailed improbable craft for hours, getting wet and muddy. A cordon pear tree growing against a warm brick wall by the back door to the kitchen with actual edible pears on it. An orchard out there too with lush grass and windfall apples full of drunken wasps in Autumn.

We discovered that the reason for such a degree of neglect and failure to modernise the farm was due to a county plan making any development pointless as, in due course, the entire valley was to be flooded to create a reservoir, so the house and everything else was going to be drowned, swallowing up the whole time warp. This meant we would have to move out just when we had settled down and everything was turning out so well. I had passed all my O Levels the year before and was going into the sixth form to concentrate on zoology and science subjects, vaguely thinking I might follow Fa into some kind of medical career.

Muz thought the best idea for our next move would be a village house near the school, so we could walk to school, with shops and church nearby. She was good at finding houses with charm and, most essentially, plenty of space for her piano, while Fa just wanted to live in a box with as few possessions as he could get away with. Luckily he was not involved in this move and Muz was able to choose a storybook house called Greenways. It was set back in a proper garden full of flowers and big trees, with an orchard on one side and, best of all, a secret, private woodland with its own rookery. The raucous sound of rooks circling the tops of trees every evening, cawing as they dived down to hop and peck at their higgledy-piggledy nests, was an unchanging ritual that gave us a profound sense of attachment to that place with enduring memories.

Ros joined us at the school, reluctantly, as she felt stifled by its austerity, just as I did, while Elaine thrived on it. She had adopted as mother figures two of the teachers, both spinsters, who had responded sympathetically to this forlorn girl so desperately craving substitute parents. Her attachment was such that she refused to join the rest of us when Muz came back, and asked to stay on as a boarder. So it was just Ros and me walking to school each morning from Greenways, taking a short cut through a field where there was a mare with a foal. Both used to come to sniff our pockets for sugar lumps or apples, always gentle and friendly. This changed one day after the foal inexplicably died and the mare, maddened by the loss, went berserk and attacked us the moment we climbed over the stile. She pinned us to the fence, slamming her body against us while rearing up, biting our heads and trying to pound us with her hooves. I had never encountered a horse behaving like this, only having seen stallions fighting in this vicious way in films. It was like being in a horror movie as the mare got her teeth around the top of my head, where, luckily, my school beret saved me from being scalped, and the beret got stuck in her mouth; this spooked her, and she charged off, champing on it, so we were able to escape, never going that way again!

There was another horror-movie incident that term. As we were walking home from school one day, a Meteor jet fighter came screeching very low over our heads and, although we were used to these planes exercising above the Sussex countryside, this one was so low we could see both the pilot and navigator quite clearly through the cockpit window. A few moments later there was an almighty explosion some miles further on and flames streaked high into the air. The plane had crashed on top of a butcher's shop in the main street of a village near to a church and one of the engines hurtled off, landing in the churchyard among gravestones. Both the pilot and navigator were killed instantly, but miraculously there were few other casualties despite the street being full of shoppers that afternoon. A story later emerged that the pilot was making a low pass over his girlfriend's house in the village to surprise her, but, misjudging the height, he was unable to pull out in time. The main street never recovered from the devastation caused to so many traditional old shops and buildings, so its original charm as a model village was lost. But a modern new shop called the International Stores rose from the ashes to provide the village with its first supermarket.

I was due to leave school that year, 1956, and my final year's studies in zoology included a course in primates at London Zoo. This was great stuff, working behind the scenes and getting up close to animals such as orang-utans, charming yet tragic animals that launched themselves into my arms like frantic orphans as soon as I opened the door of their enclosure, hugging me tightly while rubbing their banana-smeared faces all over mine. After relaxing their grip (with a little persuasion), when I looked into their eyes I could see mirrors of myself achingly linked with theirs. They may not have been *homo sapiens*, but they were more *sapiens* than many humans I knew.

These were blithe times for me and the others: having at last a home we felt bonded to, in the gentle community of a village, with no stress or demands. Andrew, now called Spindle, was being considered for a place at one of the local Rudolf Steiner schools, where young people like him were tutored with understanding and support. Muz was happy with her music and a new Labrador. Her grand piano looked splendidly at home too, in the long, low, triple-aspect drawing room at Greenways, which had overhead beams and French windows opening onto the garden. Light streamed in all day, giving a comfortable glow to the room with its slightly battered chintzy sofas and armchairs, where we sat about reading and chatting while Muz practised her sonatas.

There was a reassuring rhythm to our lives and all was proceeding without a ripple when, unexpectedly, a telegram arrived saying that Grandad had died from a heart attack. Muz went to his funeral in Bournemouth and when she came back she told us that he had left her a considerable legacy as well as a large quantity of furniture, china and ornaments. We were astonished, as none of us thought Grandad was that well off since he lived quite modestly. By coincidence, just as we were absorbing the news of this good fortune allowing Muz the freedom of having her own money, Greenways suddenly came up for sale. This seemed extraordinarily fortuitous, as it was now quite possible that Muz could buy it and we would have our very own home at last. She was just as excited as the rest of us, having longed for years to have another house that was all ours, like White Cottage. Of course, we still missed Kenya and would have chosen more than anything to go back, but Fa was pessimistic about the future, with independence now inevitable.

As soon as Fa heard about Muz's unexpected windfall, he decided we needed him back in England, to make sure any purchase as big as a house didn't go ahead without his advice on what was suitable.

First photo in China

Fa and Wendy in Burma

Wendy and Elaine in India

Wendy, Ros, Andrew and Elaine, in England

King George V Hospital, Malta

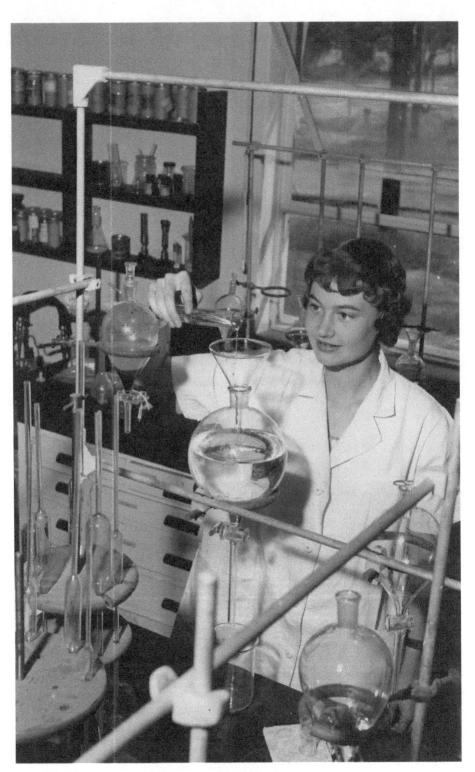

Pyrethrum Board lab at Nakuru

With my Vespa

Pearls and a faint smile

Elaine

Ros

Ward at The Royal Free Hospital, Gray's Inn Road

CHAPTER 9

Fa's arrival to check up on us and see what was going on in his absence – in particular that no important decisions were being made or money spent (even if the money belonged to Muz) – was not greeted with the usual fanfare, as this time we were all getting on remarkably well without him. We were even starting to enjoy ourselves, plugging into village life as part of a community that had its roots in centuries of reassuring tradition and mutual support.

Now in my last year at school, I was beginning to take liberties and slacken off. With the end of final exams, I began to inhale impending freedom like great gusts of oxygen drawn down so deeply into starved lungs it was making me half-crazy with giddiness. Since leaving hospital with the magic bottle of little white pills (which neither Matron nor anyone else ever asked me about), I was no longer fearful of sudden blackouts, and when the pills were finished it seemed safe to conclude that I must be cured. So I was no longer a mental case. I would be eighteen later that year and was longing to find out what lay beyond home and the school; to see who was there and what was going on. But first we had Fa coming to inspect Greenways and what was going on here at home.

We were looking forward to showing him the glories of Greenways and how it led to a private road that further on revealed miles of the kind of walking he loved: bridleways and footpaths merging with the great liberating space of open countryside under wide skies and far horizons. Walking was one of his passions and this vision at the end of our lane, we confidently imagined, could not fail to get him striding off with binoculars, exclaiming at all the birds to watch and views to gaze at.

Another attraction we'd lined up in our eagerness to impress him was one of the star features of Greenways' interior design, something few houses possessed at that time (usually only very large ones modernised by owners with money to spare and time to read *Ideal Homes* magazine). This marvel occupied the whole of the space above the long drawing room, and was a Hollywood-style master bedroom suite in eau-de-nil, with a matching eau-de-nil bathroom. This even had a bidet (very useful for washing feet), and a proper gent's dressing room leading off, which looked out over the back garden. The main bedroom had a huge bed and ranks of built-in cupboards decorated with scrollwork matching the other elegant features. We were certain that Fa, being a romantic at heart, would be seduced by the room. We hoped this would extend to his loving the rest of the house and surroundings, so everything would fall into place just as it was meant to this time.

'What are we going to give Fa to welcome him back?' Elaine, always the thoughtful one, asked.

'What about something nice for supper, his favourite things?' we suggested.

'What about *me*?' came from Spindle in his funny, cracked, teenage-breaking voice. 'Why can't I have my favourite things too?'

'Because you're not arriving back from a long time away needing to have a Welcome Home special type of supper,' Elaine told him.

'Well, when I go away to my new school and come back for the holidays, I want to have a whole bag of cream horns from the shop for my Welcome Home,' Spindle said, dropping an octave.

'We're talking about Fa,' Elaine reminded us. 'What kind of supper we're going to do for him. What he likes best.'

'Mainly kippers, steak and kidney pudding, jam roly-poly and treacle pudding,' some of us suggested. Muz nodded vaguely, then added, 'Kippers would be easiest.'

'I just *knew* you would say that,' I said, sounding rattled, as it was annoying that she didn't want to make an effort with anything more complicated, or go to the trouble of producing the steamed puddings he loved.

If a mousse or trifle was produced, he would growl that those were not 'proper puddings', such as he had been brought up with. Not that his mother did much cooking at any time during Fa's upbringing, according to Muz. 'Granny Craddock was a sitting-about type of person,' she used to say disparagingly. 'Slow of body [and mind, she would add], incurably lethargic. Daddy Craddock spoilt her and did everything for that family, then died of exhaustion.'

Having known the family for most of her life while living in the same street in Stoke Newington, Muz had candid views on Gran's perceived indolence, her own mother being unceasingly busy, darting about the house, keeping everything fresh and homely. No one in Muz's family ever sat about. Being industrious and 'getting-things-done' were guiding principles of life for her. 'Making-an-effort' was another, which became pressing at this moment of Fa's imminent arrival and the business of the Welcome Home supper.

Whoever did the cooking didn't have to wash up, and, as the eldest I had first choice; so, with Muz's lack of enthusiasm for cooking anything special, I volunteered, which meant I also got to choose what we were going to eat. I liked exercising my cooking skills, so the menu for Fa's Welcome Home supper turned into quite an elaborate affair with three courses. Each of these was very scaled down, of course, in line with modest Craddock appetites. Eating sparrow portions very slowly, allowing animated conversation to dominate over food, was the way family meals operated.

The much-anticipated three-course supper was served the evening Fa arrived, but it was a muted and unaccountably stiff affair. Fa was not his usual sparkling self, entertaining us with stories of his more eccentric patients and eventful road journeys. This time he seemed distant and distracted, no longer holding the competitions that were standard at meal times to see who could come up with the most original new word or idea. This was a ruse to get us to surf the dictionary, to learn new words and think new thoughts; at least that was the intention, but he seemed now to have lost interest. Worst of all, though, was the massively disappointing discovery that he didn't like Greenways. The seductive à *la mode* master suite that we had been sure would appeal to his aspirant inclinations, drew barely a glance as we ushered him in, throwing open the door theatrically.

He hardly noticed the king-size bed and mesmerising eau-de-nil decor, or the well-appointed gent's dressing room.

Well, at least he will see how wonderfully the acoustics work in the big beamed drawing room, we consoled ourselves. He can sit cushioned in one of the chintzy armchairs, reading his journals, with Muz's music lilting over him. He might also fall in love with the garden full of birds and the rookery in its secret wood at the far end.

Each day, while Fa was engrossed in catching up on intensive reading of his papers and journals, Muz continued valiantly to try and engage him with her music, but the mood in the house grew steadily heavier. Familiar routines marched on, as if, by methodical application, the lid could be kept on anything going wrong. The dog had to be walked, shopping done and meals cooked. Fa went for his customary long hikes and sometimes went off in the car for a whole day. 'Exploring,' he said. He didn't explain what was being explored, or where, or why. Muz's hopes that he might decide to come back to England for good on seeing the rest of us settled and happy, selling his share in the Nakuru partnership to buy another one in England, were not materialising.

We always knew when Fa was about to make one of his seminal pronouncements, as he would start off with a series of disarmingly vague, pontifical preambles, clearing his throat and fixing us with the penetrating gaze accompanied by twitchy smiles we knew and feared. It was a signal for bracing ourselves with familiar, pricking anxiety, ready to hear what was coming next.

It could hardly have been more startling. 'We're moving to East Grinstead,' he said at last, his voice booming into the tense pause as we waited to hear our fate. No one spoke. The silence went on and on. Muz sat pale and mute.

All at once: 'WHY?' burst in unison from the rest of us. 'WHY?'

Fa smiled his twitchy smile. 'I've found an ideal house in East Grinstead. It's completely new, only just built, not quite finished. The builder ran out of money, so the price has been reduced. Very good value. Much better than an old house which is always going to need keeping up.' He looked at us keenly for endorsement.

'Greenways has got five acres of land – that's where good value exists,' I said, loudly enough to make sure the point got across, 'right here in the village where most houses are on much smaller plots. Anyway, we like it here, we don't want to move.'

Muz sat impassively with her lips pressed together, looking resigned. It was obvious she had accepted being over-ridden, as usual.

'And what about school?' I went on. 'It's all right for Elaine being a boarder, but Ros and I need to be here so we can go on being day girls.'

Fa looked up. 'You can leave school straight away,' he said, making it sound like a favour. 'You don't need to stay on for your last term. It will save fees.'

Well, of course, that made sense if all of this mad farce was simply an exercise in saving money. 'And what about Spindle?' I continued, getting more incensed.

'Andrew will go to Camphill Village, which has been already arranged,' concluded Fa, smiling his big-toothed smile as everyone except me sat there too miserable to argue.

It was all fixed then, and Muz's money was going to be used by Fa to buy a horrid modern house just to satisfy his own lust for control and penny-pinching. And he was not even going to live in it himself. He went on to tell us that he would be going back to Nakuru as soon as he got us settled.

I wasn't going to leave it at that. 'How are we going to live in a house that isn't even finished?' I began, feeling suddenly hot and enraged at the sight of Fa lording it over us so exultantly with his Mephisophelean smile.

'We're going to spend the holidays working together on this new project,' he went on, having got it all worked out. 'All of us together. A family workforce. You can choose how you want the house to look, painting rooms in your own colours. You can even have wallpaper if you want to. It will be one of our best times as a family, doing things together, before the older ones start leaving school and going away. It's a great chance for all of us, being united in this new endeavour. Learning new skills, very instructive, and a healthy form of exercise. I will help, of course.'

As a kind of afterthought he added, 'By the way, the house is called High Torrs, and is on a main road near the town centre, so it will be very convenient.'

Very convenient for what? I wondered. During all this time the others had sat dumb with bewilderment, retreating into their own separate shells, and now, with Fa having finished the eulogy for his scheme, we sat looking at each other, hearts in boots; even the dog had his ears back.

'We can go and look at the house tomorrow,' Fa said, opening his journal, the matter having been settled.

When we saw High Torrs and gulped at the reality that good money had been paid for something so appallingly horrible, rough and unready, it seemed beyond reason that Fa intended us to live in this bleak block of cement sprouting from a heap of rubble and lumps of masonry. 'Why do we let him do these mad things to us?' I stamped around, raging and furious with Muz for handing over the money.

'I had to let your father have the money,' she said. 'It's in the marriage vows. All that I have is yours, and vice versa.'

'But you didn't have to let him buy this awful place,' I went on.

'Have you ever tried to stop your father doing whatever he wants?' she replied.

When it came to the dreaded day of moving into High Torrs, various items of furniture and household goods left to Muz by Grandad that had been stored in a warehouse, were now decanted from large vans into the emptiness of the grey shell that was still unfinished and unpainted. Fa's grand plan for directing a happy band of workers had produced feeble progress from a sadly unmotivated and demoralised team. But unloading the vans and laughing at some of the outlandish objects that emerged, lifted spirits all round, except for Fa, who viewed the bequest with brooding suspicion as more and more dusty old pieces were set down wherever space could be found.

When the last items had been deposited, Grandad's heavy dark furniture now occupied the rooms like slumbering elephants. Ornate clocks, unwrapped from packing cases with no mantelpieces to put them on, were parked among the elephants and proceeded to chime from unexpected corners where assortments of china and other goods lay piled up. One of the clocks was a weighty Victorian mantel-squatting object of black marble with fluted pillars under a Grecian-style pediment. We christened it the Acropolis and became very attached to it, even constructing a heavy-duty mantelpiece to accommodate it in the sitting room.

I had one of Grandad's walnut bedroom suites in my room, which crowded the room but disguised its grim outlines and I grew fond of the twirling patterns that I imagined as animal faces, while amusing myself lying in bed squinting at them.

I had left school now, leaving Elaine still boarding, where she was happy being incubated by the two broody-hen teachers who were her substitute parents, assisted by an older girl who was her crush. Ros and I spent days and weeks at High hateful Torrs up ladders, painting inside and out, wheel-barrowing interminable loads of builders' rubble to form a jagged pile on one side of the garden, where we fancied it might transform itself into a rockery if we ever got around to planting death-defying succulents in the crevices. Before Fa left, I insisted that he paid us for the work as money had been saved on the purchase. So Ros and I for once started to have a little money of our own to buy some decent clothes and small indulgences. Spindle was packed off to Camphill Village where, for the first time in his life, he was happy, and Ros was found a new school. It involved a long complicated bus journey, which she found stressful with strange men preying on her at bus stops.

Fa's final piece of advice before he left was to inform us that Grandad's old-fashioned furniture and assorted homely objects were unsuitable for a fresh new modern house and, in order to assist us, he had paid for them to be taken to the auction rooms. 'Not the Acropolis!' we cried. But he was determined to see it go, along with everything else he regarded as interloping on our territory, as if Grandad himself inhabited the ponderous pieces and was crouching like a rival lion in the midst of Fa's pride. When the vans arrived and everything was packed up, we watched the Acropolis disappearing into its many folds of wrapping paper, mournfully chiming jangled tones as the bells inside got jolted this way and that. Just like the last crows of Julius, I thought, as yet another of our treasures was dispatched.

However, nothing that Fa did now, or even the dismal experience of life at High Torrs, could touch the dizzy freedom of leaving school and having my own life to live, which felt like reaching the top of a mountain light-headed with exertion from the long climb, and revelation of limitless otherworldly views all round. Desperate to get out there and loosen ties with home, I joined the East Grinstead Youth Club, discovering, once inside, a den of deafening energy where we Rocked and Rolled every night until the doors closed, then roared off on motorbikes to race up and down the long empty roads that radiated from the town. Girls sat pillion, gathering up the skirts of flouncy frocks to avoid catching them in the wheels; arms tight around the boy in front, hair flying, eyes squeezed into slits in the wind rush, no helmets or goggles – the greatest possible way to burn off all that high-octane hormonal excess, in the absence of sex, which wasn't invented before 1960.

All the boys were on leave from National Service or waiting for assignment, most of them in blue as homage to the Battle of Britain pilots who were local heroes, famous as Archie McIndoe's pioneering plastic surgery guinea pigs at the Queen Victoria Hospital. The Guinea Pig Club met regularly at the Felbridge Arms pub, where we hung out with other bikers and regulars. The terribly disfigured faces of the guinea-pig pilots became familiar to us as we all congregated in the bar, chatting and joking. Everyone teased the pilots about their wives and girlfriends, who were always the best-looking ones; so it seemed that getting shot down in flames and horribly burnt only enhanced the extraordinary vitality of their characters and drew beautiful women to them.

All this sudden flinging of myself out into midstream East Grinstead club and pub life scandalised Muz, who was, in any case, feeling deeply unsettled by recent events. Her music no longer provided the same consoling bedrock of her life since the grand piano now stood like a displaced refugee in the sparse sitting room at High Torrs, its rooms denuded of the comforting clutter of Grandad's lumbering pieces. The sound and setting for her piano was all wrong. The move had been all wrong, her money spent on something that was never going to be a home, with all of us plotting to escape from it as soon as we could find a way. At the back of my mind I knew how short this glorious time of fast bikes and feverish dancing was going to be. This long hot summer – going off in coaches to the Orchid Ballroom in Purley where the big bands were playing, getting home late, giving my escort a quick kiss under the street lamp while Muz, woken by the explosive arrival of the bike, watched like a smouldering apparition from the doorstep, ready to let me in with furious lashings of her tongue – I knew all this was no more than a wild jubilant interlude and considerations of a career would have to follow soon.

In particular, I needed to devise some means to an income as the money I had earned labouring on High Torrs had all been spent on clothes and cups of coffee at cafés and pubs with my friends. We never drank alcohol. It was too expensive. Coffee shops were popular and fashionable and there were lots in East Grinstead, always jumping with a young chattering crowd like starlings. No one had much money; girls made their own clothes and did perms for each other with 'Toni' home-perm kits. We all turned out looking the same with tight crimped curls, but no one cared. We had Elvis and Buddy Holly and Chuck Berry and the big bands. We had short bouncy rock skirts and bosom-hugging T-shirts, and everyone had a job ready to step into.

What I wanted more than anything else was to get back to Kenya, where nostalgia pulled me with irresistible force like the ropes of the great twining lianas hanging from forest trees where we had swung and played. However far out we swung, the giant lianas always carried us back to the mother tree. I needed to save up first, and I had to think whether I still wanted to do something medical for a career, or something quite different. London shone like a beacon for all aspiring careerists and adventure seekers, so I bought myself the sort of coat I thought suitable for going for interviews in the big city and went off on the train from East Grinstead, with the address of the YWCA at Earls Court where I could rent a room. This was just like boarding school but friendlier.

When she heard I was in London, Babs invited me to meet and have tea with her at Bart's Hospital where she was now working as a ward sister. Loyalty to Muz made this awkward, but I wanted to see a big hospital from the inside, as I had become fascinated by the mighty throb of organised activity during those weeks in a mental ward at The London Hospital. Babs met me at the great door of Bart's and took me on a tour of all the many departments. Everyone knew her. I noticed the easy way she made people laugh; her popularity was unmistakable and her unaffected banter was greeted warmly wherever she went. The frivolous silliness had gone, and now at thirty-five she had that natural poise and confidence that goes with being successful in a senior job and well liked. In addition to which, she was a lively blonde with a peachy figure and a wicked smile. Bart's sisters' uniform emphasised her appeal, with the flowing gauzy cap setting off her tall slender figure. I could see now why Fa was so attracted to her, while Muz, sadly, in the long years of struggling to hold the family together, had become worn and drab. Pausing for tea in Bart's courtyard during the grand tour, Babs chatted pleasantly with refreshingly liberal views and it was difficult not to feel slightly beguiled. On we went then to visit ground-floor departments, including Casualty, where she again seemed to know everyone. She introduced me to Casualty Sister and told her I was eager and waiting with my school certificates, looking for an interesting job.

'Come and work here in my department,' Casualty Sister said. 'We could do with another receptionist in the Accident Box. It will be a crash course for life in the wider world,' she added, and we all laughed at the pun.

The commute from Earls Court to St Paul's on the tube was easy and quick, and working in the Accident Box was like being an extra on the film-set of a fast-action drama, as there was never a flat moment to stop and think what might happen next. Quick reactions and systems of working were essential parts of the job. This was the East End of London where life was rough, sometimes brutal, and accidents frequent. The whole area around Bart's and St Paul's was a wasteland of bombsites, now gradually being cleared, with new developments starting to rise up. The worst danger zones were in demolition and construction work, but strangely it was lorry drivers who were frequent casualties, either from accidents on the road, or getting sensitive parts jammed in trouser zips. I tried to work out how something as silly as zip entanglement happened so commonly, and concluded it must be that lorry drivers were always in a hurry trying to meet delivery times with not many convenient places to stop in city streets, causing careless attention to small details when snatching a moment in an obliging alleyway.

Ambulance bells clanged so loudly we could hear them far away, charging through the traffic. Every time I heard the bells I felt both anticipation and dread, wondering what new kind of trauma was about to arrive on a stretcher or trolley, banging through the double doors, where I waited on the inside with my clipboard.

I didn't work in an office, I didn't even have a desk; sitting down was not part of the job. My clipboard held printed admission forms and whenever an ambulance arrived or someone came in on foot, I was responsible for writing down their details and making sure these were accurate. Sometimes it involved trying to keep up with a trolley as porters ran with it to one of the small operating rooms where patients were resuscitated or given emergency surgery. If the patient was unconscious, I had to get details from the ambulance men as best I could. Often there would be police accompanying the more serious emergencies and what they wanted more than anything else were cups of tea and nurses to flirt with. When they discovered what a terrible blusher I was, there was no escape for me after that.

One of the topics causing alarm around that time were stories of young girls disappearing into what was called the White Slave Trade, and I was warned about it and how to look out for traps. There was a standard formula, I was told. A respectable-looking African man would introduce himself politely in the tube or on the street, saying he was a talent spotter for a model agency, and would I like to go for a photo shoot as I was exactly what they were looking for and could earn a lot of money as a model. I would then be handed a card with a telephone number. One very personable black man did approach me, introducing himself as Milton, saying that all he asked was to be allowed to take me for a coffee, handing me his number. The girls at work and the YWCA were horrified and said to give his number to the police. They of course would discover nothing on investigating since these people, if they were genuine White Slave agents, were very clever.

A friend of mine in London was sharing a flat with an Australian girl who answered an advertisement to join the crew of a yacht sailing around the Mediterranean. She was excited to be taken on after being interviewed by the owner and was then flown in a private plane to Gibraltar, where the yacht was based. She left all her possessions in her room at the flat, intending to return to London after the cruise. Weeks went by and then months, but she didn't come back. Her distraught parents flew from Australia to try to find her, but she had left no information about the yacht or its owner, no name or copy of the advertisement, nothing to go on at all. The police were sympathetic but without any leads it was a dead end, the girl's fate likely being a dead end as well. White girls were said to be prized in North African countries, which is where they were thought to end up, drugged and locked in brothels or harems, then disposed of when no longer useful.

All this time I was not distracted from the real purpose of my work, which was to save up enough money to go back to Kenya. It took six months and then I was ready to go. Fa was back in Kenya by now and had moved from the railway house to a cottage in Nakuru town at the Agricultural Society's Showground. It was close enough to the surgery for him to walk to work, so that pleased him with his obsession for keeping fit. As soon as he heard I was coming to join him, he decided that would be very convenient as he could dispense with house servants and I could be his housekeeper, saving staff wages. He hasn't changed a bit, I thought, still the same old skinflint.

I knew that I should be thinking about some kind of professional training instead of vaguely returning to Kenya and doing Fa's laundry, but I also had a pressing need for breathing space before going back to overheating my brains in a classroom. The experience of school had been so claustrophobic that I was hungry for rehabilitation, to breathe the pure oxygen of freedom and discovery. At the Sussex school there was no oxygen, only religious carbon dioxide.

Fa seemed uncommonly pleased to see me when I arrived, this time by Viscount airliner, the latest from Vickers Armstrong at Weybridge. The moment the door of the plane was opened at Nairobi and the hot dry blast eddying from Athi Plains blew in my face, I breathed deeply and rapturously, ecstatic to be home at last after four years. Fa smiled his most generous smile and kissed me enthusiastically. It was a sweet moment. I had come home. We were both at home now. It was a good feeling.

Fa's latest choice of house was a small dilapidated lean-to with a thatched roof and timber-framed mud walls, propped against the inside perimeter wall of the Showground. The thatch hung, worn and limp, over a jumble of rooms sheltering from the blistering sun and tropical rain. It was more of a shanty than a house and so utterly adorable in its craziness I instantly felt good about it, but curious as to how someone like Fa, with a passion for modern box houses, allowed himself to live in such a quaint place. The answer of course was obvious: it was cheap. That was because the whole place was rotting inside and out, literally vibrating with armies of white ants chomping their way through the wooden supports that held the mud walls together. My room was a tiny cubby-hole next to the front door, which might once have been intended for storage or a cloakroom, but got overlooked in the mad muddled way that the house had been put together. The room was perfect for me because I could see everything that was going on outside my window that, like everything else, was sagging, its gingham curtains hanging like old flags, still cheerful with a bit of a jaunty wave when the breeze caught them.

Fa was genuinely interested in discussing my options for a career. He was intuitive when something caught his interest and deduced that my preferences might lead towards research in some form, as I was always wanting to investigate things, wanting to find out what was going on and what the answers were. I had thought about this, but didn't know where to start. Fa, though, had already made enquiries and with his laboratory contacts had met a new research chemist recently recruited from England to work on a project at the Pyrethrum Board labs in Nakuru. Fa found out that he was looking for an assistant who would work to his personal instructions without preconceived ideas about the project. In other words, someone from outside the present lab team whom he could train in his own methods and way of thinking. He didn't want any smart-asses, so it seemed I might fit requirements. I went to meet the new chemist and found an instant rapport with him, resulting in the two of us becoming unlikely partners, toiling in a cramped steamy lab, working on a new method for analysing the pyrethrin content (active constituent) of pyrethrum, which was an important cash crop in Kenya. Farmers were paid on pyrethrin content rather than sack-load of dried flowers, so the figure awarded had to be very precise.

163

Every morning for an hour this erudite man, my boss, would sit at his desk in the lab, smoking a Sherlock Holmes pipe, looking at the wall with steady fixed concentration, which meant he had gone inside his head to think. I knew not to speak a word to him and the phone must remain disconnected, with the door locked, until he came out of his trance. Then we would have a cup of tea and he would tell me about the next stage of the current experiment that his thoughts had indicated. Sometimes, if an experiment went dead, he would ask me to suggest what had gone wrong, believing that my untrained mind could 'cut the crap' (as he put it) of complex processes. In his view, scientifically programmed minds too easily got stuck between fixed parameters.

While he was engrossed in thinking sessions, I was sitting at my workbench on a high stool, setting chromatographic columns and taking readings from them. Or I might be working with solvents in the many processes involving solutions of pyrethrum extract. The principal solvent used was petroleum ether. This was highly flammable, with an invisible heavy vapour having the unnerving ability to creep along a bench without being noticed until meeting a Bunsen flame. One day this led to an almighty explosion and fire in one of the main labs, with two technicians being badly burnt. The vapour from solvents as well as being flammable, was toxic, especially benzene, and I often got dizzy when evaporating solvents from flasks (a process producing an extract residue) and had to go outside for deep breaths of fresh air. Masks were not worn and concepts like Health & Safety had not yet entered the workplace.

The church youth club was still a focus for me and I never missed badminton, Scottish dancing or some of the discussion groups. Fa was happy to be left reading his journals and listening to his long-playing records. Looking after him was simple due to his frugal attitude to food and other indulgences, with the possible exception of indulgent thoughts towards Babs I suspected, who was never spoken of but whose aura inhabited the air around us like a hovering nimbus.

At badminton one evening in May 1957, a new club member turned up and introduced himself as Greg. He had arrived that week from England to join the Nakuru branch of a finance company. Nakuru was fast becoming a base for different companies supplying the ever-increasing needs of farming and businesses up and down the country. Greg was twenty-two, well spoken, tall and athletic. Good-looking in a conventional sort of way, he was eager to make friends. After that, he came to every badminton evening and sometimes picked me up from home in his car if it was raining. I had a Vespa, which in no way provided a rain-proof ride to the church hall. In his very English upright way he had first asked Fa for permission to call at the house and give me a lift. Fa liked that, and liked this Brylcreemed young man who was taking an interest in me.

One weekend Greg asked if I would like to go on a picnic with him, driving to a place south-west of Nakuru, where the steep edge of the Rift Valley had buckled millions of years ago to form a wide ravine. On each side, high cliffs rose up in sheer rock faces, where lammergeiers soared and nested, while far below gazelles grazed the short tufted grass of the wide valley. This giant chasm was popularly known as Hell's Gate, due to its immensity of scale and savagery of the harsh towering cliffs, but the area was not much visited as it was remote and difficult to find on rough tracks. This had never deterred Fa, who would go with a picnic and all of us packed into the Morris Minor to observe the lammergeiers, so I was familiar with the area and could show Greg all its wonders.

After the usual pounding and battering for a couple of hours on corrugated roads, with Greg's little Morris sportingly holding all its parts together, we reached the gazelle plains and set out our picnic. Sitting demurely on a rug in the shadow of the great cliffs, we drank our Thermos tea, watching the majestic birds gliding effortlessly in a vast blue dome of sky, as we breathed satisfying breaths of the warm air and wild mysterious peace of that great empty place. We were very restrained with each other, partly through shyness, but mainly due to contemporary middle-class censure against physical intimacy between unmarried people.

I was attracted to Greg, but not passionately. I didn't know what passion was, and courtship only from the pages of Jane Austen. Greg and I were happy to go on drives, exploring the wide volcanic landscapes that spread themselves in every direction from Nakuru, excited if we found a new picnic place or secret location far from any other passing car or feet.

I wanted Greg to meet Stephen and Joan, who were again very much part of my life and affections. I was sure they would like him, but might be disappointed that I was going out with someone involved in business rather than farming. They did tease me about this, but were far too generous-hearted to mind. They had moved to a new farm nearer Nakuru, where they were planting coffee to cash in on rising prices since Brazil's plantations had been affected by coffee berry disease.

Avondale, meanwhile, had been leased to tenants. The new farm was at Subukia, on rich red land that had been cleared on the lower slopes of Bahati forest, with a river tumbling through that ran with rainbow trout in fast rills and pools. It was a beautiful property, like Avondale, fertile and well organised. Joan's new house was a haven as before, with squashy sofas and beds, and wonderful food. There were capons and young beef, home-grown lambs, and crayfish reared in pens in the river, all served with vegetables grown on the river banks. Some of this produce was sent in perforated boxes to Nairobi, then flown to supermarkets in England.

Back in Nakuru, Greg and I after work would sometimes go down to the lake shore to watch the evening flights of flamingos circling overhead in their hundreds and thousands, amiably burbling as they flew, producing a sound like a contented communal babble. In the western sky beyond the birds, sunset would come suddenly with streaks of hot pink and burning red reflected in the blue lake water as it turned darker and cooler. All at once, as if at a signal, the squadrons of flamingos in their close-packed droves dipped and drifted down to land on their impossibly spindly legs, landing in the shallows. African night comes swiftly, like a curtain closing. There is a sudden hush, as if each living thing is holding its breath while the day snuffs out, and all at once the night sounds of insects and nocturnal animals start up in a deafening chorus, and bats come darting overhead. The temperature falls and daytime creatures go home or go to ground.

Fa was very easy-going about where I went and what time I got home, unlike Muz, fussing and standing on the doorstep waving her torch at 10 o'clock, calling out in a wavering voice, 'Are you there?' Fa was indifferent to curfews; he and I had a good understanding of each other with a minimum of demands on either side. We might as well have been two bachelors or friends sharing a house in agreeable style, so Muz's return to Kenya that summer with a complete overhaul of house rules shook us up. But I was glad to hand over laundry and cleaning duties to her, and glad to introduce her to Greg, who was guaranteed to charm her. Being exactly the kind of young man any parent would be happy for their daughter to meet, with a respectable job and background, certainly did impress her, to the extent that she seemed surprised I was sensible enough to be going steady with someone so dependable.

Elaine, Ros and Spindle had been left behind in England after being deposited with various minders, and High Torrs had been sold. I was curious to know whether there had been a loss on the £4,000 paid for it, but this was not mentioned and the reason for such a hasty sale was not discussed either, not with me anyway. I assumed Fa had felt challenged by Muz's desire to buy Greenways with her windfall and create roots in England, so he made sure the money was diverted to an easily disposable project. More of this plan took shape when Fa announced he had bought a plot of land up on the slopes of Menengai, overlooking the town and lake. An architect was already producing designs for a bungalow that was to be our new home, with the proceeds from High Torrs channelled into this inspirational scheme of Fa's, with him in charge. To get us all on side, various carrots were dangled, allowing each of us to have our own bedroom and choose the décor, with the others coming to join us as soon as the house was ready.

As it rose from a network of foundation trenches, the bungalow was exactly as might have been expected from Fa's previous record: a heavy grey blot on the bare hillside, with no distinctive features. From the start I had been suspicious after looking at the architect's simplistic drawings that all too obviously reflected instructions to produce a cut-price option. It was a curious anomaly, as Fa was meticulous about good taste when it came to his clothes. His suits and shirts, ties and shoes had always to be stylish, never drab. He made a point of looking smart and dashing; it was one of his trademarks.

My complaints about the new building looking like a bomb shelter marooned in a desert caused Fa to go out and buy two hundred tree saplings, which he planted with gallons of water and fertiliser in regimented battalions covering the whole area in front of the house. Anything planted in that climate grows phenomenally, like giant beanstalks, so in no time the house became overwhelmed, cowering behind this mighty forest, which then completely obscured the previously sensational lake views that were the sole redeeming feature of the hillside plot. Wherever property was concerned, Fa had an unerringly deadly touch.

During the time of the building saga, happy news reached us that Spindle was excelling at Camphill Village and had become something of a star, with younger boys looking up to him for advice and assistance, to which he responded with growing confidence. Fa had been paying for his upkeep at Camphill, and now that he had been recommended for a permanent place at the village, he became eligible for a grant from East Sussex County Council to enable him to stay there. The grant was subject to approval by a council-appointed psychiatrist and Spindle was duly assessed by this professional, who was a woman. With such glowing recommendations from Camphill, we never doubted the outcome, so it was hard to believe the news when it came through that the psychiatrist had turned him down for a grant despite all the favourable reports. She wrote in her report: 'This is an intelligent, articulate boy who should be with his family in Kenya. Institutional life in a different country cannot be in his best interests.' She could not have known how poisonous family life was for him – or it might have been that she was under instructions to avoid expense for the council.

Much discussion followed on the option of Spindle staying at Camphill with Fa continuing to pay for his upkeep, which was modest in comparison with boarding-school fees, but Fa was unwilling to do this, so Muz went back to England to collect him and the other two who were still there.

Elaine had left school at seventeen and had been working at the Home for Blind Babies in East Grinstead, as she was too young to start nurse training which was her career plan. Tragically, at that time, many premature babies placed in incubators were inadvertently blinded due to the high levels of oxygen piped into incubators, before harm from this procedure became known. There were several sets of twins at the home, since premature birth was a risk factor for twins; it seemed particularly sad that the extra blessing of a twin birth was followed by the tragedy of blindness.

Ros, who was thirteen, was once again pulled out of school and bucketed back to Kenya, along with Spindle and Elaine, so they all arrived at once, and it was just at this point that a life-changing event came out of nowhere to eject me from my own little reverie.

Whether it was due to the flurry of emotions caused by the family arriving, or simply some spur of timing that I had been unaware of, Greg, one evening as we were lingering at the door saying goodnight, without any warning seized my hands and asked me to marry him. I was speechless with surprise, needing some long moments to take this in. Hard-wired into my brain was the imperative to remember good manners at all times, even *in extremis*, and rather than seem rude I managed to say in a rather feeble voice, 'Yes. Yes, of course.'

I was sure Muz and Fa would think it much too soon for me to get engaged after knowing Greg for only a few months, but surprisingly they were both delighted. I sensed a certain amount of relief in their pleasure, getting a daughter off their hands so quickly, with a suitable husband having a good job and prospects.

Within days, the mighty machine of wedding plans went into action and I was being swept along. I was taken to have a formal portrait photograph of myself, posed in a studio wearing pearls and a faint smile, to be sent to Greg's parents in England. It was all happening at dizzying speed, with the wedding set for six months ahead, all very soon and strangely out of my hands. The only thing in my own hands was the ring, once a suitable one had been found.

CHAPTER 10

Wedding mania gripped the household and Muz had a brainwave, remembering there was a pattern for a knitted wedding dress she'd put away in one of the boxes at the railway house before everything was moved to the Showground. The fate of the boxes sparked immediate alarm as no one knew where they were. Fa remained entirely unconcerned, expressing satisfaction that they were not anywhere in the house as he detested clutter or any space being taken up by unnecessary objects. Muz instantly organised a search party to go round looking into all the assorted Showground buildings where any boxes might have been stored, with staff, both ours and Showground attendants, recruited to help. The search party included a random collection of dogs brought in to tackle the hordes of rats that ran out in long black columns as cattle pens and barns were opened. After much sport and flasks of boiled sweet tea being provided for sustenance, there, in some horse stables, the boxes were found, quite safe and unmolested. Muz was enormously cheered by their discovery and the excitement of opening them to reveal mouldering treasures like her Singer sewing machine, which was hauled out and vigorously oiled.

Almost toppling into one of the boxes as she rummaged through its depths, Muz called out, 'I know there are dress patterns in here somewhere. The knitted one is utterly unique. No one will ever have seen anything like it!' She chattered on happily, describing it to me. 'But the difficulty is getting the right kind of wool. I don't think we could get it sent over from England in time.'

Thank God for that, I thought.

While all this was going on, news arrived that one of Greg's friends from London was coming to join him at the same finance company in Nakuru. 'Great timing!' exclaimed Greg. 'He can be best man. No question the best man for the job.' He laughed at his little pun. 'He's a bit of a character, a cracking good sport, ex-fighter pilot and won't flinch when it comes to the speeches. You'll like him,' he added. 'You'll like Lanner. He'll give you a good thrashing at badminton and you'll like that too.' Greg was trying to provoke me as I stood there, looking unimpressed.

'Is Lanner his real name?' I asked suspiciously, feeling prickly at this sudden introduction of a best man with a peculiar name whom I'd never met.

'It's something to do with birds of prey,' Greg replied vaguely. 'All the men in the family are named after falcons or something like that. I think one of them is called Perry, which is short for Peregrine.' I began to be interested, but thought Perry sounded more promising than Lanner.

Anyway, that was it, the best man was called Lanner and he was twenty-four, which seemed quite old to me, not yet nineteen. The day he arrived, a party was arranged for that evening at Greg's house, as a welcome and to ensure that Lanner's first night in Kenya would be wild and noisy, which looked guaranteed given the number of tottering stacks of beer crates piled up ready. My instructions were to keep the party under control while Greg went to Nairobi to collect Lanner from the airport and bring him back, a round trip of about 180 miles.

Driving long distances in Africa was a normal part of life, coaxing side-valve engines to extreme feats of endurance with radiators boiling on Kenya's challenging roads. Broken fan belts and punctured sumps were all part of the motoring experience, along with rusty holes in the chassis through which dust swirled, gluing itself to skin shiny with sweat, so that one sometimes emerged at the end of a trip caked red like a Masai. Suspension systems were rudimentary, consisting of leaf springs that frequently felt compelled to spring apart miles from anywhere. Everyone carried jerry cans of spare water for boiling radiators as well as for drinking, and just as essential were spare fan belts and spare wheels, as the stony roads chewed up rubber tyres.

A girlfriend of mine called Judy, cheerfully jolting along in her little car one day while peering through dust clouds inside as well as outside, suddenly became aware of an unusually violent shuddering and grinding motion of the whole vehicle as it collapsed onto one side. She got out to have a look and saw that the wheels on that side were not there anymore. Being Judy, she had no clue as to how that could have happened. Knowing how unreliable her attention span was, I had a theory that she hit a culvert without noticing, and then went on not noticing until everything started to fall apart. As was generally the case, however, two spare wheels solved most problems. There was not a Kenya girl born who could not change a wheel, mend a puncture or leaking radiator, replace ruptured fan belts and hoses, clean spark plugs and reset points. But if it was a bust sump or brake fluid reservoir, that could be a bit more tricky.

Lanner arrived from Nairobi well into the night when the party was getting rackety and lights had been dimmed for dancing. Greg came in first, walking quickly across the room to where I was acting as DJ on the record player. 'Lanner will be here shortly. He's brushing up,' he said, reaching out to turn me around and away from the dancing couples for a few moments, so we could isolate ourselves in that bubble that couples create as their own personal exclusion zone.

A few moments later, Greg shouted, 'Here he is!' and I lifted the record player arm so the music stopped abruptly and the dancers looked up. Across the room Lanner stood in the doorway, looking dazed and tousled. He was tallish, slender and fine-boned, wearing an old flying jacket that hung loosely, seeming slightly too big for him. Greg made introductions in a general way and everyone raised glasses as Lanner was steered towards the bar that was sagging with beer bottles. A glass in his hand, Lanner was brought over to be introduced to me. Someone had started the record player again and whatever words of introduction were spoken, I heard none of them or Lanner's response. He put down his drink and held out his hand. It felt dry and steady as he held mine for a moment, hesitating slightly; he looked at me as if some kind of current had passed in a mysterious way between us. Whatever it might have been it was momentary, as he was taken off to meet other people to keep him occupied while Greg came back to dance with me.

I was disturbed by the meeting as Lanner was not the kind of person I was expecting. He wasn't like Greg, or Greg's other friends, merging seamlessly into any gathering. He did not merge, but held himself apart, very composed; not one of the crowd, he looked entirely his own man. I was uneasily aware that in the instant of our hands touching, something strange had been conveyed. It felt like a recognition or acknowledgement – but of what? It must be some kind of fanciful notion, I decided, something I was imagining, not something real.

After that evening, Lanner came to join the badminton fours at every session in the church hall. He seemed possessed of an infectious energy, which had a dynamic effect on me as I found myself running faster, jumping higher, hitting harder and feeling super-charged, while all the time the intensity of his gaze and presence was unsettling me. Badminton games became highly animated, and one evening, as we both reached for a shuttlecock at the same moment, my arm brushed against his body and I felt a shock go through me so fiercely that I had to bend over, pretending I had a stitch.

Greg seemed merely happy that we were getting on so well, but he was grumpy at times about Lanner sharing a house with him, as the privacy that we had been enjoying was lost. At weekends I used to go and put flowers in the house to brighten the place up, and now there were two of them it became more of a home as I brought extra additions like books and cushions. When Lanner saw how much I liked flowers, he began gathering bunches for me, helping to arrange them around the house.

Church Hall activities were still a central focus, with different groups organising events. I was in the church choir and we appeared on stage in various roles when variety shows were put on. Theatre productions were popular, but for anyone in the cast it was a scrum backstage, with limited space and facilities, but it was always exhilarating. Props and costumes were crammed into cupboards, often getting mixed up in the changes. It was so stifling behind the scenes and in the wings that flannels were kept in buckets of water to rinse our sweating bodies, like horses at the races.

At the end of one production, Greg was putting audience chairs away while I was backstage storing props. The lighting was dim in that confined space and as I reached up to a high shelf I felt a movement behind me. Turning round, I saw it was Lanner, so close I could see every outline of his face shadowed in that light, and could smell his skin; astringent like rubbed lemons, it was strangely arousing. We stood there, inches apart, not daring to move or breathe, just staring at each other. Unaccountably at times there can be an impetus outside one's normal control that perversely takes over, and somehow we were drawn together with such inescapable force there was no possibility of resistance. I could feel the beats of Lanner's heart and my own almost choking me in the intensity of that embrace. The power of the emotion shocked us both into immobility, like Rodin's lovers entombed in marble. We knew it was forbidden, that there was no way back, and we had done a terrible thing. It was terrible because it was a knowing betrayal of that innocent, unknowing person who was Greg. It was only a kiss, but was no ordinary kiss.

Maybe it was lucky there was no time to linger as Greg's voice came eerily from the empty hall, calling to see where we were, and the spell was broken. Lanner pulled away and went to the stage door, while I resumed putting away the props. I called back to Greg slightly out of breath, 'Just coming', and clambered out of the backstage pit to join him.

Keeping up appearances was the standard antidote for tricky situations, so that's what we did and rattled along as if nothing had happened and the most important thing was to carry on as normal. Everyone's attention was diverted as the Menengai house was almost ready for occupation, with Fa recruiting volunteers to do the painting and decorating. We were allowed to choose colours for our rooms and mine was to have white walls with a blue ceiling, so I could lie in bed imagining I was looking at the sky.

Fa, in a most unusual display of extravagance, had imported rolls of Chinese wallpaper for the sitting room, which had an oriental theme of his own design. An Italian wrought-iron specialist was commissioned to make elaborate screens to serve as room dividers for the split-level reception rooms, and space for a grand piano was included in the floor plan. We were glad to see Fa had remembered this. The floors were cedar parquet that shone with a soft glow among the jewel colours of Persian rugs he'd bought from a passing carpet salesman. He really was trying his best to make up for the High Torrs fiasco.

The Chinese wallpaper had been delayed in Mombasa and all hands were put to hanging it when the crate finally came off the train at Nakuru.

This handmade paper was to give the room its ultimate crown of beatitude and Fa was twitching with anticipation as the rolls were unfurled and paste pots filled up, ready to display Kenya's finest (and most expensive) wallpaper. Everything had been prepared with meticulous instructions so the wallpaper, which was of exceptional quality, went on smoothly with not a single bubble or crease. When half of one wall was done, Fa stood back to admire the lustrous paper of sunshine yellow with its bold, black, vertical calligraphic columns painted in traditional wide brush strokes. It had the visual effect one might encounter in a Chinese palace or temple, so was slightly out of scale in our Menengai sitting room, but was impressive in an off-beat, eccentric way, just like Fa himself.

He went on looking at it, putting his head to one side and then the other, as if weighing up the effect, when all of a sudden he leapt in the air with an ear-shattering howl before dropping to his knees, yelling and hissing through his teeth in the way he did when particularly aroused.

We all waited, stunned into silence, paste brushes drooping.

'Can't you see?' raged Fa. 'None of you has a clue. Can't you see what you've done?' he ranted on. 'If your mother was here she would know immediately. She knows the language.'

'Well, what is it?' I said, feeling cross, as everything looked perfectly all right to me.'

'It's damned well . . . look at it . . . you can't be *that* blind!' He went on shouting and hopping like a madman.

We all stood there dismally, waiting for the tirade to end.

Finally, he shrilled between clenched teeth, 'It's damned well *upside down*! It's a disaster.' He sank to his knees again, crouching on the floor as if about to sob into the parquet.

'No one is going to know that except you and Muz,' I said, 'so it doesn't matter. And, anyway, the rest of us think it's amazing and wonderful,' I went on, trying to soothe him.

Fa was having none of that, and fuming even louder, he ran at the wall and started to tear down, dementedly, one by one, all the strips of beautiful silky wallpaper.

We stood there paralysed, staring at the crumpled strips and blank wall sticky with glue. There was not enough paper left now to cover the walls if we hung the remaining strips the right way up, so what were we going to do? We went on standing there, waiting in some terror to find out.

Subsiding into quiet despair Fa looked ready to have a nervous breakdown, when Ros had an inspired idea. 'Why don't we hang the rest of the paper, what's left of it, in panels, the right way up this time, leaving strips of plain wall in between so the panels look like banners.' She went on encouragingly, 'The effect could be more elegant that way, rather than having the whole of each wall covered in such a bold design. The plain areas of wall can be painted to match and complement the banners. It would look very good.'

Fa listened and, to everyone's relief, perked up while considering this, which took some minutes, and with no other solution being proposed, he relented and actually started smiling and telling Ros it was a very clever idea. We measured the spaces between each strip so they were uniform and made sure the lettering was the right way up according to Fa's instructions, and the whole operation was done very quickly and with much satisfaction. When it was finished, everyone, including Fa, agreed that Ros was quite right about the banner design being more refined than what had been originally intended.

While all this was going on it had been easy to put wedding-dress options and other associated discussions on one side as there were more pressing topics, like what kind of cooker Muz was going to have in the new kitchen. As well as the choice of a modern all-electric cooker, she was to have fitted units – a new invention for kitchens that was just beginning to come into fashion, replacing old cupboards with doors sticking or falling off. Some of the new units were to be fixed on the wall above worktops surfaced with a magic stick-on material called Fablon. This was smooth and shiny, easy to wipe down and keep clean, unlike our old worktops, which were made of wood that needed to be scrubbed. Our Menengai kitchen was to have the latest fixtures and be fully electric with all kinds of gadgets and devices now that Fa had suddenly discovered the new thrill of extravagance.

The house with its innovations, revived hope in Muz for a proper family home at last. This, combined with plans for the wedding, propelled her into high gear, and once she had managed to complete the household with a couple of dogs, her whole outlook became transformed. When Muz was happy and not worrying about something, she started laughing again and letting down her guard against whatever new calamity might be getting ready to fall on us, which usually happened as a result of one of Fa's sudden whims. The house was another new start, with security restored now the Mau Mau emergency was over and life was getting back to a form of normality – at least for Europeans. African aspirations had yet to be satisfied and political solutions worked out.

Now we were all together again and the essential element of each house we lived in – a grand piano – had been installed in the new sitting room, orchestral evenings were resumed. Each of us (apart from Fa and Spindle) played an instrument in what had become a family quartet, giving recitals, either for Fa alone or an audience of friends. Muz had her father's viola, which she played on these occasions instead of the piano, which I played, while Elaine played her violin and Ros her cello (called Sebastian). Fa loved to have us play in the evenings after supper, which, at that time before TV and other diversions, was the normal way people relaxed and entertained each other. Spindle, who found these musical interludes tedious, would be lolling under the piano with the dogs, looking sullen but not daring to interrupt.

My nineteenth birthday was planned to be celebrated in the new house with a tea party, so I could invite my Pyrethrum Board friends and others from the church. Greg and I now had our own social circle among the influx of young people arriving in Nakuru. The town was growing fast as new businesses opened up and jobs became plenty and varied. The split-level main rooms of our house were ideal for entertaining and Muz enjoyed playing show tunes and swing-time numbers as a lively accompaniment to the socialising, so our tea parties soon became as popular as the ones we used to have in Malta.

Among the cards that arrived for my birthday was one from Lanner in which he had copied a poem, with a message in his stretched-out handwriting. The poem, by Sir Philip Sidney, starts off with the lines:

My true-love hath my heart, and I have his, By just exchange one for another given:

I hold his dear, and mine he cannot miss, There never was a better bargain driven . . .

The message with the poem was a pledge of love expressed in simple terms that in any other circumstance would melt all defences, but in this circumstance left me dismayed because I could not return the sentiment. Equally, how could I go on with wedding plans and marriage to Greg, pretending all was well when clearly it was not? And, however tenuous the presence of Lanner on the scene, it was a fact I could not deny or ignore. I needed someone to talk to who would not fly into a fluster of panic as Muz would, or alternatively tell me not to worry . . . 'It's just a little stumble that all young girls experience on the worthy path to marriage . . . etc.' Fa, when he was not riding wild horses, pursuing new quests, or cast down in pits of fuming irritation if things did not go his way, was a wise counsellor, as many of his patients would testify. Waiting for one of his more benign moods to settle upon him would be a good moment to talk. Since moving to the Menengai house he had calmed down a lot. With a few thousand feet of mountainside right outside the door, he could lope off to release all the bottled energy that inhabited his lean frame. Muz's piano playing always soothed him and now, in the Chinese sitting room, surrounded by satisfying objects of his own choice, he could allow himself to feel at peace. He liked to sit there in his new armchair, long legs stretched out, admiring the glazed alcoves he had designed with frames of wrought iron fashioned into Chinese characters, spelling out his name and favourite mottoes. Concealed lighting illuminated the decorative fretwork, a focus for calm contemplation as he sat listening to Muz playing Chopin or Debussy.

In the evenings we would sit outside on the veranda in the warm diffused light of that golden hour following the glare of all-day sunshine that is one of Africa's most special times. This was when we would have long languid conversations on events of the day or exchange latest thoughts and ideas, watching the distant, pink, moving blur of flamingos circling the lake on their evening flight. It was a good opportunity, when Fa and I were alone there one evening, to edge around to the subject of Greg and my dilemma.

'I need to ask you something,' I started rather diffidently. Fa liked being asked things, but he never responded to a question like most people, within a couple of breaths. He would look off into the distance for long moments as if preoccupied with something else, eventually coming back with a carefully considered reply, while in the meantime whoever had asked the question might have wandered off or given up waiting. This time my question hung in the air as was customary until, after a long pause, Fa answered, 'Go ahead.'

A direct approach always worked best with him. 'It's about Greg,' I said. 'I don't think my feelings for him are strong enough at the moment to go on with the engagement and get married.'

Fa showed no indication of having heard as he continued looking into the distance. I waited for him to say something. He did his throat-clearing preamble. 'The only good reason for marrying someone is because you can't live without them,' he concluded briefly.

'The question is not whether I can live without Greg. It's whether I can live *with* him,' I said.

'That's your answer then,' replied Fa, still looking off into the distance.

'How do I tell him?' I asked. There was an even longer pause while Fa considered.

'When you have to tell someone a truth that is going to break their heart, as I have to do with patients and relatives on those occasions when a diagnosis offers no hope, the burden of grief is eased if you can share that burden with them honestly and with true compassion, deeply felt and genuine.' I waited for him to go on. 'Being open and honest does not necessarily mean laying out all the stark facts of the situation, which might be too painful for others to bear.' He stopped to collect his thoughts again. 'You might think about sparing Greg too much stark fact,' he said gently.

The next time Greg and I were alone, I fortified myself, hating what I had to do and feeling like an executioner, but knowing I had to tell him the truth about my feelings and our plans. 'It's all too soon, too fast. I'm feeling muddled about it,' I explained.

A pistol shot from point-blank range could not have produced a more startled and wounded look from Greg as he began to crumple and, very upsettingly, tears spilled from his eyes.

His voice tight and uncomprehending, he said, 'But I don't understand. We love each other. We're meant to be together. We make each other happy, everyone can see that.' He sat very still for a while, then, 'You can see that, can't you, how right we are for each other? And what about our children, the ones we've talked about? We both want a big family, that's what we agreed. We did, didn't we?'

I couldn't think what to say. I felt wretched and empty. There was another long silence before he continued. 'I can wait until you're ready. We don't have to rush. Please don't go away,' he said quietly.

I went on sitting there like an idiot, dumb because I couldn't think of anything to say that would make things any better.

'Is it Lanner?' he asked.

I looked down, feeling my face flushing, feeling terrible shame.

'You are his best friend,' I said, entirely aware how lame this sounded.

'Yes, of course,' he said. 'But I have seen the way he looks at you. Do you remember that evening at your parents' when we were all standing there looking at the new painting your father had bought? You were looking at the painting, and I was looking at Lanner looking at *you*.'

I laughed and replied, 'He considers himself a bit of an art fancier and Fa's paintings would not be his choice, so he was probably trying to find something else to look at, and I just happened to be standing in the way.' We both laughed and the moment passed.

Greg continued. 'We'll still see each other, won't we, and go to parties together? We'll still be a couple? Otherwise what will we tell people?'

'Can you let me have a breathing space to get my thoughts together?' I asked.

'Yes, but not for too long,' he said, smiling now and, being the good man that he was, taking it on the chin.

Muz and the family would have to be told before anyone else and Fa, knowing the upset this would cause, saved me from the worst of it by explaining to Muz first. She, in her usual stoical way, sighed and accepted Fa's consoling words, before going off to pack up her Singer and the wedding-dress patterns.

It was much more difficult dodging the barbed gossip that flew around the small community of Nakuru; as with all tight circles, each has its female bloodhounds with sharp tongues and noses snuffling up anything with a promising aroma. Dr Craddock's daughter breaking her engagement to such a well-liked and eligible young man (while rumour had it that his best friend was involved in some way) was something unmistakably meaty to be chewed on.

Our family was used to upheavals so the news about Greg and me, after some initial flurry, was tolerated philosophically, except for Spindle's concern that there would be no wedding cake or other diversions to relieve the tedium of his own life. He was now an eager teenager, fizzing with suppressed energy, hungry for outlets, frustrated to be loafing at home while no one knew what to do with him, and there were no schools that could or would take him. Ros, his loyal friend, was now a boarder at Limuru School, and Elaine was working as a probationer at Nakuru Hospital until she was old enough to start nurse training back in England at Fa's old hospital, The London.

My parents' main strategy for Spindle seemed to be aimed at keeping him quiet and getting him to accept life as a 'mentally defective' person, living at home. This was very much the standard attitude to such people at the time, if they were not consigned to an institution. Camphill Villages were pioneers in providing an alternative for young people such as Spindle, and it was the greatest pity that he was denied this chance of support in a sheltered, nurturing environment. At home, his indignation and anger at finding himself 'written off', as he put it, with no hope for a worthwhile future, began to spill over into occasions of violence and weird behaviour that were, in reality, desperate cries for help. Muz and Fa seemed inexplicably helpless when confronted with this head-on situation. Instead of using their considerable intelligence and ingenuity to find simple employment, therapy or guidance for Spindle, they dithered and retreated into the automatic comfort zone of Christians when perplexed, shunting the problem onto God. 'The Lord will provide' was the standard mantra on such occasions, allowing perfectly capable adults to pass the buck.

Life must carry on as normally as possible – that was always the overriding principle – and our tea parties could be relied on to keep the tone steady. Friends came at weekends or after work, sitting round the table with sandwiches and cake, Muz playing requests on the piano. I had a group of girlfriends sitting demurely at the table one tea time when we noticed that Muz's melodies were accompanied by strange noises coming from under the piano, grunting animal noises with loud groans and squeals. All conversation stopped while we looked at each other anxiously. Muz carried on playing, seeming deaf to what was going on so close to her feet on the pedals. Before I had time to go and investigate, there was a piercing scream and deep-throated yell as a demented apparition shot out from under the piano and came leaping up the steps to confront us in the dining room: a figure, stark naked and smeared with something slimy and nasty, leering at us with horrid glee. It was Spindle gone raving mad and terrifying in his lunacy. Muz was the only one who could calm him, and after that he was sedated and locked in his room if we had visitors.

Spindle's deteriorating mental state with unpredictable outbursts of terrifying anger and disinhibition, was very destabilising in a household where I was trying to keep my own nerves steady after breaking up with Greg. Added to this daily tension it was impossible to avoid meeting Lanner at the many social events around town, which was uncomfortable because everyone was watching to see what we were going to do next, making us wary and edgy. We never spoke to each other in public and were careful never to be seen alone together. The guilt we both felt was too overwhelming to allow ourselves to seem happy after wounding Greg so bitterly. The outlet for our forbidden emotion was in letters written and posted; we never used the telephone.

On one side of our house there was a steep stony track worn into the mountainside that could be used as a short cut from the road below. Cars in low gear could negotiate this, avoiding rocks and potholes, but due to these obstacles it was not much used by vehicles. One night, lying in bed, I heard a car grinding up the track and could see the beam from its headlights wavering in the dark sky outside my window. It was unusual for cars to use the track at night, so I went to look. The car stopped below the garden and its lights went out. A dim figure emerged and walked across the grass through our young trees to the veranda, and when the figure got close I saw with surprise it was Lanner. I thought maybe there was some problem he had come to tell me about and, wrapping myself in a blanket, went out quietly, being careful not to disturb anyone.

I found him sitting on the steps of the veranda in the dark, smoking a cigarette. He looked up, startled to see me. He didn't say anything.

'What's up,' I whispered.

'Come and sit down,' he said. I opened the blanket and, wrapping it around both of us, we sat huddled in the darkness. He hesitated before explaining. 'I wanted to come and sit here by myself, not disturbing you or anyone else, just to feel close to you. It was enough to know you were inside, only yards from me, asleep as I thought.' He laughed softly. 'But now you're here, that's even better.'

We sat like that, warm and close, folded together in the blanket, and talked and talked. It was as if we could never come to the end of all the things we wanted to tell each other. As if we had waited all our lives for this. The great dome of sky above us, blazing with stars, moved infinitely slowly until those bright stars on the edge slipped towards the horizon and a distant sound of clanking from the mail train coming up from Nairobi rose through the early morning mist. Lanner ducked out of the blanket and wrapped it around me with his arms holding it there so tightly it felt symbolic of his desire to keep hold of me, before he disappeared into the mist, and the soft crunching of his car tyres on the track soon disappeared as well.

After that, the quiet night-time veranda, when everyone else was asleep, became a place where we could meet unobserved for as long as we liked. The engine noise of Lanner's car labouring up the hill was the signal I waited for, and sometimes if I was asleep and missed it, he would come and tap softly on my window. But he never came inside the house or to my room; that would have crossed unspoken boundaries.

Other boundaries observed but never spoken of involved a loyalty to Greg, which meant that I never took Lanner to any of the places Greg and I had made our own. But there was one place I had not been to with Greg, which was possibly the most special of all. It was so hidden away that few people knew of its existence, or how to find it, on private land in a wilderness where it was easy to get lost and roads were no more than rough tracks, with gates putting off any casual explorer.

We left the car at the foot of a rocky hill where impala flourished on the tough bleached grass, herds of them standing flicking their short tails in the heat of midday among scant Leleshwa scrub. We took water bottles and found the game path that climbed, twisting among rocks and lava shale. Our shoes, scraping and slipping on the loose surface, disturbed dik-dik and other small animals that stood startled, staring at us momentarily before scurrying off into the grey-green bush. After a slow climb the ground began to level out under some larger trees and there, in a clearing, a tiny oasis became visible. This was a natural spring, rising from rocks and spilling over into a long shallow pool. It was known locally as a hot spring but was in reality lukewarm and wonderfully refreshing, clear and slightly sulphurous.

I had taken my shoes off to test the water and was looking for hoof and paw prints around the edge to see what kind of animals were drinking there, when ripples made me look up. Lanner had eased himself into the shallow cup of the pool that was just long enough and wide enough for him, and then me, to lie side by side with our heads above the surface, while the spring bubbled contentedly around us and the air sang with cicadas. We turned our faces to the sun, absorbing its rays like a blessing as we in turn were absorbed by the sensations of the smooth gurgling water and each other.

We may have created a small world for ourselves as secret and hidden as the rock spring, but the outside world was indifferent and Lanner was posted away from Nakuru to another branch of his company within weeks. Whether as a result of the scandal caused by the broken engagement or just coincidence, I didn't know. This was a wrench, just as we were beginning to feel more comfortable with each other, but I needed to focus on work at the labs as my boss was getting ready to publish results of his research and would get tetchy with me if I lost concentration. My work was an anchor for me, as was the Menengai house with a room of my own, and I had started taking lessons on the church organ with a new and very earnest young organist who had arrived from England eager to recruit pupils. Muz often played the organ in church and I sometimes sat beside her, watching her small busy feet working the long pedals that fanned out temptingly at floor level. At keyboard level the organ had two sets of keys, one above the other, with banks of ivory stops that could be pulled out for extra volume or effect. My fingers fidgeted to get at those stops and keys, and I wanted to have my own feet dipping among the pedals, creating rich tones.

Tom, the new organist, had thick black hair, dense and oily as Elvis Presley's, with heavy black-rimmed glasses emphasising the effect. I was fascinated by the texture and quantity of this hair, and sitting on the organ bench next to him I tried squinting down his collar to see if it extended down his chest and back, but as he always wore a tight collar and tie, this tended to impede my efforts. Not so fascinating was his gruesome breath that engulfed me with noxious fumes as he swayed back and forth on the keys. When I complained to Muz about it, she said it was my own fault for being so nosy and getting too close.

Despite Muz's flippant dismissal of the bad-breath complaint, seeing it as irrelevant to the more serious business of learning to play the organ, I felt I needed to weigh up the pros and cons of becoming a proficient organist with the downside of becoming infected with some as yet unidentified deadly form of mouth fungus. But this debate was overtaken by Tom himself suddenly declaring that our lessons would have to end because he was going out with Elaine (that certainly was a surprise), and she didn't want us sitting so close together on the organ bench all alone in the church. Well, she's welcome to his fumes, I thought.

After that, Ros and I used to wait until we heard Tom's car arriving back from an evening out with Elaine and then we'd scramble to the open bathroom window to spy on them as they sat inhaling each other's emanations, pressed together in the front seats under the gloom of the car port. On one occasion it was too dark to see properly and Ros got a torch to use as a spotlight so we could illuminate what they were doing and embarrass them. It was a bit of a fumble getting the torch adjusted for maximum focus, but it worked spectacularly as they were caught in an embrace. However, in our efforts leaning out of the window to get a good view, all the tooth mugs and other clutter on the windowsill fell out with loud clattering noises. The entwined lovers in the car went into contortions trying to get untwined as they looked up, catching Ros and me disappearing behind the window. Elaine was furious, and Ros and I were forbidden to do any more spying. Of course, the action in the car may have been Tom valiantly giving Elaine some energetic resuscitation after asphyxiating her with his breath.

Lanner had now been posted to a branch office in Molo and I bought a Ford Anglia (for fifty pounds) so I could go and see him on those weekends when he was not back in Nakuru for sports or parties at the Rift Valley Club.

We never went back to the rock spring. We didn't need to. It was one of those singular interludes that come along, perhaps once or twice in a lifetime, with their own perfect completeness. Africa had entered Lanner's blood that day, and so had I.

CHAPTER 11

September 1958 was a landmark for me as I had my twentieth birthday that month and Lanner had invited me for dinner at his house in Molo, just the two of us. I would stay overnight as it was too dangerous to drive back by myself afterwards, too far, and unseasonal rain had turned the roads into ribbons of mud. It took several hours to get there in time for dinner, my little Anglia in low gear, groaning and wheels spinning as it edged up the Molo hills. Rain lashed down, turning the mud liquid so it more easily splattered up onto the windscreen, with the wipers squeaking to and fro in a frenzy trying to clear enough of a fan-shaped space to see ahead. Slithering into the ditch was my worst fear, as it would be almost impossible to get out by myself; but Anglias were champion in the most dire of circumstances, having real guts to keep going and keep out of ditches.

I arrived in the dark by 8 o'clock, wet and dishevelled but safely there, more than ready for a hot bath and alcoholic revival in front of a mighty crackling fire with Lanner beside me.

He had asked me some time before what I would like for dinner and my request had been roast chicken followed by peaches and cream, which his cook put ready for him to serve. It was the best kind of celebration and we may have had wine or even champagne, but that didn't seem important as I was inebriated enough by the thrill of the occasion, being alone with Lanner for a whole evening when, as usual, we were completely absorbed in each other, talking and being close but always restrained, too inhibited to give full freedom to our feelings. Girls were scared of becoming pregnant and men were scared of making girls pregnant and having to marry them. Men like Lanner often had the belief that respecting a girl meant sex was off limits unless intending to marry, and after what had happened with Greg we were both wary on the subject of marriage. I had no doubt that loving each other as completely as we did would lead in a natural way to marriage, and we did talk about children and the future, but casually, cagey about tempting fate.

Molo stands at high altitude and is piercingly cold at night, so it seemed more than natural to sleep in the same bed, keeping warm at the same time as keeping chaste. Some girls I knew slept in the fullest sense with their boyfriends, but it was a risk before the pill became available. The pill was in fact being prescribed at that time, but ironically was used as a fertility treatment. Artificial suppression of ovulation followed by stopping the pill was thought to induce pregnancy, and was often successful.

That night at the Molo house was long and full of powerful sensations. I had never slept in the same bed with a man before and while Lanner subsided quickly into a calm untroubled sleep, I lay awake, intently aware of the warm smell and shape of him close beside me, as unaccustomed as the sounds of the night in that high plateau: rain dripping steadily from the eaves, and forest hyraxes screeching with that unearthly sound, surprisingly loud and shrill for such a small creature. There was a *kaross* (coverlet) spread over the bed for warmth, made from animal pelts stitched together, as furry as the hyraxes, and the heaviness of it gradually slowed my breathing so that at last I slept.

The drive back from Molo was all downhill, like a ski slope, except that it was mud instead of snow, with the car slaloming from side to side as good as any joyride, especially when meeting vehicles coming up and sometimes bouncing off them like dodgems. The dents and scrapes on my little Anglia became part of its character after a few years banging around the countryside.

Weekends were still mainly taken up with visits to Fa's patients, with me going along as gate-opener and car-pusher as usual. One of the places we visited often was Soysambu Estates, that spreads itself over thousands of acres of dry ranch land in a spectacular part of the Rift. It even has its own flamingo lake, a jewel-like pocket of water, captured inside the lip of a small crater. The crater rises in a high mound on one side with bumps resembling the features of a man's face in silhouette, lying down as if asleep. This mound, clearly visible from the main road going to Nairobi, was known as 'The Sleeping Warrior' in affectionate memory of Lord (Hugh) Delamere, whose pioneering efforts had developed the ranch from uninhabited bush at the beginning of the twentieth century. The land had been uninhabited because the cattle of Masai nomads who traditionally roamed that area, failed to thrive, and they had named the land 'Elmenteita' – 'the place where the rhino has no milk'. When this puzzle was investigated by Lord Delamere, a cobalt deficiency in the soil was discovered and cobalt licks introduced so that cattle and other animals could breed and thrive again.

Soysambu was now the home of Lord Delamere's son Tom, who was an old man in poor health, often visited by Fa who was his doctor. When we first started visiting the family, Tom was still married to Lady Mary, but a new interest, Diana Colville, was often there and my parents had been quite startled by the situation when they were staying over one weekend. Sitting at dinner with other guests, Diana suddenly stood up halfway through the final course, announcing that she was ready for bed, and indicating that Tom must be too. She went to help him from his chair and, murmuring goodnight to the guests, they left, arm in arm. Lady Mary carried on without a pause as if this was quite normal, and my parents concluded it must be so in aristocratic circles, as not an eyebrow twitched among the guests, no one apart from them appearing to think there was anything unusual about it.

Not long after this, Tom and Lady Mary divorced and Diana became the new Lady Delamere. Her previous marriages had not produced any children, and while she was married to Gilbert Colville they had adopted a daughter, Deborah, who was known as Snoo. Soysambu was a lonely place for children and Ros, who was the same age as Snoo, was invited to go and play with her. I sometimes went too and would spend the day chatting to house guests who seemed perpetually to populate that household and were a very curious assortment of people, from impoverished jockeys to wealthy aristocrats.

Diana herself was unfailingly hospitable and very lively company. I liked her and was intrigued by her. She didn't care in the slightest for anyone's opinion, which I admired. But it was not her hauteur that set her apart;

191

she had a compelling magnetism that captivated those around her. While appearing light-hearted and carefree, she had also a calculating quality; a paradox, as she went about in a devil-may-care manner but was not careless in dispensing her powers. She was always carefully groomed and elegant, even in casual clothes, moving about a room with ease and grace, her movements and chatter flowing in the same way effortlessly. I used to observe her from my worm's eye view, crouched on the floor, playing with the children. She and Tom clearly adored each other; affectionate banter thrown between them the whole time.

'You silly old fool,' Diana scolded him. 'You've gone and put the vet's instructions somewhere idiotic where the dogs will get them and chew them up.'

Tom dismissively: 'Tell Paulie to go and look for them, then.'

'It's Paulie's afternoon off, you know perfectly well. She's gone to her room to get some peace and quiet.'

'Well, send someone to get her out.'

'Christ, Tom, who the bloody hell do you think you are, the bloody King of Siam!'

Paulie was Miss Edna Paulson, an old friend of Fa's from early days at the London Hospital where she worked as a medical secretary. Later on she joined us in Malta and more recently had come to Kenya, where she became Diana's PA.

When Gilbert Colville died, boxes of items belonging to Diana were delivered to Soysambu and Paulie helped Diana unpack and sort through them. One of the boxes held old photographs and letters from the time of her notorious affair with Lord Errol and among these was a photo in a silver frame signed in affectionate terms by Lord Errol. Paulie asked what she should do with it.

'Throw it away with the rest of the stuff,' was Diana's casual reply.

Her sometimes artless or arch remarks were all part of that insouciant spirit and sparkle, which set her apart from others. She was kind and generous to me, never dismissive, though she might easily have thought a girl as gauche as I was could not be worth noticing.

Taking tea with Tom was the highlight of any visit. He always had marmalade sandwiches, which he shared with me and the dogs were allowed to lick our fingers, something that would never be allowed at home. Marmalade at teatime and dogs joining in would be seen by Muz and Fa as very lax behaviour.

'People as old and noble as Lord D are allowed to do what they like,' said Muz. 'Ordinary people like us don't mix breakfast with teatime.' What a silly affected answer, I thought, and went to eat spoonfuls of marmalade straight out of the jar in the larder in protest. Ros joined me and we shut ourselves in with the marmalade jar, hiding from Elaine who would have informed on us. Shutting ourselves in the larder, eating forbidden spoonfuls of this and that, was a regular pastime for Ros and me. A favourite cocktail was made from vinegar mixed with sugar and salt, diluted sufficiently to avoid stinging eyes and noses. We would put the concoction in an empty jar and go and sip it in the garden, swooning over the acid taste and smell. Had there been any alcohol in the house, we might have sneaked some of that to get high on, but with both parents being teetotal we had to make do with vinegar.

Spindle was now sixteen, with behaviour that was getting more bizarre and violent, even to the extent of attacking Ros one day when she had inadvertently annoyed him, gouging her face with his nails so badly that she was left with a permanent scar down one cheek. Another day they were out in the garden digging a patch of ground with a *jembe* (hoe), which is heavy like a pickaxe. One of the garden boys was bending over weeding another patch when Spindle suddenly grabbed the *jembe* and threw it at his head. Luckily he ducked and the *jembe* went flying past, but had the sharp metal hit him it could have caused serious injury or might even have killed him.

After this incident it was decided that Spindle's mental condition had deteriorated to such an extent that he would have to go to the Mathari asylum in Nairobi, to be held in a secure environment where he could be assessed by a psychiatrist and given treatment. This treatment was called electroconvulsive therapy, otherwise known as ECT (shock treatment).

When we went to see him after he'd had a course of these shocks, which induce epileptic fits, we found him in a state of abject terror and misery, like a beaten animal. Just as shocking was the communal cage he was kept in with hordes of other mentally disturbed people, all Africans apart from him, climbing the bars of the cage, yelling and gibbering, while more timid ones like Spindle cowered in a corner. The ECT had been successful in the sense of pounding him into submission, but the next dilemma for Muz and Fa was what to do with him as he needed some form of rehab, which could not be provided at home or anywhere in Kenya.

Fa had heard about a juvenile unit at a mental hospital in a place called Epsom in England. This sounded suitable as Spindle could be among other young people, and possibly psychiatrists there would know of new treatments or therapy that could help him, so it was decided to send him there.

Spindle later told me what happened next. He had thought his life was going to be saved when we came to see him in the terrible madhouse of Mathari, feeling sure we had come to take him home now that the appalling ordeal of the ECT was over. It was administered with no anaesthetic; patients were simply strapped down and electrodes applied to their heads, with shocks being given until their bodies went into convulsions. The pain and terror is beyond imagining and would surely now be classified as a form of torture.

However, Spindle remained lucid and kept his nerve throughout all this horror, relying on the prospect of being released from Mathari as soon as he'd finished the treatment. He had enough self-awareness to realise that he needed help to 'get better', as he saw it, and agonised over what was wrong with him and why he couldn't be normal like other boys his age, who were getting on with their lives, growing up and doing interesting things. 'How soon do you think the doctors will find a cure for me?' he asked frequently. He was as baffled as anyone else by his inability to fit into mainstream life, and all the other deficiencies he recognised in himself, which were constantly highlighted by Fa's criticism and mockery. Muz used to try and compensate by giving him treats such as sweets and cakes, but he didn't need childish indulgences. What he needed was Muz fighting his corner against Fa and getting him back into a place like Camphill, where he might again find security and purpose.

Spindle's narrative continues as he describes the day of his release from Mathari, when his suitcase was produced and his clothes bundled into it while being told he was leaving. He expected to see Fa and Muz waiting outside, but instead there was a van with no windows, and a driver who opened the back doors and told him to get inside. No one said anything or explained where they were going. Spindle thought it might be a taxi taking him back to Nakuru, but without any windows he couldn't look out for landmarks. He was surprised to find that, after a short drive, the van stopped and the doors opened again, this time onto a wide stretch of tarmac. When his eyes had adjusted to the sunlight, he saw they were at an airport, and the van had stopped beside a big plane. Before he could work out what this was about, he was grabbed by a man in a white coat and pushed up the steps of the plane, then strapped into a seat at the back. The man in the white coat sat next to him, but would not answer any questions except that they were going to England and Spindle would be going to a new hospital when they got there. He found the long flight frustrating as he wasn't allowed to look out of the window or walk around without the man holding firmly onto his arm as if he were a prisoner. When at last they arrived, he was handed over to another man in a white coat and driven off in a van once more. He had thought maybe Fa and Muz had gone back to England and would be meeting him there, but he found he was on his own, with no idea where he was being taken or what was going to happen next.

What happened next was in no way reassuring. When the van arrived at its destination, he was escorted into the forbidding fortress of an enormous prison-like hospital with clanging doors and hundreds of people in pyjamas shuffling about with nurses herding them. He was taken to a ward and locked in with a crowd of demented old men. There was no one anywhere near his age in the ward, but he was glad of this, because younger men were often more dangerous and violent. He had learnt to survive among mad people by keeping to himself and holding onto a core of belief that the ordeal was temporary and he would go home as soon as he'd finished whatever new treatment had been ordered for him. Much more worrying for him this time was that none of the staff would listen or talk to him when he tried to find out where he was, and what kind of treatment was planned. He remembered he had writing paper and a pencil in his suitcase. Muz had put them there when he went to Mathari, telling him to remember to write home whenever he could. The staff would post the letters for him, she said. Spindle thought he must have been put into the van at Mathari by mistake, instead of a taxi taking him home, and no one at home knew what had happened. If he could get a letter to us we would come and rescue him.

Spindle thought the safest place to write a letter was under his bed, where he would not be interrupted by other inmates. So he settled down to write, which was a laborious process for him as his writing skills were not well developed, but they were adequate. He began writing, but staff looking for him and finding him under the bed, viewed this behaviour as highly suspect and suggestive of subversive tendencies – inmates did not hide under beds writing: this was not the way mental patients usually behaved. Added to which, pencils were forbidden as they could be used for poking eyes out. So the pencil and writing pad were confiscated and Spindle was put under watch for suspicious behaviour. He decided, much as I had done years before when confronted by a similarly bewildering situation, to lie low and say nothing, waiting for a metaphorical hole in the wall to appear, providing a means of escape.

At home in Nakuru no mention was made of this sudden transporting of Spindle to England, or the special juvenile unit where he was supposed to end up, if it ever existed. Ros was away at Limuru School and Elaine was happily occupied assembling her trousseau since becoming engaged to Tom the organist, whose dead-dog breath in some curious way she must have found seductive. I was still trying to sort out my life with Lanner, which was increasingly fraught as he was moved around every few months to places further and further away. Greg, by contrast, was not being moved at all and remained in Nakuru in a more senior position than before, with a new girlfriend. I was pleased about this as it helped to relieve my guilt. He was always very civil to me and so was his girlfriend, who I had to acknowledge was several leagues higher up the scale of good sense and sophistication than I was ever likely to be.

She was some years older than Greg, dark with glowing skin and curves in all the right places, unlike me, one of the whippet-thin Craddocks. There was a problem with this new girlfriend, however. She was married and was not separated from her husband. Surprisingly, the husband seemed to take a benevolent view of Greg and his wife behaving like a married couple with him as the interloper. I watched from the sidelines intrigued as the three of them, with extraordinary gracefulness, wove an intricate *pas de trois*, manoeuvring around each other while appearing entirely unabashed.

For Lanner and me the manoeuvring was of an altogether different quality as we seemed destined to spend longer and longer apart, struggling to see each other, driving hundreds of miles on hideous roads, sometimes meeting halfway if there was any sort of respectable hotel or wayside stopping place with beds free of bugs. Separate rooms and beds, of course. Every aspect of our relationship seemed to be spiked with frustration. When Lanner was posted to a small town near Mount Kenya, a full day's drive away, he would sometimes leave for the weekend after work on a Friday, driving through the night so we could spend Saturday together, when he would be tired and strained, before leaving again on Sunday.

I think he was often very lonely in these far outposts, where he was on his own, manning a small branch office, with few other people for company. It was not healthy for a man of twenty-five to be so alone and, although Lanner was by nature a self-contained, private person, strong-willed and independent, I could sense cracks. Many of these isolated small towns had clubs for members of the widely dispersed white community to meet and socialise at weekends, when drinking was one of the principal activities. The many long evenings that a young man might spend alone in impersonal lodgings in these circumstances too often led to the companionship of a whisky bottle.

To offset this and fill the long evenings, we wrote letters that did not always arrive, but the correspondence became a testament to the hope that fate would in due time reverse our fortunes. We wrote poems and quoted those by more competent poets that better expressed our sentiments. Not all of these helped us to feel encouraged and a verse by Andrew Marvel came to haunt us after Lanner quoted it in one of his letters:

Therefore the love which doth us bind
But Fate so enviously debars,
Is the Conjunction of the Mind,
And opposition of the Stars.

197

Despite so many obstacles, I wanted to believe, and was determined to believe, that all we needed as an anchor to our relationship was the will to keep faith with each other. As Fa was fond of saying, 'All that is required for success against adversity is the will to succeed'; which was a great antidote to the Marvel quote, I hoped.

Lanner himself, whenever lifting a glass to our future, would give a toast: 'Here's to winning through'. But for me those words seemed to hint at doubts, and whenever he said them my heart did a flip.

A modern telephone service, so much taken for granted now with the added benefit of mobile phones, would have transformed communications for us. Telephones in remote rural communities operated a party-line system with everyone listening in, which provided a bonanza for gossips, so we left that for emergencies.

Good news on the other hand could not wait and when the phone rang at home one evening, I didn't care how many people were listening on Lanner's line as he told me that his annual leave allocation had come through and we could spend a whole two weeks together. We could drive down to the coast and find a quiet place to stay on one of the flawless white-sand beaches that stretch for miles north and south of Mombasa. This palm-fringed coastline with its exquisite coral reefs was untouched by tourism or big hotels, and those that did exist catered for local (mainly white) people on holiday or honeymoon. I had never been to the coast as beach holidays were not on Fa's list of approved ways to spend leisure time, so Lanner's suggestion was thrilling; not just seeing the coast, but having all that time together.

His latest car was a new model DKW, much better adapted to Kenya's untarmacked roads than his previous gutsy but limited Morris. We met in Nairobi and set off down the Mombasa road, which ran parallel with the railway line most of the way for hundreds of miles. Elephants strolled across the road, which could be a hazard but also a delight, and when we arrived at one of the Tsavo Park gates we turned off and drove to a lodge for the night. The lodge was no more than a simple collection of thatched huts around a communal cooking fire, thoughtfully supplied with metal mesh to hold pots. A small group of visitors had already arrived and installed themselves. The camp staff told us that they were from the BBC, taking the famous 'radio doctor' Charles Hill on safari, to record him observing wild animals for a documentary that would later be broadcast in England. It was dusk when we arrived and lesser crew members were attempting to produce an elaborate three-course meal from the one cooking fire, while at the same time setting up a long table with unwrapped china and sets of cutlery, even stretching to candlesticks holding lighted candles that spluttered in a haze of flying insects. The great doctor, meanwhile, reclined some way off, surrounded by his entourage in camp chairs with drinks, waiting for dinner to be served.

I offered to help the perspiring cooks who had the first course of soup ready, but no toast, as this presented too much of a technical problem on an open fire. They thought I might have a solution, but normally we didn't bother with such refinements as toast on safari. Then I remembered I had packed one of Fa's wire flywhisks, which possibly might adapt itself into a toasting implement. Showing the crew how to scrape some embers to the edge of the fire, then placing a slice of bread on the mesh of the whisk, holding it above the embers – *voilà* – a piece of toast could be induced to appear. Any residual bits of squashed fly on the mesh would shrivel up during the toasting process, so no one would know. By this method a satisfying pile of toast was able to present itself next to the soup on the table of the famous doctor and his attendants, while Lanner and I, after assisting the cooks with subsequent courses, feasted on the leftovers.

Lanner was one of those drivers addicted to speed. By a skilful use of gears aimed to achieve maximum revs and engine performance, he subscribed to the theory held by many East African drivers that driving fast enabled a vehicle to fly over the tops of corrugations, producing a smooth ride instead of one with occupants rattling around like peas in a tin. Flying along like this, only occasionally bouncing off the top of a bump, I glanced at Lanner and caught a wide-lipped tight smile on his face as he gripped the wheel, staring ahead. It was the fighter pilot shooting clouds again, urging his craft to ever greater bursts of speed. At one point on the road near Mombasa there was a sudden sharp bend with no warning sign, and as we approached the bend it became obvious that when we got there we would be going straight on, with no chance of taking the corner. By lucky chance, there was nothing coming towards us as we shot across the road and the car flew like an arrow over a deep ditch, before crashing down and carving a wide furrow through undergrowth and a mealie patch, then sinking with some ominous grating noises into a small field of ploughed earth.

As the car settled into the sod, wheezing and groaning, we sat stupefied. Lanner realising he had nearly killed us both with his recklessness, was unusually silent. We were both stunned, trying to compose ourselves, when within moments, as ever in Africa, curious faces came to peer at us through the wrecked maize, happy to see us alive so they could pull and push us out for a handful of coins. Paper money was still distrusted by many of the people living in small impoverished communities along the coast. They wanted something more substantial that could not be eaten by goats or white ants and could be jingled reassuringly in their pockets.

After collecting some lengths of rusty corrugated-iron roofing panels to lay on poles bridging the ditch, we were hauled back onto the road again – now in a somewhat subdued state, driving from then on rather cautiously as if the car was a convalescent patient recovering from some as yet undiagnosed injury that might at any moment disclose itself in a sudden collapse. DKW cars however, in robust German fashion, we discovered do not countenance collapsing on the road, despite such ill treatment.

A night in hot, steamy Mombasa, heavy with the smell of fermenting vegetation and diesel fumes, was enough to send us quickly north on the road to Malindi, where we found the small, modest, thatched rooms of Lawford's Hotel scattered along the beach under palms as ideal as anyone could imagine. Inside the reef, the lagoon shimmered with hardly a ripple on limpid turquoise water washing over white sand, with no one in sight. We swam and then walked for miles along the beach, while underfoot the powdery sand felt like icing sugar, crunchy and squeaky. That night, as we stood at the edge of the water watching the moon throw a wide silver pathway across the sea to our feet, like a drawbridge to dreams, I shivered with a sudden foreboding and Lanner put an arm around me. 'We must never, ever, let go of each other,' he said.

Exploring up and down that strip of coast, where in places tangled forest spreads itself down to the water's edge, we found signposts to the mysterious Gedi ruins, an ancient Arab-style settlement where no inscriptions or bones record its history. All that is left are remnants of skilfully built stone walls and arches, standing silent among twisted roots and trunks of trees that reach up, blocking out the sun. A sense of eternal twilight hangs over the ruins, adding to their mystery and slightly sinister character. Grateful to escape the clammy heat and gloomy forest pressing on all sides, we went on to find, a few miles further south, the extraordinary rock formations and tranquillity of Turtle Bay at Watamu. Here, no hotels or tourists existed, only occasional visitors like us buying a ride from local fishermen to go out goggling on the reef, which was still pristine in its perfect, vivid, marine world.

The deeply satisfying joy of each day was disturbed only by the knowledge that an agony of parting lay ahead, and there was no promise of another time like this for at least a year. Local holidays for expatriate staff were short, as their main holiday was home leave for three months every three years, and Lanner was only just starting his second year.

Saying goodbye in Nairobi felt like an amputation, and the drive back to Nakuru on a road where so many landmarks held memories, provided nothing but emptiness. All we could look forward to were more letters, the first of which from Lanner came with the worst kind of news, as he had been told on his return that he was being posted to Lindi in the far south of Tanganyika, eight hundred miles away. It seemed almost intentionally cruel.

By strange coincidence, Tom, Elaine's fiancé, was posted at the same time to Mwanza, another mosquito-infested outpost of colonial commerce, so Elaine and I were both bereft and became prone as time passed, to fits of jitters when letters were slow or failed to arrive. Whether it was the unreliable post or Lanner's deteriorating state of mind, languishing in the squalid armpit that was Lindi, after a few months his letters dried up altogether and telegrams brought no response. I heard through friends that he had been ill and his parents had flown from England to be with him, which was far from reassuring. I decided to go and see for myself what was going on and bought a bus ticket to Dar es Salaam. This cost 100 shillings (£5) and the journey took six days and nights on a meandering route from Nairobi. No bus service operated onwards from Dar, so I had to book an East African Airways flight that made the trip to Lindi once a week.

The bus journey from Nairobi was tortuous, calling at every town and village along the way. Many of these visits were errands to pick up or deliver items the bus driver was carrying for people, or in some places merely to visit friends and relations. These stops were accompanied by much socialising and drinking at local bars with me, the only European, being treated with much courtesy and graciousness, so that I was never allowed to buy my own Coke or fly-encrusted maize-meal cakes. The bus driver felt it was his responsibility to look after me as a young white girl travelling alone, insisting I sit up front with him to avoid being 'troubled', as he put it, by any undesirables sitting further back. He stopped frequently for everyone to get off for pee breaks, which he recognised would be awkward for me, as all the other women, when they got off, merely hitched up their skirts at the side of the road, squatting in a line while the men stood around nonchalantly relieving themselves. The driver would look out for a patch of bush or clump of trees not too far from the road before stopping; then, inspecting the site first to make sure there were no animals or hidden hazards lurking, he escorted me to it, quickly hurrying back to the bus as soon as I indicated approval of the chosen patch, so as not to embarrass me.

I had expected there would be a change of drivers somewhere along the way, but the same one drove night and day with no sleep stops, which worried me. No one else seemed bothered, probably because I was the only person who stayed on the bus the whole way, noticing signs of fatigue in the driver when occasionally the bus veered off the road, or he got more irritated than usual if someone started an argument and scuffles broke out. In some ways the bus resembled a travelling circus, with an assortment of animals on board or on the roof-rack in flimsy baskets tied together with sisal string: chickens, dogs, rabbits, hog-tied goats; other unidentified furry or feathered livestock being taken along as picnic food if we stopped anywhere with cooking fires. These stops could last for an hour or several hours, depending how much eating and drinking was going on. I usually took the chance to lie down somewhere for a sleep as it was impossible to do that on the bus sitting bolt upright on a metal seat, jolting and rattling with constant explosive bursts of noise from the exhaust, and the driver singing like a fog horn to keep himself awake.

Lack of sleep was one of the worst aspects of the long journey, but worst of all was not being able to brush my teeth or have a proper wash, as clean water had to be kept for drinking. The only bottled drinks available were Cokes or sodas. Bottled water was not a sellable item; people would have thought it crazy to spend money on water in bottles when it could be had free out of a tap. I refilled my water bottle at public standpipes in villages, but there was no public washroom with a nice clean loo to be found, even in large towns. Hidden down back alleys there would be communal latrines providing some basic shelter and privacy, but inside these the smell was overpowering, along with the putrid squidgy mess all around a gaping hole where one had to squat over a dark pit, so I preferred to wait for the driver to escort me to a quiet spot out in the bush.

The journey seemed to roll into extended time, with days and nights merging in a blur as the driver held up grease-stained maps for us to see where we had got to. Dar seemed no closer as the interminable dirt roads stretched out in front, choking us with gritty dust clouds blasting in through the open windows. There were places where the road had subsided or, even worse, when crossing dry riverbeds we sometimes got stuck and everyone had to get out and push in the steamy heat. One of these dramas happened during the night and the driver decided to wait till morning to do the pushing in daylight, when it would be easier and safer. It was grand being able to sleep, lying out on the soft sand of the river bed, with a multitude of stars overhead and perfect peacefulness, except for the occasional whining of mosquitoes and squawks from children and night animals.

The next day, after all the passengers had sweated and heaved to get the bus moving again, we emerged from dry scrub along the river bank to find ourselves crossing some vast flat plains, featureless from horizon to horizon, empty of life, or so it seemed. The bus thundered on as the sun rose and the road in front danced with an undulating mirage distorting anything that might be coming up in front. After some hours of this sweltering progress, up ahead a group of figures appeared, bobbing in the mirage. These were five Masai *morani* (warriors) standing by the road, propped on their spears, waving us down. The driver stopped and the Masai, after exchanging greetings, started to climb in, but were told they could not come on board with their spears. It was against bus policy due to incidents that had occurred in the past when fights broke out. A loud and ferocious altercation followed, with passengers joining in and everyone getting very animated, until it was suggested that I should be put in charge of the spears, which would be held in a pile next to my seat, with the Masai sitting at the back. As soon as this solution was proposed, there were smiles all round and I became the unlikely custodian of the spears until they were reclaimed when the Masai got off some way ahead.

Arriving at last in Dar was like waking from a dream-like state of unreality as the whole journey had been completely outside any normal experience. I was sad to say goodbye to the bus driver, who had looked after me with such kindness, expecting nothing in return. He was concerned about the next stage and who would look after me now, so I explained that I was getting on a plane and there would be two pilots and maybe a hostess responsible for passengers to make sure everyone was looked after. We shook hands and he wished me '*safari njema*' (good journey), as I thanked him and wished him the same.

After finding a cheap hotel to have a wash and change of clothes and at last clean my teeth, I felt better about presenting myself at the airport for the short flight to Lindi. If I thought that other passengers might shrink from my previous dishevelled appearance, I need not have worried, as the only other passenger was a dog. This was an Alsatian in a large crate, staring dolefully through the cracks at me, so I talked to him in what I hoped was a reassuring voice and he wagged his tail and lay down, sensibly deciding all was well and he could relax.

As soon as we were airborne, one of the pilots came back into the cabin inviting me to join them in the cockpit, which could not have been a more extravagant thrill as he waved me towards his seat, asking if I would like to do a little flying. No persuasion was needed. I couldn't wait to get my hands on the controls as he showed me how they worked, the basics of which I already knew from weekend flights at Nakuru Gliding Club, where I was learning to fly gliders. The Dakota, of course, was different and I had my first surprise, discovering its sensitivity of response, even to a light touch. The pilots protested: 'Not so ham-fisted, go easy, she's a bird not a bucket,' and I soon got the idea after a few dips and surges.

I had a thought. 'Does our route take us over the Rufiji Delta?'

'Why?'

'Because I've always wanted to see the wreck of the *Königsberg*. Very few people have seen it. You can't get to it by land. It's the famous German battleship which scuttled itself in the delta in the First World War, and the crew heroically salvaged the ship's guns, manhandling them over hundreds of miles till they could be handed in to General von Lettow-Vorbeck, the German commander. It's a very dramatic story,' I finished in a rush.

Without much time to think about it, as the delta was coming up fast, the pilots said, 'Let's do it,' and one of them took over the controls, reducing altitude to search along the great river opening up below. The widening delta that covered an immense area of impenetrable mangrove swamps and grey mud flats was clearly visible ahead until, right on cue, the skeleton hulk of the *Königsberg* came into view, lying on its side in the mud. We circled a few times to get a good look, the pilots never having seen it before, and then, careful to avoid losing time, continued on to Lindi.

I had sent a telegram to Lanner with the date and time of my arrival but had no reply, so I was nervous as well as tense with anticipation on this last leg of my epic safari to see him.

'You have someone meeting you, haven't you?' the pilots asked as we approached Lindi. 'The town is fourteen miles from the airstrip and it will be dark in an hour. We have to go on to Masasi with the dog before it gets dark.'

'Oh, yes,' I said confidently. 'I've sent a telegram.' Arriving in late evening, the sun was low in the sky, turning to gold the wide flat sisal plantations extending out for hundreds of acres on all sides of the airstrip. This was a dirt strip with a hut at one end but no sign of anyone, or any waiting vehicle. The pilots didn't want to leave me there on my own. 'Don't worry,' I said. 'I can always spend the night in the hut.' We laughed uneasily and I watched the plane trundle off down the strip until it was lost in a cloud of dust.

I stood beside my suitcase, contemplating whether to set off walking to Lindi town, hoping I might meet someone who could give me a lift. It would be better to be doing something with a purpose rather than hanging around by the hut. While I was thinking about it and checking my torch to make sure the batteries hadn't died, I noticed a plume of dust rising in the distance, and as it came closer I recognised a speeding car, which incredibly sounded like a DKW.

Chapter 12

The car stopped some yards from the hut, its wheels crunching and creating a dust storm, which on clearing revealed Lanner standing beside the driver's door, looking like a stranger. I stood by the hut with my suitcase, hesitating, uncertain what to do next as he didn't move or say anything. The few yards separating us might as well have been as wide as the Grand Canyon, such was the gulf between us. After several long moments, Lanner took a cigarette from his pocket, and as he stooped to light it I felt my heart lurch at the familiar gesture, unable to stop myself taking a few steps forward. He straightened, inhaling slowly with a long pull, the cigarette between his lips, his face expressionless. Silence stretched out, heavy with unspoken words, as he fingered the cigarette; then, looking steadily at me, he said, 'Why are you here?'

'To see you, of course. I sent you a telegram.'

'I only got the telegram yesterday. You didn't give me much time. Or much choice,' he said, looking at me with the same steady expression through the haze of tobacco smoke.

'You stopped writing or replying to my letters. I was worried. I didn't know what was happening.' I paused. 'And I heard you had been ill.'

I suddenly felt dizzy and drained after so many days without proper food or sleep and must have gone pale, because Lanner's tone changed as he went to open the boot of the car, taking my suitcase to put it inside.

'Where are you staying?' he asked.

'With you, I thought.'

'You can't stay with me, it isn't suitable,' he replied quickly. 'I'll see if the UMCA Mission can find you a bed. You better get in.'

The DKW felt and smelt just as it had before, and this familiarity instead of being consoling made things worse, because it felt welcoming, in contrast to Lanner's mood which was cool and detached, holding me at arm's length.

The drive to Lindi was awkward as Lanner remained silent, resisting all my attempts to break through his reserve to try and find out what had happened, causing him to behave as if we were strangers. Nothing seemed to work this time, as previously, when he went into one of his closed moods, a bit of light-hearted joking around would usually bring him back; or, failing that, just leaving him to mull on his own. But I was in no mood for indulgent mulling or careless humour; feeling stressed and exhausted, all I could think of was somewhere to lie down and close my eyes, hoping the Mission might have hot water and a bath as well as a bed.

In fading light, we reached Lindi town and stopped beside the looming grey shape of a large and very plain stone church with a matching grey residential block beside it. Lanner told me to wait in the car while he went to see if a visitor bed was available. I sat in the car, wishing I had stayed on the plane with the dog going to Masasi.

After several minutes he came out with two of the missionary women, who took my case and my hand as if I was an orphan being delivered to their door, which was not far from how I felt at that moment, watching Lanner driving off, doing a quick getaway. The women were young and didn't look like missionaries. They didn't behave like missionaries either, as they took me inside to where several jolly-faced people were sitting round, having sundowners. Quickly pulling up a chair for me and pressing a gin and tonic into my hand, someone said, 'Here you are, drink this, beats anything south of the Equator for body and soul revival!'

This was not normal missionary-speak. I was going to have to readjust my thoughts to contribute anything as a visitor in this upbeat environment, but need not have worried too much as the carefree hospitality seemed to come easily to them; making others feel comfortable and welcome was part of their creed, just as they assumed I was there to walk the path of daily Christian practice with them. The grey church next door wasn't there as an appendage; it was central to their lives, and bells would ring at different times of the day for rituals of worship or contemplation. This had never been part of my church experience in Nakuru. The missionaries explained this was due to their church being 'high', while ours in Nakuru was probably 'low' church. It was the first time I had come across high and low paths to righteousness, and wondered where Jesus fitted in; from biblical accounts seeming to be oblivious to rank, going out in boats with fishermen or chatting to beggars, just as comfortably as joining in debates with high priests at the synagogue.

Living as part of the UMCA community was a comforting diversion for me, while waiting a week for the next plane out of Lindi, which Lanner had said I must make sure to be on. During that long week, and possibly to avoid seeming like a complete cad, he invited me for lunch one day, coming to pick me up and driving out the few miles to where he lived in a fair-sized rented bungalow, which I noted had at least one empty spare bedroom.

I'd decided beforehand that I would act naturally over lunch with casual friendliness, as if we had never been more than acquaintances, hoping this might help him to feel less defensive, and with no pressure we might even rediscover the effortless rapport that had come so easily before. He responded by becoming less guarded, and relaxed enough to settle down with a pile of week-old newspapers, offering me some to read, so that we sat companionably like players in a set piece, each of us carefully polite, avoiding eye contact, studiously ignoring the one subject that loomed between us like the Berlin Wall.

After lunch had passed in this contrived play-acting and Lanner had retreated behind the papers once again, my own reserve started to dissolve, as I could see how the day was going to end if we went on like this. Nothing would be explained and my emotions would be left in limbo, perhaps for ever. Lanner's emotions were clearly elsewhere or locked up. I didn't want to find myself asking any important questions standing on the doorstep of the Mission when he dropped me off. I put down my old copy of *The Sunday Times* with enough loud rustling to make him look up. I was impatient now and riled as I faced him.

'I understand that we won't be seeing each other again, but I would be grateful for an explanation, and a lift to the airstrip when I leave.'

He looked at me with an intensity I knew well, and knew it signalled (like Fa with his own version of that kind of penetrating look) some kind of seminal statement.

'I think you must know by now, or must realise, that you have been seriously mistaken in coming down here,' he said. 'It's important to get things clear.'

'Yes, that is exactly what I mean. But I need to be clear as well. You haven't explained what has gone wrong between us, why you are behaving like this, as if we are strangers, while you and I both know perfectly well how it was before. You are not being honest with me. What I need to be clear about is what has happened, what has made you change?'

I waited for him to speak, but he remained impassive, as if nothing could reach or touch him anymore. At last, but still betraying no emotion, he said, 'There is only one thing for each of us to understand.'

'Yes, what's that?' I was impatient now.

'I have things to attend to here. Obligations.' There was a long pause while he seemed to fumble for words, before going on, 'You must make your own life. Today is not just the end of the chapter, it is the end of the book.'

That was savage, I thought, but at least I know now, even if there is still no explanation.

He didn't respond to my request for a lift, and later, when he took me back to the Mission, I asked him again. I didn't want to reveal how short of money I was since paying for my lodging and other unexpected expenses as, during the previous week, I had developed a fever and the missionaries had called a doctor in case it was malaria. The doctor, of course, needed paying in cash. It was bad enough having to hide my hurt and grief so I could keep some sense of pride, and needing to ask a favour of Lanner was shaming, but a short trip to the airstrip I thought was not too much to expect of a twenty-six-year-old man with a car, good safe job and money to spare, after a loving and trusting relationship lasting nearly two years.

None of this registered with Lanner as he explained that he had to meet the mail boat at the harbour on the morning I was leaving, and there were plenty of taxi drivers who would be glad of the fare.

Disappointingly, we parted on that dreary note and when I arrived at the airstrip a couple of days later (as the only passenger once again), the taxi driver, seeing that no one else was around, demanded an outrageous sum for my fare, which was a great deal more than had been agreed. I resisted and he became threatening, which alarmed me, as I was not in a situation to defend myself. It is easy to disappear in Africa and I thought it was better to pay up and be rid of him; added to which I was still feeling fragile after the double assaults of fever and Lanner's hostility, so I gave in, despite knowing I would now struggle to find what was needed for the long journey ahead.

It was just like one of those disturbing dreams, in which you are urgently trying to get somewhere, as scenery and circumstances keep shifting and drifting into blind alleys, while all efforts to get back on track lead to yet more confusion and sense of panic at getting lost and never being able to find a way back to familiar territory again.

By chance, at one point in this harrowing odyssey, a young English charity worker who had been out on some remote rural project, joined the bus, and seeing the state I was in, dirty, starving and penniless, immediately took care of me, sharing what food he had and keeping at bay the worst ravages of the trip. There was no kind, attentive bus driver with us this time, only a series of maniacs.

Arriving in Nairobi, my new friend took me to the house of Dr Charters, who was a friend of Fa's, suggesting I might stay a night or two with them to recover, before getting a lift to Nakuru. Dr Charters was alarmed at seeing me so debilitated, immediately phoning Fa, who seemed unaware of any of the circumstances of my situation and was surprised to receive the call. He expected that if I went away on a trip I would be more than capable of looking after myself and getting back home without any extra help. He suggested putting me on the next bus to Nakuru. With Dr Charters paying for the ticket I imagine Fa would have assumed, since it was explained that I had no money.

When I got home, still on wobbly legs from my ordeals, I found the family in turmoil. No one noticed or was in a mood to notice my pallor and emaciation, which Dr Charters had thought should be noted in a letter which he gave me to hand to Fa on my return. Everyone was much more concerned about Elaine, whose fiancé Tom had written from distant Mwanza, breaking off their engagement without any credible explanation, except that he had changed his mind. Elaine was distraught and everyone was rallying round, trying to make her feel better. Was there something about the isolation and melancholy of these far outposts that sent young professional men half out of their minds?

I needed two things immediately. First, some money – fast. Then a new start to my life. For the first I sold my car and for the second I decided to buy a ticket to England. It was essential, now, to get my feet onto a ladder leading to some kind of qualification and career, so that any future hopes of mine would not be reliant on faithless chancers like Lanner.

Without much money and Fa unwilling to fund me, I needed a course that provided paid employment alongside training, and I wanted a change from lab work. Nursing was an option, though not very appealing as it offered derisory pay for years of servitude with very little intellectual reward – or so I thought. But I was still interested in medical subjects, and nursing could provide a measure of satisfaction in a medical environment. Elaine was starting her nurse training at the London Hospital in September and, not to be outdone by her, I applied to the Royal Free Hospital for their next intake, so I could be out of Kenya and far away from Lanner to wipe him from memory as quickly as possible.

My friends in Nakuru, big Maggie, little Maggie, Pixie and Jane, were all indignant, seeing how gaunt and faded I had become, wasting away, they said, with sickness from a broken heart. The cure, they insisted, was the same as falling off a horse: you have to get straight back on, any horse, so you get your nerve back. Big Maggie was the organising one. 'We've booked you onto our table at the Hospital Ball,' she said. 'We've got tickets for you and a blind date. He's on leave from the Kenya Regiment and needs a partner, so we've fixed him up with you.'

'Don't be ridiculous,' I said. 'The last thing I need is being picked up off the floor like Cinderella, having to spend all night dancing with some oaf I've never met. And anyway, I haven't got anything to wear.'

'Don't be so wet,' Maggie said. 'You know that girl Virginia from the Players [theatre] who's leaving? Her husband has got promotion or something. Well, she's selling a whole heap of dresses she doesn't want and we've been to have a look. There's a fab strapless evening dress she's never worn because it's too small, but that's lucky for you being so skinny, it's perfect. Go and see for yourself.' 'I'm completely broke,' I said. 'I can't buy dresses.

I've got to buy a plane ticket to London.'

'You need to treat yourself. Show Lanner's friends what an idiot he is, throwing you away. They'll notice. You'll make them notice.'

This last remark had a certain appeal as an act of defiance with positive action thrown in. I could slay dragons in a strapless dress. I was model-thin and tall. I went to see the dress, which looked expensively elegant in leaf-green glazed fabric with a full skirt, very stylish. The new strapless fashion was daring, as it was the first time bare shoulders had come out in public to be shown off without producing too many gasps. We were on the cusp of the sixties and social attitudes were changing.

As soon as Virginia zipped me into the dress and its tight waist slipped into place, fitting perfectly, I was transformed. Even the bold green design looked right on me, which was entirely unexpected. Craddock girls did not normally wear bright or conspicuous colours, let alone reveal bare shoulders – which might get them noticed in a non-Christian way.

Virginia was so pleased with the effect and my response, she let me have the dress for almost nothing, as in any case it would have been difficult to find anyone else that size who might be likely to buy it.

Fa and Muz needed some persuading when I showed it to them, but what concerned them more was the identity of my blind date as I was still under twenty-one (only just), so the suitability of any escort needed to be established. Dr Charters' letter may have startled them into thinking there could have been some element of parental neglect in failing to keep themselves informed of my whereabouts and perilous encounters on the Tanganyika road.

They had not shown any particular concern when I set off on the quest to find Lanner, and when I returned in some degree of disarray, no questions were asked or anxieties raised. No one seemed interested to know what had happened and I was too bruised to want to expose those sensitivities in an atmosphere of indifference, but this was not unusual in our family. Weakness was seen as failure. Even genuine illnesses were frowned upon, as if doctors' children were not supposed to get sick, or, as Ros put it,

'Not *allowed* to get sick.'

Elaine's broken engagement was seen in a different light as Tom's family had already forged bonds with her, so the ramifications were more complicated, especially as no explanation for his cold feet had been discovered, leaving both families frustrated and questioning his state of mind. If anyone had asked me about Lanner's similarly perplexing behaviour, it might have illuminated the plight of young employees despatched to these lonely posts, where keeping hold of a sane perspective may prove too much of a challenge for even the most level-headed of them.

I was hoping that Fa wouldn't go all pedantic and insist on vetting my blind date, but as soon as he heard it was Adam Hill, the eldest son of a well-known local farming family, who were also patients of his, he was all charm. I already knew Adam's father, Cen Hill, through my work at the Pyrethrum Board, running field trials at the farm. Cen always invited me in for a cup of tea after we'd finished counting ticks on dipped cattle, which was laborious thirsty work. The cups of tea were very reviving, as were the many animated conversations we had about politics and Cen's early days in Kenya. He had arrived as a young assistant to his uncle Jack David (related to the cookery pioneer Elizabeth David) on this same farm in 1922. His eldest son, Adam, my blind date, had been away at agricultural college and, more recently, National Service in the Kenya Regiment.

On the evening of the ball, Adam arrived to pick me up in a battered old Land Rover, which scored plenty of points with me, so that was a good start. Coming inside to introduce himself, he first took Muz's hand, bending to kiss it, which might have seemed affected, but he carried it off with the ease of someone to such manners born. Taking my hand next, he kissed it too, before shaking hands more formally with Fa. He spoke in pleasantly cultured tones, very polished, in contrast to the scruffy state of the Land Rover, as he stood tall in his DJ with the complete composure that good manners always seem to bestow. I could see Fa and Muz looking impressed, but I was not prepared to be so easily taken in, especially by a stranger, and especially with Lanner's image in front of me every minute of every day as an icon of manliness, undented by recent experience.

I was happy to have a polite escort to take me to the ball, and one that wasn't bad-looking either, as I assessed all six foot of Adam standing there lean and fit, twenty-one years old, his hair the colour of jet, like Fa's, but thick and wavy, while Fa's was fine and straight. Fa then did something uncharacteristic: after a few light coughs and twitches, he offered Adam a drink, which was very unusual in our teetotal household. Alcohol was allowed only on rare occasions for exceptionally honoured guests and kept locked in a cupboard to which only Fa had the key. I could see him leading Adam off to sit him down and engage him in some lofty conversation, monopolising him as Fa often did if a new interest caught his attention.

Adam is my date, not Fa's, I thought indignantly and commented loudly that we must not be late for the ball, glancing in a pointed way at the gold Omega watch I was wearing, that Lanner had given me for my twentieth birthday. I started for the door and Adam opened it for me, assuring Fa and Muz that he would bring me back before midnight, wishing them goodnight with elaborate courtesy.

I had to hitch up the skirts of my long dress to climb into the passenger seat of the Land Rover and Adam helped me, both of us laughing at such volumes of rustling fabric with layers of petticoats underneath. When he got in the other side, before driving off he turned to me and, with what seemed genuine sincerity, paid me several extravagant compliments, saying that it was an honour to be my escort. Then, taking my hand, he kissed it again, as if to seal the sentiment.

He was a very good, supple dancer and I loved dancing (which Lanner did not), so that was a refreshing change, and the evening restored my usual vitality, with all the energy of a live band and good company. Adam was very attentive and charming all evening, getting me home by midnight as promised.

The next morning I lay in bed looking at my sky-blue ceiling, which always made me feel good. The ball had been invigorating, giving me new impetus that was in large part thanks to Adam for dusting away the doldrums with his vibrant dancing and personality. As I lay there, absorbed in the calming effect of the ceiling and my thoughts, I had to decide whether to accept his invitation for another date.

After being suitably restrained while meeting Fa and Muz, as soon as we got to the ballroom Adam had relaxed and become his normal self as an unabashed extrovert, entertaining and theatrical, a bit of an exhibitionist, knowing and known by almost everyone, a natural party catalyser. Not my type at all. I preferred quiet thinkers who would never take to the floor as a solo act demonstrating a Highland Fling as Adam did; his dinner jacket tied around his waist as a kilt, making everyone laugh and clap as he pirouetted and twirled his arms high above his head. He was very light on his feet and surprisingly graceful in his movements. This was someone whose measure I had yet to gauge and didn't know if I really wanted to. The chemistry between Lanner and me had been overwhelming to such a degree it was like bonding glue, so powerful that nothing and no one could ever dissolve it, I remained convinced.

I had known Lanner in all his ways, every nuance and gesture of him, his moods and mindfulness, the way his skin felt and smelt, which seemed to meld with mine so that we became two halves of one entity when we touched. I knew the patterns of his thinking, or so I thought, until he closed himself to me. Any subconscious search that might spring from human longing for completeness with another person began and ended with Lanner. I didn't want to explore any other relationship potential. I was content now to discover my own personal spectrum of possibilities, getting out into a wider sphere where big things happened, where anything was possible – and the centre of that sphere was London. Not Lanner, or the family, or a new distraction like Adam.

When he called to ask if I would like to go out riding with him on the farm, my resolve wobbled a bit as I had to admit I was tempted. I still enjoyed riding, usually confined to weekends at the Hemsteds' farm at Subukia, but these had become less frequent since long-distance weekends with Lanner had taken over. Occasionally, he and I visited the Hemsteds together, but there was always a sense that Stephen and Joan thought I could do better than entangle myself with young men who spent most of their lives in offices wearing suits, instead of shirt sleeves outside in the sunshine with fields full of productive cattle and crops. I loved their farm so much, why wasn't I going out with farmers' boys who could offer me the open lifestyle much more suited to my inclinations, they wondered – and so did I. But Adam was not the one, or it was too soon. The timing was wrong.

Remembering to be polite but not too polite, I made excuses to Adam and felt a twinge of guilt when he sounded surprised at being turned down, and then even more surprised at my refusal to consider any alternatives. I explained I was leaving soon and had too much to do, which was true. But he persisted. 'There's your twenty-first birthday party coming up. You must need a partner for that?'

Oh bother, I thought, he knows about the party. 'Well, of course you would be welcome to come,' I said rather ungraciously.

Much to my surprise, Muz and Fa had decided to give a party for my twenty-first, which was to be quite a lavish affair with printed invitations sent out. These stated the dress code was evening dress with dinner and dancing, all to take place in Fa's ornate Chinese reception rooms. Any overspill could drift out onto the long veranda or stroll among Chinese lanterns on the lawn. All kinds of innovative ideas were suggested as plans gathered pace.

Was there going to be alcohol as well? I held my breath, waiting to hear. Elaine's engagement party had offered tea or squash with sandwiches, so I was inclined to be sceptical. Amazingly, yes, we were to have some kind of fizzy alcoholic drink at my party. Not some weird concoction disguised as champagne, I hoped. The Hemsteds would not be taken in by any substitution of cheap fizz and neither would others like Fa's partner, Dick Johnson, who was coming with his new wife. The new wife, disturbingly, was a large domineering woman who wore striped tents and turbans. We were all stunned when adorable Dick suddenly married this steamroller who we feared might crush him to death one day, inadvertently tripping over his slender form as she boomed into a room, tent and turban tails flowing like bright sails.

In the event, she was not at the party for some reason and this allowed Dick and Muz to sit on the sofa flirting unashamedly. Dick's marriage had not taken any of the edge off their passion for each other, I noticed. I always felt elated when Muz relaxed enough to enjoy being admired and show her true feelings, which Dick could unlock simply by touching her hand and smiling at her. Muz later said she could easily have run off with Dick during the long years when there had been many opportunities for consoling each other. Since Muz had been displaced in Fa's affections by Babs, there was Dick, lonely and loving her, so she might easily have responded, but she explained her marriage vows could not allow this. A great pity, I thought, as Fa appeared not to have the same view of his own marriage vows.

I wore the glorious green strapless dress for my party and noticed how the style suited me, with my long hair draped over bare shoulders. Lanner would have scowled at such exposure; he had conformist ideas about modesty for girls, as well as disliking make-up or any artifice. But Adam loved the dress and was very attentive to me all through the party, disarming everyone with his spark and wit, so that by the end of the evening it seemed he had established himself firmly as a fixture in my orbit.

The next day he came to help us clear up and a photo shows us all, afterwards, slouched in chairs on the veranda, looking pale with fatigue after the exertions of the night before. Adam was relaxed, smoking a pipe this time instead of cigarettes. I liked the easy way he held the stem of his pipe between his lips and teeth, small curls of smoke escaping now and then. I found it soothing, and the mellow scent of his Sweet Nut tobacco was pleasing too.

Undaunted by my previous negative response to his invitations, Adam said he was holding a swimming party the next Saturday at the farm and lots of people would be going, so he hoped I would accept an invitation this time. I asked who would be there and he mentioned several people I knew, which seemed reassuring.

Every day in the Rift Valley is a sunny day and September is a hot month, so a swimming party with a picnic sounded appealing. When Saturday arrived and I drove the five miles out of town to meet Adam at the farm, I thought it must be the wrong day as there was no sign of other cars, or other people. Adam looked embarrassed, admitting that no one else had turned up yet, which immediately made me suspicious. But he assured me all was in order and we would be driving to the swimming pool further away on a hillside at the top of the farm in his Land Rover with the picnic, and would probably find everyone else already there.

I discovered, when we arrived, that the swimming pool was a raised, circular, concrete water tank in a field, with pipes from the tank supplying cattle troughs further down by gravity. A clever arrangement, but the swimming party was not so cleverly arranged, I thought, looking at the surrounding area of dry grass splatted with cowpats. Adam appeared not to notice these or the all-too-obvious absence of other guests and, spreading a tarpaulin on the ground for me to sit on, he scrambled up the side of the tank and plunged in, shorts and all. 'Come on,' he shouted happily. 'I won't look while you're changing.'

A rock had been placed helpfully by the tank wall for those less athletic like me to get a foot up, and none too enthusiastically I hauled myself to the concrete edge to look over and see how clean the water looked. Adam seemed unconcerned about dead rats and other debris floating in the tank, which he flicked out, assuring me the water was quite pure and was what they drank out of the taps down at the house. Bath water came from the river, which was less reliable, he explained, with effluent being drained into it from farms and homesteads along the way.

Only slightly appeased by his assurances I joined him in the deep water, which was too dark to see down to the bottom, and we splashed around in the strong sunlight until hunger drove us out to lie, wet and drying, on the tarpaulin, eating hard-boiled eggs and slabs of dense grainy bread provided by Benjie, the Hills' cook. I later discovered that Benjie presided over a kitchen as black and filthy as any hole in Calcutta, and food coming out of it needed to be viewed with caution. In Kenya, farmhouse kitchens were built as separate entities several yards from the main house to avoid the whole lot going up in flames each time the wood-burning Dover stove caught fire. A flaming chunk of wood or ember would fall out, sparks would fly up into the thatch, and the only thing to hope was that it happened after dinner had been served instead of before.

My birthday was on 18 September and I was due to report for duty at the Royal Free Hospital Preliminary School of Nursing, College Crescent, Primrose Hill, London, on 5 October, so there was no time for any more dates or parties or anything else much, except once again packing a suitcase and saying goodbye to Kenya and all my friends and family, possibly for as long as three years or more, which was the length of time required for training and qualifying.

CHAPTER 13

Going back to a classroom at the age of twenty-one, with most of the other students still in their teens, was an uneasy experience. I felt very old and uncomfortable sleeping in a dormitory with several other girls, which was like boarding school all over again, but friendlier this time, and Primrose Hill was one of the more charming parts of London to have as a base for exploring. There were thirty of us at College Crescent, which was to be our home and classroom for three months while we were trained in the basics of nursing, before going onto the wards at the main branch of the Royal Free Hospital in Gray's Inn Road.

Before a single book or antiseptic bottle was opened, we were lined up in front of two flinty-faced Sister Tutors to present ourselves for inspection, wearing our new uniforms. These had to be faultless, with sleeves and hems long enough to disguise any disturbing sight of feminine arms or legs that might cause excitement on the men's wards. Hair had to be shining clean and, if long, swept back into a French pleat or bun with no strands escaping, or, if short, must be neat and not reach our collars. Fingernails were to be trimmed short and ultra-clean, while absolutely no abomination of make-up or jewellery of any kind was allowed. Engagement rings, if anyone was so forward as to be engaged, had to be worn on an inconspicuous chain around the neck, out of sight. Marriage was not permitted until the third year, and then only with Matron's permission. Our posture, like soldiers, was required to be upright, standing tall with no slouching, ready to carry stacks of bedpans, blankets or other nursing paraphernalia in a professional-looking way.

Three regulation dresses were supplied in blue and white striped heavy-duty cotton to be worn with black stockings. Tights had not been invented and stockings were worn with suspenders, which Heaven help us must never be seen while bending over to adjust bed wheels or help a patient with slippers. Later, when we got onto the wards, we found it was a contest for male patients bored out of their wits lying in bed, to try and get us up stepladders, reaching to open or close the high windows, remove a cobweb or change a light bulb. We would have thought it shameful to consider only our own safety when something like this needed doing, which was all part of making wards run smoothly with attention to every detail.

The Sister Tutors were imposingly tall stern women in navy uniforms worn with fluted white caps. Our own caps were the new American-style triangular pillboxes perched on our heads, cute but fiddly to fix in place with kirby-grips. Many senior nurses such as the tutors had experienced war conditions at home or abroad and had no tolerance of sloppy standards or namby-pambyism. These formidable women were to be our instructors and disciplinarians for the three-month preliminary nursing course, during which any unsuitable girls would be weeded out. SRN training for men was at a very early stage and we had none at College Crescent, but they had their own route into nursing by joining one of the armed services, where they could train as male orderlies and then become charge nurses. This was a very useful role on male wards where these CNs were highly regarded.

Standing in line, trying not to fidget in our stiff new uniforms, it was clear from that moment that we were expected to represent the highest order of professional practice and look the part, however uncomfortable, unbecoming or constricting this classic style of nurse's uniform felt. The dresses had three rows of wide tucks above the hem, so that one or more of these could be let out to make a dress longer if any of us happened to grow taller. Hems had to be five inches below the knee, measured with a ruler.

On top of these dresses we had starched white aprons, the bibs held in place with concealed safety pins, and our waists held in place by wide belts stiffened with starch and petersham webbing, making them solid and shiny as bone. First-year students had white belts, second years had striped belts, and third years the coveted blue belt that meant they had nearly finished and would soon be staff nurses with a flattering blue uniform and silver buckle.

Meanwhile for us at the lowest level, like horses being fastened into unyielding harness for the first time, we suffered hideous discomforts, in particular having to wear tight, black lace-up shoes called Oxfords. These were so narrow across toes like mine (rather spread out due to walking barefoot most of my childhood), it was an agony forcing healthy feet to mould to the shape of these unhealthy shoes. As soon as we got onto the wards, I made an appointment to go and see Matron, a fearsome woman appropriately called Miss Hardman, to ask if I could be allowed to have Clarks' black lace-ups, which were made of softer leather with a wider fitting.

She glared at me. 'Nurse Craddock, you are not yet six months into your training and you are already complaining,' she said, her face like stone.

Being older than most of the other girls, with some knocked-about experience of life and trained by Fa to be forthright, I was not going to be put down.

'Having to be on our feet all day means we need comfortable shoes, which is just as important as good boots for soldiers. Which the army takes seriously,' I added.

Matron stiffened. 'Clarks do not make nurses' shoes,' she said, as if I might have suggested getting shoes from Woolworths.

That's the whole point, I thought. The horrid Oxford shoes churned out by Dickensian hospital outfitters no longer suit the way young feet have developed, while Clarks make comfortable shoes for modern feet, I tried to explain, but realised the subject was not open to debate with this type of hospital matron whose mind was of the old school – regimental, immovable, impervious to logic – so I decided a tactical withdrawal might be wiser than getting branded as a trouble-maker so early on.

As if the shoes were not discomfort enough, our stiff white collars were another form of torture. These were detachable for washing (and yet more starching), fastened to our dresses with studs for easy removal when going to the laundry. Due to the excessive amounts of starch used,

223

the collars had sharp edges that dug into our necks, causing red marks and sometimes rashes, but no one complained for fear of being marked down as unsuitable for nursing if any sort of allergy or weakness was detected.

We were all given physical health checks and TB tests to make sure we were up to the standard of fitness required, and as soon as these were done and we had passed the uniform parade, day one of training started. This was spent cleaning lavatories; every lavatory in the college had to be cleaned over and over until that test was passed as well. It might be thought there could be any number of ways to clean a lavatory, but not if you were being taught the Royal Free way, which was up there with all the other fine arts of nursing practice, resulting in the consequence that to this day I am an expert lavatory cleaner and not the least bit squeamish about it. Once you have learnt how to do something expertly, there is a peculiar satisfaction in doing it that way every time from then on. In Royal Free terms, this extended to every procedure being programmed into us, so we were able to go out later as qualified nurses knowing what we were doing, feeling confident and able to cope in any situation. .

At College Crescent, each procedure and routine was taught in a set pattern so we learnt to do these methodically, practising our skills on each other, including injections, using sterile water. Before we actually plunged the needle into anyone else, we were given oranges to practise on, as these were thought to be the closest approximation to real flesh. It was a test of nerve for those girls who had a fear of needles and needed a bit of a push to get stuck in. At this point, camaraderie began to develop as personalities asserted themselves, with the stronger ones helping the others over difficult bits. We started to make friends and create our own amusements, going out to coffee bars and noticing how our uniforms attracted attention; everyone wanted to be friendly with girls from College Crescent. We were easily recognised in the rather dashing cloaks that were our outdoor uniform. These were navy blue lined with scarlet, billowing as we walked. If it was cold, we wrapped the cloaks around ourselves against the wind and they were very warm. We also discovered they were a useful protection in more ways than one, as it was almost unheard of for anyone to attack a nurse in uniform, such was the respect and affection we attracted, with smiles and greetings everywhere we went. This was a surprise to me and very gratifying for all of us, as we sometimes struggled to keep up with the demanding routines and class work.

One of the highlights of life during these three months was being let out on days off to go walking and exploring, with spacious suburbs all around and places like Hampstead Heath as good as being out in the countryside, while nowhere in London was very far away by bus or tube. We were paid ten pounds a month with free board and lodging, but the pay was not much more than pocket money for covering fares and other necessities like stockings and chemist items, as well as writing materials and postage. Most expensive of all were study books and these were well outside my budget. The standard nursing textbook was Balliere's definitive guide to every aspect of nursing practice, an impressive tome the tutors said was essential for passing exams and each of us must have a copy, in addition to several other reference books. Most girls got their parents to buy these books and I wrote to Fa, thinking he would want to make sure I had the recommended texts, and would understand from his own student days that these had to be got hold of somehow. He would expect me to do well, and helping to pay for the books would be small change to him.

Letters were achingly slow getting to Africa and coming back again, but I always wrote home every week and either Muz, or occasionally Fa, replied. In the case of the books, Fa had an inspired idea, being sure it must be possible to get cheap second-hand ones. He knew someone who might help to find some old copies. By this method, in due course a parcel arrived with some vintage books, including one with instructions on brewing ancient remedies. I showed this to Sister Tutor, thinking it would amuse her, but she wasn't impressed. 'If you don't get the proper books you will never pass your exams,' she said impatiently. 'You must go to Foyles and get yourself properly equipped.'

I went to Foyles, but seeing the price of a Balliere's, in thick hardback, I counted what was in my purse and bought a more modest-looking SRN handbook with floppy covers that claimed it had all the relevant information. So I put my faith in that and when, later on, I needed more amplification on a particular subject, I went to the hospital library, which Fa had suggested as an afterthought when I told him about the job-lot of books, including the one on boiling roots.

While such out-dated remedies were no longer part of the nursing curriculum, we did learn how to make and apply poultices. The substance used came out of a tin marked 'Antiphlogistine' and was like putty, with a pleasingly pungent smell. I used to think the smell was just as therapeutic as the poultice itself. Using a spatula to scoop the paste out of its tin, we slapped a big wodge of it onto a square of lint, which was then folded over to enclose the poultice. This was heated on top of one of the stainless-steel sterilisers used for boiling instruments, and when it had reached a temperature just bearable to touch but not sufficient to cause a burn, it was pressed onto the affected part, whether a rheumatic joint or chesty chest or badly infected boil, and the whole lot bandaged up so the poultice stayed on. This was soothing as well as therapeutic.

Bandaging was one of the fine arts we practised on each other, with no one wanting to volunteer for a full head and chest bandage as this was too uncomfortably close to a feeling of Egyptian mummification and ruined the day's hairstyle. Bandages when taken off, had to be washed and rolled up again on a contraption with a winding handle, so archaic it gave us fits of giggles as some of the inexpert windings produced weird sausage shapes.

Along with poultices and bandages, we were shown how to fill a hot-water bottle safely to place in the bed of a new patient, making it warm and cosy for them; or for patients returning to their beds after surgery, hot-water bottles were comforting as well as pain-relieving. There is nothing like a warm bottle for easing aches and pains generally and it was a great pity when they were banned by Health & Safety rules, along with a whole raft of other useful and important aids to well-being, such as nurses being responsible for keeping everything shiningly clean, avoiding cross-infection.

Class work, sitting at desks, was all about anatomy and physiology, drugs and diseases, with regular test papers along the way. After becoming competent in the basics, we were packed into a coach to go and spend a morning on the wards at Gray's Inn Road, to experience the real world of high-pressure nursing. It was a bit terrifying at first, as the wards were the old-style Nightingale barrack-like rooms with high ceilings and long lines of beds, fifteen on each side, with very little privacy. The original building had in fact been built as a military barracks during Napoleonic times, later being taken over as a hospital. This was in 1828 when a surgeon, William Marsden, after finding a woman dying in a doorway, too poor to afford medical care, founded (with Queen Victoria's approval) a free hospital, the first of its kind to offer this service to the poor of London. The history and ethos of the hospital appealed very much to my own sentiments in wanting to help and look after people, much like Fa with his altruistic leanings.

Before we were allowed to touch a patient or practise any of our newly acquired skills, the noble art of bed-making had first to be demonstrated to perfection. Bed-making was up there among the most hallowed of techniques, producing perfect 'hospital corners' and correct use of the draw sheet, with pillows arranged as an 'armchair' for maximum comfort. The turn-down of the top sheet had to be sixteen inches exactly, measured with a ruler until we could judge it correctly by eye. Once we had passed the bed test, we could then rise up to learn about doing what were called 'obs' (observations): recording temperatures, pulse rates, blood pressures and monitoring drips; but crucially, talking to patients, asking how they were feeling and noting how they looked. On my first ward, the Sister said, 'If a patient looks pale and anxious, with a grey tinge and a bit breathless, they could be on the verge of a heart attack, so it's vital you recognise this and act on it.' Heart attacks were frequent and much feared without modern drugs, and many of these patients were in poor shape, some of them coming from Rowton House, a hostel for tramps in a back street behind the hospital.

These men may have looked disreputable, but were known as 'Gentlemen of the Road', and were treated with much kindness and respect. The hostel was the base from which they set forth on their customary walkabouts, and it was common to see tramps trudging along roads, not just in London but far and wide. They had a fierce pride in being independent and keeping to themselves, somehow seeming to exist on mugs of tea and slabs of bread and jam handed out from back doors, where they were regulars, having also a bottle of something alcoholic stowed away in a pocket of the shapeless, ancient greatcoat that was their trademark all-weather wear. These, together with hobnail boots, marked them out as Gentlemen of the Road, and when they were brought into hospital with pneumonia from the chronic exposure of their lifestyle, it took a mighty effort to remove clothing and boots which had not been taken off for months. Socks would be stuck firm, with dirt and congealed oozings to the skin of their feet, so we had to get them to sit patiently soaking these in a bowl of warm water with plenty of antiseptic till the socks could be peeled off. The Ward Sister helpfully suggested we might wear masks at these times when removing boots, socks and other rancid clothes.

Sometimes, gentlemen were brought in with alcoholic poisoning or DTs (delirium tremens). It required two porters, one on either side of the bed, to restrain the violent convulsions and manic bellowing provoked by the terrible hallucinations accompanying DTs, while doctors administered an injection of formaldehyde, which was the antidote. If the disruption was too great while all this was going on, the bed with its occupant would be wheeled into the corridor and we would stand out there helping and mopping up until things calmed down. After being injected, formaldehyde seemed to seep out of the skin of the DT patient and had a horrible sickly smell, unlike any other kind of smell, so nasty that, combined with the whole experience of attending DTs, it remains embedded in memory.

Sister was surprisingly tolerant in these situations, but what she could not tolerate was unseemly behaviour: if any gentleman, forgetting where he was, blew his nose on the sheet or, leaning over the side of the bed, spat on the floor, he would not escape a few whacks of her tongue and the apologies would be abject.

Work at the Pyrethrum Board labs had been mentally and technically demanding, but this new kind of work was physical in its demands and these were extreme. I found myself getting increasingly thinner with the daily output of energy, but was not particularly concerned, as I no longer had to try and look like the kind of curvy person Lanner might want to be seen with. I was still grieving for him with all the emotional effects of a bereavement, and this affected my appetite, so I was probably not eating enough to avoid losing weight – not that Craddock appetites were ever more than minuscule.

Despite the finality of Lanner's parting thrust, closing the book on me, I still looked for a letter from him each morning at breakfast when the mail was distributed. I couldn't believe that he felt nothing after all that we had shared together, the challenges we had faced and overcome, the pledges we had made, the many letters and poems we'd written to each other. His to me I kept stored in the same old suitcase which, having covered so many thousands of miles on my various travels, was beginning to wear thin. Like various other parts of my life, I thought, as I stuck Elastoplast patches over cracks on the cardboard flanks of the old case.

Lanner had a very elegant calfskin writing case, which I admired and envied, wishing I had one of my own. The case had a lock, so private letters could be kept safely inside, together with all writing requirements: envelopes and Basildon Bond with pens and blotting paper, all neatly fitting into separate compartments. The case, when closed, served as a useful writing surface as I often saw him use it this way sitting in a chair with the case on his knees, and I wondered now if my letters were still kept inside as they always had been. His letters now formed part of my own small collection of valuables which included the gold watch and a gold ring set with amber stones that was another gift from him. It was a family ring and looked as though it had been designed for a man, being of wide, heavy gold, but was such a small size it must have been made for a very small man. This was a bit of a mystery, since Lanner didn't know its history or how it came to be in his stud box, which is where I found it one day. I tried it on and it fitted perfectly, so he said this was symbolic and I should keep it as a love token.

When I had a closer look at the ring, I saw that it had an inscription inside, a poignant one, indicating that it was a mourning ring. So the symbolism was not a happy one and wearing it reminded me of the apprehension I had felt when reading the Marvel poem. I showed Lanner the inscription, which he had never seen before, and knew nothing about it, except that his family had a connection in some way with the family of Earl Haig. The inscription reads:

Jane Haig died 26 March 1877 aged 38

Looking at the ring again and feeling the weight of it in my palm, and the way the amber stones glowed, I thought about Jane Haig and whoever it was who had loved her enough to have this ring made to be worn in her memory. I wondered if Lanner had anything of mine to keep, apart from the letters, or if he would want to keep anything. I had nothing of value like the ring or the watch to give him, and wondered if it was my lack of substance in any area that finally bored him when there was nothing left to offer. The withering emptiness of our last encounter at Lindi and the finality of his dismissal was still unexplained.

But he miscalculated. The book he referred to at Lindi as being closed – '*Not just the end of the chapter, but the end of the book*' – did not close itself. However forcibly he might have pressed its covers together, the book reopened itself for a sequel later on.

Meanwhile, at College Crescent no letter arrived in his distinctive flowing handwriting. However, another kind of letter did arrive, with writing in strangely squashed-up vertical strokes, the opposite of Lanner's. I didn't recognise this unusual writing spread across a big envelope with a fat letter inside, and was very surprised to find it was from Adam. It was full of news of his activities in the Regiment, which was still mopping up Mau Mau, and news of the farm and friends, with many pages of how much he was missing me and how he hoped I would write to him. The immediate effect was to make me feel very homesick and lonely, which had so far been fended off with the strenuous routines of College Crescent and on the wards, leaving not a moment to feel distracted. Adam's letter was enormously comforting and encouraging, once I had got over the initial impact of news from home with all its poignant associations. Suddenly I felt connected to him and the anchor of continuity with Kenya that I craved. I replied with pleasure and gratitude, feeling now a measure of genuine affection for him in response to his spontaneity of concern and desire to continue our friendship.

Still no letter came from Lanner, but hard work is always a solace and it may have been that subconsciously I had chosen nursing precisely because it offered this form of sublimation. Our mornings started at 7.30 a.m., whether in the classroom or on the wards, where there were three shifts in each twenty-four-hour period. Day shifts ran from 7.30 to 3.30, alternating with 1.30 to 10.30, allowing an overlap in the afternoon for important handovers, with reports on each patient, and tutorials. These were given by the Ward Sister, who also gave instructions for the next shift, so we all knew exactly what we were supposed to be doing. Some of us might be allocated as 'specials', which meant special attention to any seriously ill patient. The night shift ran from 10 p.m. to 8 a.m., with three months' night duty each year.

Ward Sisters had formidable reputations, suffering no fools or sloppy attitudes. The needs and details of each patient and system were their intimate concern and their eyes were everywhere. Staff Nurses came next in line of authority and could be just as exacting. One in particular, Staff Nurse Harrington, not much older than I was, coming to inspect what I was doing on my first ward, was so dissatisfied with the way I was stacking clean towels in the linen room, she insisted that I fetch a ruler and line up the edges of each pile to an extreme degree of precision. It was not as if we had legions of staff to carry out these tasks; stretched to our limits, we were perpetually chivvied to work faster, feet in tight shoes flitting up and down those cavernous wards, never sitting down except for meals. Running was forbidden, except in cases of fire or haemorrhage.

During our first year, the start of each morning was still devoted to cleaning, except that now on the wards West Indian cleaners scrubbed the lavatories as well as floors and sluices, and carried out general cleaning work. Student nurses cleaned lockers, bed-tables and all parts of the beds, including the wheels that had to be turned so they all faced the same way, like soldiers, 'eyes-right', with none sticking out, looking untidy or causing someone to trip. As soon as the cleaning was finished, we changed into clean aprons ready for proper nursing routines that started with the bedpan round. Sterilised metal pans, hot from the sluice machine, were piled onto trolleys and given out to each patient. Curtains were pulled around beds and help given to heave a patient onto a pan, with a nurse on each side if they were unable to climb on by themselves. Any more uncomfortable or impractical position for these particular bodily functions, perched on one of the grossly uncomfortable pans on a wobbly mattress, is hard to imagine, and I felt sorry for patients who failed to perform in the time allowed. The penalty was an enema, with their names added to a list of enemas allocated to us as another of the morning tasks. Commodes were not part of ward equipment, possibly due to lack of space as the beds were much closer together than would be allowed now. Male patients of course, had bottles, which they kept in their beds out of sight, a convenience not available to females.

After bedpans came the 'back round', a routine designed to prevent bedsores, which was very effective on the whole. Bed-bound patients were turned to lie on one side, exposing their lower back area: the part most vulnerable to pressure from lying immobile for extended periods. Gloves were not used except in theatre and for very dirty jobs, so with our bare hands, using surgical spirit, we rubbed and massaged those lower spine areas energetically enough for the skin to take on a rosy glow, indicating that healthy blood supply had been restored. Men in particular loved this. Curtains were not drawn for the procedure and after attending to each back, we moved on to elbows and then heels, rolling up bedclothes at the end of the bed to expose feet. Each foot would be lifted up in turn for the heel to be rubbed and massaged in the same way as backs.

On my first ward, which was Men's Medical, I was doing backs and heels for the first time when I came to the bed of a cockney sailor called Ernie, who was one of the regulars, in and out of hospital with chronic diabetes. He was an irrepressible comedian, always clowning around, teasing the nurses, keeping the other men entertained with a running commentary on all our rushed activities. It was my luck to have Ernie on my list. After finishing his back massage accompanied by a flow of remarks on my skill or lack of it, made worse by my terrible blushing, which was still one of my incurable shames, I went to roll up the bedclothes at the end of the bed to do his heels.

He's tucked his feet up out of sight to embarrass me, I thought, rolling the bedclothes further up. Still no feet appeared. The ward went silent with expectation, no doubt having seen this joke played many times before on unsuspecting new nurses. I went on rolling, thinking, these feet must be here somewhere. Then, shockingly, I uncovered two short stumps and the ward convulsed – 'Ol' Ernie, ee ain't got no legs, fools 'em every time, Ha Ha' – with whistles and cat-calls, while I stood there trying to apologise to Ernie with pathetic good manners, looking utterly foolish. 'Go on rollin' up the sheet,' the other patients called out. 'You'll find 'is other stump. Ee likes 'avin' that one rubbed an' all.' Ernie lay there saying not a word, a beatific smile spreading across his face.

The rising commotion stopped suddenly as someone called out, 'Cavey, cavey, war-hoss picked up.' Sister sitting at her desk in the middle of the ward had stood up, neck craning, to see what the clamour was about. She strode over to where I was standing, struck dumb beside Ernie's bed.

'If you had taken the trouble to read his notes, Nurse Craddock, you would have seen that Able Seaman Drummond has a double amputation due to diabetic necrosis.'

Well, I thought, when do we ever get time to read patients' notes, especially when we've only just started.

After passing basic-level exams at College Crescent, we were sent full-time onto the wards at Gray's Inn Road, but the nurses' home was full so we lived in a converted hotel in Highbury, with coaches taking us to and from the hospital for our shifts. The Belmont Hotel was quite grand in pre-war style; spacious and comfortable, it was just around the corner from the Arsenal football ground, and when crowds surged out after a match, struggling to get through them was like trying to part the waves of the Red Sea.

The hotel was our home for a year, presided over by Home Sister, whose sole occupation was to attend to our needs and welfare. Unlike ward sisters, whom Ernie and his mates aptly classed as war horses, Home Sister was a cosy older woman who thoughtfully put friends together sharing rooms, and I had my two friends from College Crescent, Beth and Andrena, sharing with me. Andrena was Australian, from a place called Wagga Wagga, which no one had ever heard of. Beth's family was Welsh, living in North Wales, in a small town with an equally foreign-sounding name. I was glad neither of my friends came from places with English names, since I came from a small town called Nakuru that no one had heard of either. I didn't think of myself as English, feeling far more at home in Africa than England, so the bond between the three of us may have been because we were all foreigners in the drab environment that was the East End of London in 1960.

The hospital served what were still very poor districts, and Islington, where the Royal Free had its Liverpool Road branch, was one of the poorest, with families living in conditions of severe deprivation crammed into squalid tenement buildings. Some families lived in just one or two dark, grimy rooms with no running water, only a single communal tap out on the landing of each floor, so water had to be collected in buckets. Later in my training, I went 'out on the district', as it was called, accompanying the Health Visitor or District Nurse for experience of the wider world of nursing. We used to climb the dark, mouldy stairs of these tenements to inspect new babies that had arrived into these slum pits already full of hollow-eyed, scrawny children dressed in rags, while the mother lay in bed exhausted, trying to hold the new baby to her breast with thin white arms, papery pale.

Often there would be no clothes for the latest arrival, which had to make do with being wrapped in an old towel, and the Health Visitor would bring baby clothes provided by the WRVS (Women's Royal Voluntary Service). The next time we visited, instead of seeing the baby wearing these new clothes, sometimes the mother would look coy and admit that the child's father had sold them to buy drink. Broken windows were stuffed with newspapers to keep out the cold and bitter winds, with no heating inside these mean rooms. Some had tiny fireplaces and children would be sent to pick up pieces of coal that had fallen from coal lorries or carts in the street. There might be a gas ring with a meter providing a shilling's worth of gas (if there were any coins to spare for the meter), enough for boiling a kettle or cooking. But cooked food was often an unaffordable luxury for poor families, who lived on bread and 'dripping', which was rendered-down fat they could buy cheaply from the butcher.

On our way to and from the Belmont we passed through these run-down areas, which had neat rows of Victorian terraced houses alongside the tenements, but there was never anyone out in the street looking well dressed, except policemen, who always patrolled in twos. Women in slippers and pinafores shuffled along, their hair permanently in curlers, with shopping wrapped in newspaper inside string bags. Plastic bags were still waiting to be invented, and no one owned a car.

With the Arsenal football ground a centre of popularity on one side of the Belmont, on the other side, and not so well attended, was a rather grim-looking Victorian church. I went to see what time services were held as I missed church activities and the friendliness of St Christopher's in Nakuru. I saw that matins was held on Sunday mornings and arrived the next Sunday, wearing my one good coat, looking forward to meeting new people and becoming part of a congregation again. The door was open, but no uplifting peals of organ music rang out as I went inside, squinting through the gloom. I looked around; there was no one else there, yet the service had been clearly advertised on the board outside. As I was turning to go, a wispy voice rose from the chancel and startled me. Then I saw that the voice belonged to an old man dressed in black priest's robes, indistinguishable from other dark objects in the dim light, which is why I hadn't seen him up there. He came down the aisle and, without introducing himself or explaining anything, rather impatiently indicated that I should sit in the front pew, all by myself, while he stood at the chancel steps to conduct the service, urging me to sing as loudly as I could to make up for such a depleted congregation.

It was one of those surreal situations, not knowing whether to go along with the absurdity of it just to see what happened next, or run away. While I was thinking about it, Father Cuthbert (as I later found he was called) took up position and announced the first hymn, fixing his eye on me to make sure I'd heard. I fumbled for the hymn book on its wooden ledge in front of me, disturbing a thick layer of dust that swirled up, making me cough, so it was a few moments before I was ready to sing. I was not shy about singing after so many years in choirs at church and school, and tackled the first line of the hymn, belting it out to humour the old priest, but the dust cloud choked me again and I had to sit down abruptly. Father Cuthbert came and stood at the end of the pew, waiting for me to stop spluttering.

With a reproachful look, waving his hand dismissively, he said with slow emphasis: 'I don't think … you … are … going to be one of us,' and turned to walk back, very slowly, through the chancel to the vestry. Waiting respectfully as he left, I noticed from his back view how threadbare his robes were and how broken he seemed; having nursed the church through the war, his congregation had now deserted him, I thought, and felt sorry for him.

Back at the Belmont, the maids, who were all local girls, laughed when I told them how I had gone to church and found myself the only one there apart from the priest. 'Oh, yes, old Father Cuthbert, yes, he's gone daft in the head, it was the war that done it. The church is supposed to be closed, but he has a key and opens it on Sundays, just in case some poor sod like you wanders in.'

The maids and chefs had all worked at the Belmont when it was a hotel, so we were treated like hotel guests, with great food and service, a completely unexpected indulgence as most of Britain was only just emerging from post-war austerity and luxuries were rare. Breakfasts were generous to an extreme, with bacon and eggs and piles of hot buttered toast. We were encouraged to eat plenty to stoke up energy levels for the day ahead, so no one ever missed breakfast. This was also a cheerful time, catching up with friends and opening our post, delivered by the maids to our tables. Some months into 1960, a thin envelope arrived in Muz's handwriting that did not include her usual weekly letter. Instead, a small newspaper cutting fell out when I opened the envelope. As soon as I read the tiny print, I felt sick and couldn't eat the rest of my breakfast. The cutting was from the *East African Standard* newspaper, announcing the engagement of Lanner to a girl in Nairobi whom I'd never heard of. The marriage was to take place in Nairobi Cathedral within the year.

I felt outraged and mortified that he could attach himself to someone else so soon after sending me away; not only that, but marrying her without a qualm. No long-drawn-out agonising of endless love poems and letters with their promises. But this girl, I had to concede, had enough *savoir-faire* to get him onto his knees, while I had been too dreamy and dim – and the only way for me to avoid spending the rest of my life distressing myself over him was to accept that my own destiny was elsewhere. I must now salute his success, leave him behind, and look ahead to a rewarding career, putting an end to this useless aching. But I felt angry, not just with him, but with Muz for sending the newspaper cutting so thoughtlessly without any note about how I might feel. That was something else I had to accept: that she and Fa were never going to show more than a passing interest in my friendships or relationships; they were too wrapped up in their own preoccupation with Babs.

CHAPTER 14

Every three months we were moved to a new ward or department to experience a range of different skills, and Andrena, on our next move, was put onto night duty. She was expecting to join other night nurses on the top floor of the Belmont, reserved for sleeping during the day, well away from noisy activities downstairs. But Home Sister came to explain that the top floor was full, so Andrena would have to stay in the same room with us and we would have to be as quiet as possible to avoid waking her during the day. This turned out to be impossible as, however carefully Beth and I tip-toed around trying not to disturb her lying in bed with daylight glittering through the curtains, nothing could block out noise from clattering feet and loud voices in the corridor, with radios and record players blaring in neighbouring rooms. She could only doze on and off, becoming increasingly exhausted and desperate as lack of sleep turned her healthy Australian golden-girl looks into a gaunt-faced shadow of what she had been. Home Sister was sympathetic but surprisingly inert in finding any solution. Andrena, realising there was no prospect of relief and feeling she was close to cracking up, decided to resign. She took her resignation letter personally to Matron's office so that she could confront Miss Hardman with the intolerable situation of being forced to leave simply due to a lack of sufficient night-nurse rooms. Miss Hardman, predictably, was unmoved, merely commenting that if Andrena truly cherished her vocation, she would put up with any inconvenience.

It was ironic that a glossy book published that year, featuring scenes of Royal Free nurses at work on the wards, had a photo of Andrena on the front cover looking like just the sort of nurse anyone would dream of having at their bedside. The Sister on her first ward, Annie Zunz, had given her an outstanding report for those first three months and we all thought she was heading to be top nurse of the year. She was the clever one among us, with brains and skill, beauty and personality, none of which seemed to count for anything with Matron, who appeared only to be looking for robots.

Beth and I were bereft, as the three of us had been like strands of a cord, each contributing different qualities to the friendship, but there was no time to get maudlin about it while we were being moved to new wards with new shifts and new, terrifying Ward Sisters. I was sent to Women's Surgical, another one of the old barrack-style wards around a central courtyard, but higher up the block, to be more easily accessible to operating theatres at the top. These occupied the entire top floor, with anaesthetic rooms, recovery rooms, rooms for storage of equipment, staff changing rooms, surgeons' rest rooms; the whole like a small empire presided over by masked and gowned figures hurrying on long corridors, with a constant flow of trolleys adding to the disturbing sense of urgency and pressure. Operating lists started early and could go on all day, with patients being shuttled to and from the wards. A nurse from the ward always accompanied the patient she had been assigned to, running beside the trolley, holding the patient's hand and their notes. We would stay with our patient in the anaesthetic room to reassure him or her until the anaesthetic took hold and they had 'gone under'. Later on, it would be the same nurse going back to collect the patient afterwards, bringing them back to the ward with post-op instructions, both verbal and written out.

In between all this hustle, we still managed to squeeze in a surprisingly full social life. Beth, through her Welsh contacts, had met an urbane older man of at least thirty, who was taking her to the theatre, opera and grand balls. She was spending all her free time with him, dashing in and out of our room to change into evening gowns, of which she had several shimmering creations squashed into our small, shared wardrobe. To make up for abandoning me in favour of this new flashy lifestyle, as I had no handy contacts in London, and no cash allowance for spreading myself among the hot spots, Beth introduced me to one of her ex-boyfriends in the expanding circle of Welsh diaspora living in London. Displaced from their heart-tugging valleys and mountains, they felt more at home when they could get together, singing and speaking in Welsh.

The friend Beth introduced me to was Conrad Oak, more of a Thomas Hardy name than Dylan Thomas, I thought. The most thrilling thing about him, apart from the perfection of his physique, was his vintage MG sports car; while not so thrilling was the way it kept breaking down, most frequently at critical moments like crossing London Bridge or hurtling around Hyde Park Corner. These breakdowns were commonplace to Conrad who was a mechanical engineer; not in the least discomforted to be standing hunched over the engine for as long as it took, while I sat on the kerb, refusing to sit idly inside. There were times when the steam rising from my collar was caused not by evaporation from a steady drizzle of rain but frustration, as I could find my way around the interior of a car engine just as well as he could, apart from which my fingers were more dextrous than his in cramped spaces. But he had a weird idea that two heads were a crowd under one bonnet, so I let him get on with it, while trying to make my neck shorter, shrinking down into my steaming collar as the rain continued the steady drip that always seemed to accompany these breakdowns.

Conrad's day job was with London County Council as an engineer involved in maintenance of the various exhibition halls, including Olympia, which the council was responsible for, so we would often be driving between these sites when he had a call-out. His engineering persona was the income-provider that allowed him to indulge another entirely unexpected side of his life that I only gradually became aware of. I had accepted without thinking that any former escort of an exquisite girl like Beth would have his own share of arresting attributes complementing hers. So, on first being introduced to him, his startling beauty did not surprise me so much as why a man with this notable quality would choose mechanical engineering as a career, rather than one of the visual arts. It was a little while before the less visible side of his life began to emerge.

I was flattered that Beth thought me sufficiently qualified in looks to be an acceptable companion for Conrad, and even more flattered that he thought so too – especially as he, a Celt, was of that build more comfortably suited to slight Welsh girls I assumed, while I was tall. Conrad was not tall, but all his details were perfect. It was hard not to stare. At first I had to keep remembering not to do so and stop myself reaching out to touch his hair, crisp with dark curls like Dionysus. He had the strong jaw-line and craggy features of those Welshmen who might just as easily have written poetry as gone down the mine, or both. His close friend was a Welsh painter called Andrew Vicari, whose cluttered studio was a hang-out for a louche set of painters, living bohemian lifestyles. I used to go there with Conrad for long, languid evenings, debating the many compelling issues of the day, arguing and drinking cheap Chianti, while Andrew cooked and swore and held forth like some legendary figure titanic in the proportions of his body and mind.

He said I looked like Nefertiti, with my high cheekbones and dark eyes, and thought these features might be useful in one of his Egyptian compositions. He was currently working on an epic depiction of the Last Supper that was being painted on a series of panels several yards long and several feet high, destined for an exhibition in New York. All these panels were accumulating in the studio, stacked up, waiting for the last one to be finished so the whole lot could be crated and shipped off. Conrad's hands were being used as models for the Apostles, so all the hands were the same, while various male friends modelled other parts. With his prodigious energy and creative drive, Andrew was at the same time preparing work for a London exhibition. When this opened, the preview clashed with my hospital shifts, so I wasn't able to go to the opening, which disappointed Conrad who said he wanted to see my face as I went in. The exhibition was in a building on one of the corners of Piccadilly, and passing by a few days later, sitting high up on the top deck of a bus, I was hardly able to miss the long banner with Andrew's name across it. Running down the stairs, I got off at the next stop and walked back. The high doorway with its banner looked inviting and seemed to be having the same effect on others coming in from the street. It was dark at first as we went in, then at a further doorway there was a spotlight picking out an image so striking it made us all stop and gasp. This was a massive and powerfully shocking oil painting, the fierce light making it seem alive and electrifying in the impact of its size and unexpected raw shamelessness. It was a full-length male nude, larger than life, its harsh body tones brushed with burnt umber, sparing no detail. Unmistakably, it was Conrad. I knew he modelled for Andrew and knew they were working on something to give the exhibition a focal point. Full-frontal nudity, especially male nudity, displayed in public in this brazen form and, moreover, enlarged to make sure nothing was missed, was still shocking in 1961. Most shocking, though, for me was to see Conrad, my own intimate friend, exposed in this way for the world to gaze at. He had not wanted me to wander into the exhibition by myself, and now I could see why.

Several years later on, I wondered what had become of Andrew, and looking on the internet, found that he was reported to be living in France. Some of his paintings were shown, along with a profile, but not the epic *Last Supper* or nude Conrad!

Back at the hospital we were being moved around again. Rooms at the Gray's Inn Road Nurses' Home became free and Beth and I were told to move there from the Belmont. It was a sad parting, leaving that tight community, which had consoled us on losing Andrena. One good thing about moving was that we now had our own separate rooms and there was a telephone on each floor of the home, which was a luxury. When the phone rang, whoever was nearby answered it. This could lead to some interesting crossed wires, with the voice of someone else's boyfriend encouraging cheeky conversations. The rooms were warm and comfortable and we had kettles for tea or coffee, providing a social ritual between shifts as we crowded into each other's rooms to unwind.

There was a canteen on the ground floor, the opposite of Belmont waitress service, but much jollier. Best of all, we had only a short walk to reach the wards instead of the half-hour commute on a bus or coach. King's Cross tube was down the road and the number 73 bus went from there to the West End with all its smart shops, and theatres where we could get cheap tickets for the Gods (seats high up with a restricted view) if we queued long enough. Soho and Leicester Square were thumping with energy both above the pavements and below, where we crammed into packed clubs such as the 2i's in Old Compton Street, listening to new bands just starting out. The liberating rhythms that sprang from their voices and instruments stirred us with arousing sensations, opening up fresh uncharted territory for music and society in general. There was jazz in hot smoky cellars throbbing with jam sessions, and intense flamenco in one very small dark cellar deep under the pavement in Leicester Square. Everyone smoked, which made the air fuggy and dense, but the music drew people who were serious about the quality of the bands and dancers, and no one was getting drunk or taking drugs, at least not in any obvious way.

In between shifts, this was where many of us could be found, with or without partners. I never felt unsafe if I was on my own anywhere in London except at King's Cross. There, the prostitutes would come up and hiss close into my face if I strayed onto their patch while I was standing outside the tube waiting to meet up with a friend. I soon learnt never to loiter anywhere on pavements in seedy districts. Later, when I worked on Ward 10 at the Hampstead branch of the Royal Free, looking after women recovering from septic abortions, I got to know many of the patients, who were mainly prostitutes, and most of these were regulars in and out of the ward. After becoming pregnant, which was one of the constant hazards of their work, having a back-street abortion was the only choice before the NHS became more lenient. Hearing their stories, which they told with wry wit and a complete lack of self-pity, I came to admire them and look on prostitution in a new way.

Meanwhile at Gray's Inn Road on Women's Surgical I was on another new path, learning about surgical procedures. These varied from routine to acute, and when major operations were performed, the aftercare could be very demanding. This was before Intensive Care Units or High Dependency wards existed. Those patients needing intensive care were placed close to Sister's desk in the middle of the ward so she could monitor and keep a close eye on them, supervising the nursing team.

The high standards of medical and nursing care routinely expected were not always assisted by a lingering post-war attitude of being miserly with resources, which led to surprising shortages of some pieces of equipment that now would be seen as essential, such as aspirators, called 'suckers'. These were life-saving for clearing blocked airways and should have been readily available at all times, especially following throat surgery. My new ward had one sucker that was shared with the next-door ward whose sister, a small ferocious Irishwoman called Sister

Kerrigan, guarded it in her own ward like a holy relic that she fiercely resented having to share. I was looking after a woman just back from theatre after having her tonsils out who suddenly haemorrhaged and started choking. Getting another nurse to stay with her, I ran for the sucker. Hoping not to meet Sister Kerrigan, I went straight to where the sucker was kept and seized the whole thing, which consisted of a large glass jar with tubing connected to an electric motor on a pedestal. Running as fast as I could with the dead weight of this contraption held in my arms, I thought I'd got away with it, when a rasping Irish voice shouted from behind, 'Stop at once. That apparatus does not leave my ward without permission.' I didn't stop. I was too scared and in too much of a hurry to get back to the haemorrhaging woman. Sister Kerrigan ran behind me, furious steps pounding the lino, but I knew when she entered my ward it would be my own Sister who confronted her and they would lock horns, while I escaped to plug in the sucker at the woman's bedside to suck out the blood which was choking her, assisted by the other nurse who had stood in for me while I was doing the sprint.

The incident was not without consequence as, in revenge, Sister Kerrigan got me transferred to her ward, 'So that I would learn some lessons', she said. This was in many ways not a punishment but an honour as, despite her ferocity, or perhaps because of it, in pursuit of her patients' welfare, she was an outstanding Ward Sister in charge of a specialist ward where important work was being done.

Walking onto her ward for the first time would be startling for most people as all the patients were yellow, their faces, eyes and skin all over their bodies deeply jaundiced due to liver failure, giving them a bronzed look. These were Professor Sheila Sherlock's patients, volunteers for her pioneering work on liver disease and transplants. She was becoming famous for her research and progress in understanding the processes leading to liver failure. Sister Kerrigan made sure the nursing of these patients matched the excellence of the medical care and that they felt valued for their contribution to this important work. She was fiercely protective of her yellow men, lying in their rows of beds, their bulging livers making them look pregnant. All of them were on a short path to death from liver failure, in most cases caused by alcoholic cirrhosis, their hopes pinned on

Sheila Sherlock, who was carrying out the first liver transplants, which were still being developed at this stage. Sister Kerrigan viewed me with deep suspicion when I first arrived on her ward – as if I might turn wild and defy her authority if not kept under control, her fierce eyes drilling into me and her shrill Irish voice following each move. It was unnerving to begin with, until I discovered a warm and lively character inside the fiery exterior, waiting to communicate itself when she felt my loyalty and competence could be trusted. 'Nurse Craddock, you will do what I say and say what I do when you yourself, if you ever get that far, show the half-wit heathen girls who are getting into nursing these days how to be doing the job.'

Since Beth and I had moved to the main nurses' home we saw less of each other now we were in single rooms far apart, but there were so many new faces all around I was never short of friends and one of these was a very bouncy girl called Susie, or Soose, or sometimes other names that she made up for herself. She had a prodigious imagination and fearless spirit, leading to all kinds of escapades that she dreamed up, added to which she was a compulsive actress. She could not have been more different from Beth. Her parents ran a pub in south London where she had grown up, earning pocket money by entertaining customers, which was encouraged by her parents. From an early age she would be hoisted onto tables in the bar to sing and dance and when she got older she did recitals; most notable of these, she told me, were theatrical renderings of the poem 'Eskimo Nell', which was enormously popular with the punters, who paid extra if she dramatised the verses with actions.

'Do you want me to show you?' she asked, eager as any performer sensing an audience. I had never heard of 'Eskimo Nell', the title suggesting a rousing but innocuous tale of igloo folk, so I was unprepared when Susie launched into an epic rhyme of such extreme vulgarity and language never normally spoken aloud it left me speechless. She mistook my amazement for an expression of wonder and paused, before offering enthusiastically: 'I could teach you. You can make good money in pubs and everyone wants to buy you a drink and be mates. Well,' pausing again, 'not all of the girls goes for it, they get grit-faced if it's their blokes all over you. But,' she added, 'it's a barrel of laughs and you come out with stacks of notes stuffed down your bra and stockings. You can't beat that, can you?'

I liked Susie a lot and discovered she had many sides to her. There was an annual competition among London hospital nursing schools, with a silver cup for the winning team, and Susie was assembling a Royal Free team to enter. 'You're on the team,' she said, giving me no chance to think whether I wanted to be on it or not. 'It'll be a lark. We'll beat Middlesex.' They were the current holders of the cup. Susie had that kind of irresistible energy and enthusiasm that sweeps others along and opens doors. With nothing but a smile, I thought, she could charm traffic lights to turn green, or clouds to scud away, bringing out the sun. She charmed unlovely features like the antediluvian sluice room machines when these turned obstinate and the heavy doors got stuck. But sluice rooms could also be the undoing of Susie.

Unloading bedpans from the mighty machines allowed moments of respite from busier activities out on the ward, and while junior nurses like us were doing this, volumes of banter went on, relieving stress and tedium. Susie was always up for a laugh and we discovered that if we made her laugh too much she would lose control, wetting herself, which caused general hysteria, and it became a game, trapping her in the sluice room, making her laugh. But nothing ever seemed to embarrass or bother her and, being Susie, she just stepped out of her knickers, throwing them in the bin with a laugh and a wink: 'No knickers, who cares!'

Susie's insouciance helped to overcome jitters the rest of us were seized with when our team came up for scrutiny in the nursing competition. The judges were senior tutors from other hospitals, in their tall starched caps, watching every movement under a spotlight of set procedures to be carried out faultlessly. It was worse than doing final exams. At least in those the practical tests allowed for occasional errors, but the competition allowed no leeway and we were racked with nerves all the way through. All except for Susie who, brimming with confidence, sailed along, smiling the whole time. It was probably the smiling that gave our team an edge as, true to Susie's prediction, we won – much to the surprise of Miss Hardman who was so impressed she allowed us to have a taxi, paid for by the hospital, to go and collect the trophy from the Middlesex Hospital. Returning with the silver cup, a little ceremony was held in the nursing school classrooms down in the basement of the hospital; nothing fancy of course, in case we got swelled heads.

Basic routines were the same on all wards, with a high point each morning at nine o'clock when Consultants did their rounds. Everything had to be ready punctually on the stroke of the clock and perfectly arranged with a degree of reverence fit for visiting royalty, so elevated was Consultant status. All patients must be sitting up in bed, with their pillows and back rests sloping at the same angle, top sheets turned down sixteen inches exactly and smoothed out. Bed covers similarly smooth and tidy, with hospital corners, bed wheels all lined up. Absolutely no bedpans were allowed during rounds, bodily functions being strictly suspended during this ritual, which commanded an almost religious sense of deference and formality, as all eyes watched for the entourage to make its entrance. This would sweep in through the double doors, the Consultant in front with his registrar, followed by house officers and then medical students, all in white coats, to be met by Sister and her senior staff nurse in charge of the trolley of patients' notes that was wheeled round as the group proceeded from bed to bed.

A student nurse would be waiting ready to stand at the foot of each bed as the procession slowly moved along. Her job was to recite the patient's name, age and diagnosis, with latest 'obs', and be ready for questions on anything the Consultant might ask about the patient's condition, before he turned to Sister to get her comments. Then it would be the medical students' turn to be quizzed. Some consultants were inclined to theatrics, booming at nervous students, taking a perverse delight in picking on the less outgoing ones or catching out the know-all ones.

'Nurses know much more about patients than you do,' one Consultant enjoyed telling the assembled medical students, fixing his eye on the student nurse standing uneasily at the end of the bed, saying to her, 'Please be kind enough to tell these clever young doctors about the complications that might be expected following surgery in this case.'

All this was stated in a loud voice, with the patient listening anxiously to every word; not only the patient, but all the neighbouring ones as well. When it came to my turn, if I tried to lower my voice when giving out a sensitive diagnosis to spare a patient's feelings, the Consultant would interrupt, 'Speak up, Nurse, what did you say, haemorrhoids, was it? Let's have a look then.' And curtains would be drawn round while the white coats crowded inside, the nurse helping the shrinking patient roll down his pyjamas to expose the offending parts to general scrutiny.

No one ever complained about any aspect of hospital care; it was accepted that Consultants and senior doctors knew best and whatever they said was treated as gospel. From the degree of reverence shown to them, it might have been thought they were possessed of almost mystical powers, speaking a medical language unintelligible to ordinary people, conducting visitations to the wards like Roman emperors followed by their legions. This grand status caused many of them to behave in a distant, even disdainful manner very different from the more casual familiarity adopted now. In 1961, people had modest expectations of services provided by the State and were so grateful to have free medical care that this new experience was still held in awe with genuine appreciation. It would have been thought ungrateful or unreasonable to complain or make demands. Medical and surgical mistakes were made, sometimes fatal ones, but there was a philosophical view that doctors were always doing their best even when they failed, and that it should not be held against them.

All this time Adam was still writing long letters to me, infrequently, but it was always exciting to see his writing on an envelope with a long letter inside. These were written on crinkly blue airmail paper, full of news in a witty style and now with many loving declarations, though we had agreed there was to be no commitment to each other and we were free to explore new interests if they came along. I had a semi-detached relationship with Conrad, who was spending more time with his bohemian circle, a strange mix of uninhibited intellects with exotic tastes and sluttish behaviour.

A friend of mine from school, Penny, wrote to say she was living in London and would like to meet up. Her flat was in Cromwell Road and we were to meet there for tea. I was on my way by tube when a man sitting next to me turned, looking rather embarrassed. He apologised and said, 'I hope you don't mind. I don't want to seem rude, but I'm very sensitive to certain types of extra-sensory communication and it seems that I'm getting some sort of message coming from you.'

Oh Lord, I thought, another creep. That's a new chat-up line. I looked at him furiously, hoping to shut him up. He continued amiably, speaking in a cultured voice, which surprised me as he didn't look like the usual kind of nuisance person encountered on public transport. I pretended not to hear. Ignore him, I thought. Get off at the next stop. But wait until the last minute and sprint for the door so he can't follow.

I got off and ran to the escalator, only glancing behind to check he wasn't there once I was halfway up. There was no sign of him, so I took the next escalator down to connect with another tube and all was well, though I felt unnerved all the way to Penny's flat. I had not seen her since leaving school and there was a lot to catch up on, with cups of tea and talking about the toxic brand of puritanism that had been practised on us at the school, where we had both been miserable. We were interrupted when the phone rang and Penny went to answer it. 'It's for you,' she said, sounding surprised. I was even more surprised, wondering how anyone knew where I was.

'Hello,' I said. Then froze. The voice on the other end was the man from the tube.

'Sincere apologies,' he said breezily. 'This is an unforgivable intrusion, I know. But I saw that you left the train suddenly before the correct stop and wondered if you were all right and had got to your friend's flat safely?'

'How did you get this number?' I said, outraged and tense with shock, but trying not to sound shaky.

He went on unabashed. 'You remember I was picking up waves from you in the tube. The name of your friend as well as her address and phone number conveyed themselves to me as they passed through your mind. I was not able to avoid picking this up.'

I was incredulous. How could he possibly have found out any of this? I didn't have a piece of paper in my hands with details written down that he could have glanced at. But I may have been reminding myself of Penny's address, so was it possible that he really was a mind reader? I put the phone down quickly before he had a chance to say anything more.

Penny had a car and said she would drive me back to the hospital to make sure I got there safely, and if the man happened to be waiting outside, we could confront him and threaten to report him to the police if he carried on harassing me.

I felt better when I got back, as there was a parcel from Adam and inside was a record of songs from the film *South Pacific*, which had just come out, with a note telling me to listen to one of the songs. He said the song put into words, much better than he could, his feelings about me. It was called, 'Younger than Springtime', and was poignant, flattering and romantic. I began to wonder if he was getting serious about me, and whether I was beginning to get serious about him.

Muz had come back to England to check on poor Spindle, who seemed to have vanished into the dark demented depths of Epsom's loony bin with no word of how he was or even if he was still alive. Elaine and I had no idea he was there, otherwise we could have visited him, but news of his departure from Mathari and incarceration at Epsom had somehow failed to be passed on to us. Muz was renting a drab thirties bay-windowed house in Reigate, which was not too far from Epsom and was convenient for Ros, who had started a pre-diploma course at Croydon Art College. The one good thing about the Reigate house was that it had enough space for all of us to be together for occasional weekends so we could be a family again, minus Fa, but it was reassuring to have a home to go to when I could afford the train fare.

My pay as a student nurse covered most basic necessities, including bus fares, but not train fares. Some girls had an allowance from their parents topping up the pay, but Fa didn't see any need for this. One of the reasons he approved of nurse training for Elaine and me was that we could be self-supporting. Beth's expensive clothes and lifestyle came from a family with deep pockets, while most of the rest of us lived sparsely on a budget of £2 a week with ten shillings saved. If anything was left over for a treat, it would be something like a Mars bar or a Babycham at the end of the week. We became expert at inventing economies and one of these was a way of disguising holes in our black stockings so we didn't have to buy new ones too often. When a hole appeared, we put black ink on our legs to disguise it. This worked very well, except when we were out of uniform and not wearing stockings. Going around with black spots on our legs didn't look so good out in the street or on buses if we had been in too much of a hurry to rub the ink off.

When Muz went to check on Spindle, which was the first thing she did after arriving, she was horrified to find him extremely distressed, not just emotionally but also physically, with injuries caused by a male nurse who was sexually abusing him. Spindle was able to describe exactly how and when this abuse was happening. The nurse was on permanent night duty, so it happened frequently and the only relief Spindle got was when the nurse had nights off. Spindle showed Muz the pot of lubrication that the nurse kept handy in the bedside locker and with this evidence she went immediately to the senior psychiatrist in charge of the hospital to tell him that she would be reporting this illegal activity to the police. The SP persuaded her that it should be dealt with as an internal disciplinary matter, and the nurse would be moved to another ward while investigations were carried out. Spindle was called to give evidence to the investigating panel and Muz was allowed to attend. She said Spindle, despite being heavily sedated (in an effort to muddle him, she suspected), gave his evidence lucidly in a clear voice with honesty and candour. There could be no doubt that his testimony was genuine and his indignation about what had been done to him was compelling. The nurse adamantly denied everything and pointed out that Spindle was certified insane, so his evidence could not be treated as valid.

The outcome was dismally predictable. The disciplinary panel, not wanting any unsavoury findings, ruled that Spindle's evidence could not be relied on in view of his mental state. The nurse was exonerated and Spindle was in effect 'sacked' and moved to another hospital. Muz was disgusted, but hoped good might come of the disgraceful episode if fresh insights on treatment for Spindle came to light at the new hospital. Perhaps some kind of occupational therapy might be provided there to brighten his life, instead of leaving him pathetically caged and drugged as at Epsom.

The new hospital that Spindle was moved to was Netherne, another vast amorphous institution in Surrey whose primary purpose seemed to be keeping mad people safely locked up out of sight. Muz did her best, pestering the psychiatrists to get him off drugs and onto psychotherapy instead, hoping this might help. She became engrossed in fighting Spindle's case, possibly out of guilt for abandoning him all that time after Mathari. She visited him faithfully at Netherne, buying him new clothes and gradually getting him to calm down enough to go home occasionally for a day or weekend.

Back at my own hospital I was moved to the Theatre Wing, where student nurses started on the lowest rung, scrubbing dirty instruments after operations and learning how to pack these into the autoclaves (sterilisers). One of the surgeons with lists at the wing was a towering figure called George Qvist, who was famous for performing heroic surgery on patients with advanced cancer. He had a formidable reputation, working at a fast and furious pace and losing his temper if anyone in the team failed to keep up. As I was still too junior to scrub for such an eminent surgeon, I was given the role of 'dirty nurse', which meant being gowned up but unsterile, standing a couple of paces behind the great man, holding a bowl ready to receive any discarded organs or tissue. On one occasion I was too slow with the bowl as he turned, holding high in his gloved hands something gory and dripping that he had just removed. It was a whole stomach and my bowl was not quick enough to catch it as he roared with impatience and threw the whole spongy mass, with forceps still attached, in my direction; but I dodged and it flew past, hitting the wall behind with a loud squelch, hanging there grotesquely for a second before flopping to the floor with a blubbery sound as blood splattered out, and everyone glared at me for failing to catch it in time.

'Leave it,' shouted one of the surgical team, turning back to the inert patient, where Mr Qvist was busy delving for more portions of malignant tissue.

Operating theatres were possibly less regulated at that time, or some surgeons more eccentric than would be tolerated now. One of the gynaecologists used to bring his African violets in their pots to sit along the windowsill in theatre while he was doing his lists, absorbing the bright lights and steamy air which he fancied was good for them.

I did rise up to being scrub nurse in due course, but never enjoyed theatre work as the pace was too pressurised and stressful. I preferred looking after conscious patients and having conversations with them, which couldn't happen with unconscious ones in theatre.

Adding to my jitters at this time, there was a knock on my door one evening in the nurses' home, with someone calling, 'Telephone for you.' I went to the phone thinking it might be Conrad, but the next moment there was a horrible sense of *déjà vu* as I recognised the voice of the man from the tube. Greeting me like an old friend, he said, 'Hello! Have I found you again?'

'Why are you phoning me?' I tried to shout, but choked on the words and instead all that came out was a sort of mumble.

Seeming not to notice, he went on smoothly, 'I wanted to apologise for my intrusion the other day and explain that I am a normal respectable professional man, not in the habit of behaving in the way that I did. But you should know that you yourself have unusual powers, psychic ones, which may connect unexpectedly sometimes.' He continued, 'I was startled by this, which led to my impertinent remarks, for which I apologise.' There was a pause as I stayed silent, not trusting myself to speak, then he said, 'I felt that I owed you an explanation. I hope you will understand.'

He spoke in a way that was both disarming and disturbing. I knew that I had occasional minor psychic moments, but not the sort that broadcast personal information to strangers on the tube. He continued, as if assuming I had accepted his apology and explanation, 'To reassure you, I must tell you about myself. I am a researcher for a television series currently going out on air. You can check with my colleagues, they would all vouch for me.' He waited for me to say something, but I still felt too spooked to reply. He said, more hesitantly this time, 'I wondered if you might like to visit the studios – maybe you would like to join the studio audience for one of our programmes?'

I was trying to work out the implications of this surprising invitation when he suggested, 'Bring a couple of friends along. It's a good opportunity to meet some of the personalities in television that normally you see only on a screen. Much more interesting meeting them face to face.'

I took a deep breath. 'You better tell me your name.'

The name he gave seemed ordinary enough, and he went on to tell me a bit more about himself, which sounded normal and plausible. I began to relax a little. 'You can leave a message for me at the studios if you like,' he continued, giving me a number. 'You can tell me which days you're free and if you would like to bring any friends. When you've checked with them, of course.' He sounded genuinely diffident about asking me and whether I would accept. Not waiting to hear my reply, he gave me the phone number again, repeating it slowly for me to remember. I just said, 'Thank you', and hung up.

I had a friend from Kenya called Des Hamill, now living in London and working as a TV newsreader, and thought I could ask him if he would check out this guy through his contacts. My friends at the hospital were intrigued by the whole mysterious encounter and the connections with television, which were seen as glamorous.

It was just at this point that Fa wrote from Kenya with an invitation to visit and, most surprising, coming from him, he even offered to pay my fare. He wanted to go on a trip around Lake Victoria on a ship doing a tour of all the ports and places of interest along the shore. He must be lonely, I thought, or hatching some new plan he wants me to broker with the family. Regardless of his motives, the main attraction for me was the chance to see Adam again. After more than a year of letters, the pangs of absence were becoming more insistent. I accepted Fa's offer quickly by telegram before he had a chance to change his mind and within a couple of months, having got clearance for taking my annual holiday allowance of two weeks, was on my way.

CHAPTER 15

Gatwick airport at this time was a small rural outpost with one long runway (the far end providing cover for courting couples where it rambled out into waste ground) and a big shed where passengers assembled. The mass assembly of travelling public later to be encountered at Gatwick was postponed for the time being. An independent airline called Hunting-Clan was running a regular service of Viking aircraft to Nairobi, taking three days en route. It was the cheapest option, as Fa was paying, but no less exciting for that, while possibly more so as this budget airline stopped at a fair number of places for refuelling and overnight stays.

Arriving at the big shed, there was no mistaking other Kenya travellers bunched together at one end with their *kikapus* (sisal baskets) tied up with string, and suitcases no more respectable than mine. There were about twenty of us waiting for the flight and one woman had a whole salmon wrapped in ice packs and newspapers stuffed into her *kikapu*, hoping it would last the journey. As temperatures rose the nearer we got to Nairobi, the presence of the salmon decomposing among the melted ice packs added to the discomforts on board as putrid puddles leaked around our feet. In the absence of air conditioning, the interior of the cabin became stifling with various pervasive aromas mixed into our recycled breaths, as we droned on through an eddying haze of heat thermals once we had left England well behind.

Our first stop was Nice, where the airport spectacularly occupies a prime position along the seafront, with its runway ending at the sea. As soon as we landed and the door was opened, a warm breeze drifted in, and outside were avenues of palms with wide walkways where people were strolling in bright sunshine, wonderfully different from the pale version we had left behind in England. I felt liberated, turning my face to the sun, feeling that at last I was on my way home.

The Viking had twin propellers and, due to its lack of pressurisation, flew no higher than nine thousand feet. Frequent refuelling meant that we stopped every few hours along the route, often at remote places, where fuel was pumped by hand from forty-gallon drums, and we were lucky if there was any shelter where we could stand or sit out of the sun. Refreshments were provided in an equally haphazard way, or not at all. The Viking didn't fly at night and our first night stop was in Malta, still a dear place to me, full of nostalgia for the happiest of times living on Marsamxett harbour where we had our first real home, with *Merlin* our sailing dinghy moored outside. After landing at Luqa airport, a bus took us to lodgings where we were glad to have a wash and a walk, giving our legs some relief from cramped seats all day. The evening air was infused with orange blossom, that scent always bringing back to me our first days in Malta at Boschetto, walking each evening in the cool of the orange groves. I would have liked to spend longer in Malta, visiting friends and familiar places, but there was no time to linger as we were off early next day, flying south-east across the sea to Benghazi.

After refuelling, we flew along the North African coast to Mersa Matruh, then turned south to meet the great, wide, green waterway of the Nile, which served as a route map. Each time we took off again, the plane rose into a sky shimmering with heat, bleached of colour by the sun's glare which was intense, the small plane dipping and rising in thermals, props droning manfully through the heavy atmosphere.

Our second night was spent on the Nile at Wadi Halfa, in a houseboat. This looked romantic on first sight among papyrus reeds, but was soon found to be swarming with mosquitoes, its timbers eaten away with age and years of decay as it creaked and sank low in the green water, straining to bear the weight of all of us climbing on board loaded with suitcases. Staff in white robes and bare feet rallied round to help us get settled in cabins reeking with the smell of rotting vegetation, while unidentified sounds of scratching and scuttling came from cracks among the planks underfoot. We were too tired to care, and having been served a supper of hot brown soup and hot brown stew, we fell into bunks, keeping our clothes on and pulling the rusty sheets over our faces to keep out the hordes of busy mosquitoes.

When the broad ribbon of water that was the Nile began to seep out into vast swamps, we made for Juba and then at last Nairobi, where Fa was waiting with his big smile wider than ever. He was touchingly glad to see me and I sensed for the first time his loneliness and how separation from the family was affecting him.

The Menengai house, which for him had been a dream of perfection with all his own ideas incorporated into its design, had now been sold, as too big or too extravagant for him to live there on his own. What had happened to Muz's beautiful Blüthner grand piano, I couldn't bear to ask. Her Morris Minor had been shipped to England to save her having to buy a car when she came back to check on Spindle. When it arrived at Tilbury, she went to collect it off the ship and was standing on the quay watching it being unloaded, dangling on the end of a crane high in the air, when somehow it slipped off the ropes and crashed down, ending in a crumpled heap, a complete write-off. Another Craddock disaster.

Fa was now living in a house attached to Nakuru War Memorial Hospital, where it was useful having a doctor close by for emergencies. He had invited Adam for dinner the night of my arrival, which was considerate of him, but Adam was already there when we drove up, not being able to wait for dinner, unwilling to arrive primly on the doorstep at 8 o'clock in a suit.

We were both overcome with emotion at seeing each other again and Fa tactfully went off to do his rounds at the hospital so we could be alone. The elation and ecstasy we felt, being close enough to talk and touch after eighteen months apart, was to be very brief as the next day Fa and I were setting off for the long drive to Lake Victoria in Uganda, with hardly time for me to wash the sweat and dust off my clothes. It was planned that I would see Adam again briefly when we returned, before leaving to fly back with the two weeks of my holiday gone in a blur of travel stops.

Most of the roads in East Africa were still primitive, and Fa's Peugeot made slow progress. He was a dithery driver, always looking along the sides of the road instead of in front, stopping at the merest glimpse of any small brown birds (known in our family as SBBs) flitting among the trees, when he would stamp on the brake abruptly and fumble for his binoculars.

'Oh, do have a look at that cisticola,' he would urge, as I waited impatiently for him to drive off again, or tried to see if there might be a turaco or some other more interesting bird hopping into sight. During earlier days in Kenya we had friends, John and Helen Start, who were bird enthusiasts, just as excitable as Fa at the sight of any SBB skulking in the undergrowth. John and Helen had a farm at Molo, sublime in its high altitude situation, the purity of air crystal-clear, with a cool crispness of early mornings when pastures were soft with dew and the coats of cattle and horses shone with the fat of the land. Helen ran the dairy and would have on her table big round golden pats of butter from her Jersey herd, with jugs of yellow cream and food that had been cooked with all this goodness melted into it. She was one of those bright, capable, hard-working farmer's wives, like so many others among those pioneering settler women building up productive farms in the highlands and lowlands. Helen came from the Millington family who, along with the Ryans, were some of the earliest European immigrants setting up farms in Molo.

The road to Lake Victoria took a climbing route through dense indigenous forest around the lower slopes of Mount Elgon, where there were shy animals to be spotted, hesitating in shadows at the side of the road, ears alerted to the sound of the car's engine, with, of course, new birds to identify at every turn. Fa was enthralled. We did see turacos this time and many other rare sights, like golden orioles.

Whether it was caused by the constantly varying changes in altitude or some other factor, hardly had we descended from the heights of the mountain, emerging onto tribal lands below, than I was suddenly overcome by extreme sickness and dizziness, unable to stand or walk steadily, which quickly became something Fa recognised as acute labyrinthitis. Realising it would now be impossible to continue the trip, he decided we must get back to Nakuru without delay so I could be admitted to hospital for treatment and rehydration. He didn't make me feel guilty about this disappointment, seeming genuinely concerned just to get me to hospital as quickly as possible.

It was a relief when, after several hundred bumpy miles at rapid speed, I could lie down in a cool, clean hospital bed, with Bunny Griffiths called to advise. Fa couldn't attend to me himself as it was not ethical for doctors to treat members of their own family. Despite Bunny's chronic alcoholism, he was continuing to practise, as in between bouts he was still a very skilled, experienced doctor. It all depended on whether he was sober or not at the moment he was needed. This time, although appearing less red-eyed and blotchy than was often the case when recovering from a binge, his hands were shaking as he wrote out the dose of Stemetil (an anti-emetic). It was too much for someone as underweight as I was then, and side-effects were immediate, causing spasms of my neck and jaw, so that I couldn't move my neck or open my mouth. It was like having lockjaw, while at the same time my neck was bent backwards at an unnatural and painful angle. Fa was dismayed to see me now in this worse state, not being able to eat or drink or even talk, except through clenched teeth. He suggested an antidote, but this was slow in taking effect and meanwhile he sent a telegram to Miss Hardman at the Royal Free, explaining the situation, as I would not be able to return until fully recovered. She replied in a surprisingly sympathetic way (considering how unsympathetic she had been to Andrena), which no doubt was due to Fa impressing her with his medical credentials.

An immediate effect of my unexpected return was the extra time that Adam and I could now spend together as he sprang to my bedside, visiting every day, being very attentive and loving in his concern. A good friend, Esther Hopcraft, happened to be a patient in the same ward and was very kind, fetching and carrying, and sitting beside my bed reading to me as I couldn't move or do anything for myself for some while.

Esther and Jack Hopcraft were patients of Fa's and had been very hospitable to us as a family when we were all together in Nakuru in the fifties, so we knew them well. They had four children – Peter, Jane, John and David – all of them having inherited their parents' astonishing good looks. The four were now grown up and associated in one way or another with MRA (Moral Re-Armament) in various parts of the world. Fa was an admirer of MRA, which was based on Christian principles, but he never became a full member because it was too painful for him to hand over the generous donations required to further the work of the group. These donations led in due course to MRA becoming a very wealthy organisation so that, to us, its whole ethos began to seem dubious.

Other patients of Fa's were Hugh and Pat McCubbin, who lived along the road from the hospital, and took me to stay with them when I was well enough to leave hospital and needed a place to recuperate. Pat was Jewish, her mother having left Germany in good time before the war, taking Pat as a small child with her, leaving behind their entire family, who later perished in the Holocaust. These family members had been very against Pat's mother leaving and abandoning a valuable business she owned. They thought she was mad to give it all up to start a new life in England, knowing no one and speaking no English, but wisely she had seen the warning signs in Germany with the rise of Hitler, and by leaving in time their lives were saved. After the war Hugh, who was by then a British Army Officer serving in Palestine, met Pat who was also in uniform, a young, vivacious, dark-haired girl who was highly capable and an asset in every sense. So he married her.

They had three boys: Norman, Richard and Steven; a loving, harmonious family in a big house with a garden full of trees like a park all around it. Hugh was Financial Director of the KFA (Kenya Farmers' Association) that had its main office and base in Nakuru. Their household was a very nurturing place for me to recover and they welcomed Adam as one of the family, so we were able to spend time there, getting to know each other better and finding that we shared many interests and laughed at the same things. Adam was now a student at Egerton Agricultural College, Njoro, intending to join his father on the family farm when he had finished the two-year course. After National Service, he had thought seriously about taking a commission in the British Army and going to Sandhurst, but his father wanted him back on the farm which, as the eldest son, he felt was an obligation, and he was devoted to the farm so it seemed an obvious choice.

Later on, during conversations about this choice, he said what he had really wanted to be was an actor, studying drama at RADA in London, but his parents would never have approved, the stage as a career being thought most unsuitable and risqué. For years he still felt a hunger for it, agonising that he had missed his vocation, many times appearing in amateur productions (sometimes with professionals), always showing exceptional skill as an actor and having a powerful stage presence. He could stand centre stage, all alone, holding an audience with the passion of a speech or comic turn; a rare gift. His name would be top of the invitation list as a social asset at parties, always in demand as a born entertainer and clever mimic. I had never met anyone like this before and he was good for me, an antidote to all the Christian inhibition that had infected me all my life, and I was flattered that someone as popular as he was could be attracted to someone as ordinary as me. Any confidence I might have had earlier in my life went to zero at the Sussex school, and later nose-dived again with the crisis of Lanner's rejection. Where Lanner and I had both been reticent characters, seeming to fit together in a shared quiet intensity, Adam and I were very different. Never wanting to be the centre of attention, I was happy to watch and listen, but I wasn't a complete introvert; I could enjoy a party as much as anyone. Adam was good company when we were alone just as much as in a crowd, our happiest times often on our own together exploring those areas of common interest that centred around our love for Kenya and the countryside pursuits we both enjoyed with our large circle of friends.

Like most other young Kenya-born men of his age, Adam had been brought up with guns from the time he could hold one to his shoulder and recite the poem: '*Never, ever, let your gun/pointed be at anyone . . .*', which had to be learnt by heart before being allowed to fire a single shot. He was addicted to hunting, polo and fishing, impatient to introduce me to these activities and to his close friend Tony Seth-Smith, whose parents had both been professional hunters, among the last of the legendary 'White Hunters'. Tony's mother, Kathleen, was possibly unique in this hierarchy as a professional hunter. The Seth-Smith farms at Njoro lay beyond the wide dry plains of the Rift Valley, their land merging with thick forest where the earth turns red and deep and fertile; a natural paradise for animals of all kinds, as well as the Wanderobo people, living lives supported entirely by their habitat.

Tony was away at Oxford during the time that I was recovering at the McCubbins', so I was unable to meet him then, but Adam took me to be introduced to his parents, Cenydd (Cen) and Alison Hill. Cen had arrived in Kenya aged twenty-two in 1920 to help his uncle Jack David on the farm they called Glanjoro, as a tribute to their Welsh roots. I had already met Cen while working for the Pyrethrum Board and had found him charming and flirtatious, so was looking forward to meeting him again. With this encouraging connection I was surprised when he seemed not to remember me at all, while Alison was quite frosty. Encountering cold handshakes was unusual in Kenya society as the settler community was known for its generosity of spirit, so this was puzzling.

I didn't know what to make of Alison Hill, who was a stiff, angular woman, upright and uptight as she stood there, thin and wiry as a coat hanger, her skin kippered by the sun. She wore twill trousers with an old faded shirt almost transparent it was so worn out. I felt awkward not knowing what was expected of me, and wrong-footed in assuming that, as long as I displayed good manners, all would be well. Whether they were disappointed that I wasn't the kind of girlfriend they expected for their eldest son, or their reaction was always this way with girlfriends, I was left mystified.

Theirs was a curious household where dogs occupied high status, sprawled on the carpet, scratching and licking themselves, scrabbling to leap up at any sound of a footstep outside, provoking an enraged chorus of swearing from both Alison and Cen as they swatted at the dogs to shut up. Despite most conversation being centred on the health and welfare of these and other animals on the farm, the dogs were thin as racks.

Trying to balance a cup of very weak tea on my lap while sitting uneasily on the edge of an armchair sagging low to the floor, which involved contortions folding up my legs to stay decent, I looked around the room as the conversation shifted to those many absorbing subjects farmers obsess themselves with, all the while puffing away on Sportsman cigarettes.

In the Hills' sitting room, apart from the collection of ancient armchairs with chintz worn grubby from generations of dogs relieving their itches along the sides, an occasional glow of polished mahogany shone in the dim light, shaded from any direct light by a wide veranda outside.

At the far end of the room was a handsome French armoire with decorative brasswork beside a long dining table with a window to one side. The open window had a piece of chicken wire stretched across it, the only window in the room with this feature. At the other end of the room some fine figurines stood on a heavy stone mantelpiece, looking slightly insecure and incongruous perched there so delicately in their bone china Staffordshire poses. Like the Hills themselves, I thought, maintaining this fragile gentility in the midst of the blood and guts life that was Africa.

Afterwards, Adam felt the tea party had gone well and his parents had liked me, to the extent that approval had been given for him to show me around the farm. He had been looking forward to this but would not go ahead without their permission. The 'swimming party', I gathered had taken place at a time when they were away. This time was different for me, as I felt comfortable and happy going back to admire the grand view from the water tank where we had picnicked that first time, and was now part of our joint history together.

I loved everything about the farm, its spaciousness and the dry heat that rose up from fields of maize and *wimbe* (millet). I loved the slow-moving herds of Friesians as they were rounded up for milking at portable bails out in the fields, a hundred cows to each bail. These outdoor milking units were moved to a fresh piece of ground every few days, the cows staying undisturbed in the field with clean grass under their feet when they were milked. A soft wind blew as they stood in the stalls, dipping their heads into metal troughs where there would be a scoop of dairy nuts to chew. The milkers whistled and cooed gently to the cows as they worked, a sound that is so much part of that life tending cattle in Africa, while in the background there was the steady, rhythmic throb of the milking machine and the generator going 'put-put-put'. Adam chatted and laughed with the milkers, introducing them to me by name, which none of them missed as having some significance in that I would be expected to remember their names, where a casual visitor might not. The same gentle wind was ruffling maize stalks in another field as I breathed in the sound and feel of all these sensations. This was a life I wanted to share.

Later, before taking me back to the McCubbins', Adam stopped to check on a borehole his father had asked him to look at. Seeing all was well, we closed the gate behind us and, pausing beside it, looked back across the field to the green belt of trees following the course of the Njoro river that formed the western boundary of the farm. A river stocked with trout, where I might cast a fly some time later on, I thought. Leaning on the gate, absorbing the view and the contentment of that moment, Adam turned to me and said, 'If we still feel the same way about each other next year when you come back . . . I think we should get married.' I waited for him to go on, thinking he might translate this easy-going statement into more of a formal proposal, but he stopped and there was a pause as he looked at me for my reaction.

I had been taken by surprise. It seemed a bit off- hand mentioning marriage so casually and I wanted to test his seriousness. 'Why don't we get married straight away instead of waiting?' I suggested. 'I can tell the hospital I'm not coming back. Muz can pack up my things and send them on.'

'We can't do that,' Adam said. 'I have to get my diploma before coming to work on the farm. And you need to get qualified in case I'm ever out of work, and nursing will always be useful.'

I wanted to establish something before anymore was said. 'Can we get engaged then?'

'Not until I've been to see your father to ask for your hand in marriage,' Adam, always the epitome of correctness said as he took my hand, giving me a wink and a smile. 'This is the hand I will be asking for.'

'We can call on our way back now,' I said, wanting to hold onto the momentum of the moment, and feeling it would be impossible to keep the news from the McCubbins when I got back to their house. Possibly, also, after my experience with Lanner, wanting to make sure this time there were no get-out clauses that might suggest themselves during any delay which offered a chance to reconsider.

'Yes, why not?' Adam, still smiling, drew me in for a kiss, sealing the intention.

It was sundown and I knew Fa would be sitting on his veranda reading the *Lancet* or *BMJ*, enjoying the scents and sounds of evening, when birds flew down to drink at the birdbath and all would be still and hushed. He looked up as we walked round the side of the house, rising from his chair, smiling his big smile, pleased to see us. He offered Adam a beer and was about to pour lemonade for me but I made an excuse, saying

I wanted to go on to the McCubbins' house which was a few hundred yards further on, and would see him later as both he and Adam had been invited for dinner.

Dinner that night became a celebration. Pat, who was a genius in the kitchen, ensured it was an engagement feast of grand proportions, with champagne produced by Hugh. The only downside was my imminent return to England and another long separation before there could be any more celebrations. With no time to buy a ring, it was decided best to keep the engagement unofficial, and we would tell just close friends, our families, and the Hemsteds.

Adam was anxious to tell his parents without delay as it would cause a major fall-out if they got wind of it before he had been to see them. Luckily it was the weekend, so we duly went on the Sunday morning to tell them. I was apprehensive about their reaction after the previous meeting, which had seemed uncomfortably sticky to me, but Adam dismissed my doubts. 'What are you worrying about? Of course they'll be happy for us and will give their approval,' he said. 'How could they not approve?'

After arriving mid-morning in time for coffee, it quickly became evident my misgivings were not misplaced, as no sooner had coffee been poured and we were sitting down making the customary remarks about weather and other compelling issues of the day, than Adam, too impatient to wait, got to his feet, suddenly announcing in the middle of Cen's observations on crop forecasts, that we were engaged. The news could not have caused more consternation had he whipped out a pistol and fired several shots through the ceiling. One of the servants coming in at that moment to empty the ashtrays was shouted at so violently he dropped the tray he was carrying and bolted out of the room. This woke the dogs, who leapt about barking, which added to the general commotion. Everyone sat with strained faces, waiting for the noise to die down.

Cen was the first to speak. 'Don't be a fool, Adam. You're much too young to get married. And,' he added pointedly, 'you can't afford it.'

Adam was still standing as he replied affably, 'We've got plenty of time. The wedding won't be till next year or the year after, and I'll have time to save up.'

'Not on the wages you'll be getting here,' Cen added.

Alison said in a stiff voice, 'You hardly know each other. It's all much too soon. I'm surprised Dr Craddock has given his approval for such a hasty arrangement.'

'It's not hasty,' I said. 'We've been writing to each other for eighteen months.'

I might as well have said we had been sleeping together for eighteen months for the effect this remark produced.

'Well,' said Alison, recovering herself, 'you'd better stay to lunch then.'

She went to ring the bell for Pedro, the houseboy, telling him, '*Ongesa chakula mbili*' (another two for lunch).

This seemed to settle the discussion into a slightly more amicable mood as they began enquiring into my background and situation: who I knew, where I had been born, where I had been to school and so on. I realised my answers were falling short in several areas and my credentials from a social angle were not sounding impressive, but I was determined to stand my ground and not be made to feel inadequate.

When we were called to lunch, I looked again at the window that had chicken wire stretched across the open space, thinking it looked a bit crude, bulging and held loosely in place with tacks. Immediately in front of the window was a serving table on which Pedro placed a small joint of meat for Cen to carve. While the rest of us were taking our places and Pedro was waving flies off the joint, waiting for Cen to start carving, there was a rampage outside the window as half a dozen scrawny cats, alerted by the smell of the roasted meat, came running, jumping and clawing at the wire. Failing to get a hold and bunching themselves below the window, maddened with hunger, they threw themselves at the wire with such force it exploded inwards, as with one bound they seized the joint and made off with it. Cen was left brandishing the carving knife, trying to spear one of the cats that was a bit slower than the others. He and Alison were darting about, shouting and swearing, cursing Pedro for failing to beat off the cats. Adam seemed unmoved by the spectacle, as if it was quite normal, patiently explaining to me that these were farm cats, kept to catch rats around the house and barns, so they were deliberately kept hungry to encourage them to be good ratters.

While Adam was involved in this explanation, having gestured me to stay put and ignore what was going on, the dogs, once more aroused, were let out to pursue the cats who sensibly had swarmed up a tree with their prize, where they were tearing at it, growling like panthers. Cen went out to throw stones at them, thinking they might release the meat, while Alison, with a sigh, went off to the larder, returning with a tin of Spam as a replacement for the lost joint.

'Do come back and carve,' Alison shouted out of the window to Cen, indicating the small pink lump of Spam waiting to be sliced into wafer-thin pieces. Once this was done, Pedro came back with an entrée dish where the two potatoes cooked for the parents' lunch had been halved to provide one half for each of us, while another entrée dish held some amorphous vegetables that had been boiled long enough to erase any identity they might once have had. A scoop of pale gravy was ladled over the Spam as the vegetables were added to it, and this was my introduction to meals with my prospective in-laws. Pudding, however, was junket made luscious with cream from the dairy, the high point of the meal after the excitement of the cats' raid. I looked across the table to Adam on the other side, while his parents sat one at each end, a very spaced-out arrangement. He gazed happily back at me, everything seeming to be well in order, with my presence already accepted, as the conversation settled down to banalities.

The Hemsteds and McCubbins had warned me about the eccentricities of Adam's parents and this I now understood with some amusement, but also some serious doubts about how I was going to fit in, and what degree of subservience might be required to achieve this. Adam's tender gaze swept aside these doubts, and we were so locked in that concourse of loving glances and toes touching under the table, nothing else seemed to matter very much. The only thing that mattered was the pain of leaving with so few days left together.

If I stayed any longer I would have to repeat a whole year of training and although the effects of the illness had not fully worn off and I was still a bit unsteady and delicate, the journey back and my return to work had to be faced. So it was a very strained parting at Nairobi and a very long three days' return flight, retracing the outward journey which back then had been a much happier one with its prospects and better health.

But my good fortune now was to have made a quick recovery and to be returning to England engaged to Adam, confident of my feelings for him and his for me. There was a whole future to plan and look forward to.

CHAPTER 16

The news of my engagement was not greeted with any rapturous response back in Reigate, as Elaine was still unengaged after being jilted by Tom and no one wanted her to feel she was being left behind. She herself, having such a charitable nature, was genuinely glad for me, while relying on God to reveal another bridegroom waiting patiently around the corner. Muz was unable to summon much enthusiasm for my news in the absence of a ring or announcement in the newspapers, saying it couldn't be a proper engagement while it remained informal. Her own mood was low, with Fa away and Babs insisting on visiting to 'check' on her in what was allegedly a spirit of friendship and support, but it jangled every nerve in her body when Babs arrived all gung-ho, chirping, 'Here I am to cheer you up!'

'Your mother looks thin and anxious, she needs feeding up,' Babs said to me, arriving one weekend when I was home.

'She doesn't need feeding,' I murmured under my breath. 'She's already fed up.' Fed up with you, I thought, coming here all bright and jaunty, full of sugary excuses, while the real reason for coming was to hear me talk about Fa.

Babs' arrivals were always theatrical, her car crunching into the back of someone else's or scraping the gatepost as she leant out of the window, one hand steering, driving up waving and breathless with exclamations. The car would be loaded with bags full of peculiar items of food and her laundry, which she brought along to wash over the weekend while cooking meals for Muz. All these bags would be bundled through the door in a fluster of bonhomie as she prepared to reorganise the household around her plans for our welfare. This time, among all the other packages, were eggs, milk and brandy. 'I'm making eggnog for you all; it's just what you need, packed with goodness!' she exclaimed, whisking up half a dozen eggs with milk and glugs of brandy, not even stopping to have a cup of tea first.

The eggnog was poured into glasses and handed round. 'You have to swallow it down in one go, like oysters. It's very reviving,' she said, throwing her head back, upending her glass to slide its contents down her throat. 'Ambrosial!' she cried, smiling triumphantly at the rest of us holding our glasses uncertainly, while we looked at Muz to see what she was going to do. I decided to be bold and swallow my sample of yellow gloop so Muz would not be left in the position of next one to follow Babs. It was an odd sensation slurping the slimy mass which, contrary to expectations, did not go down easily and the brandy made me choke, so my exhibition failed to be encouraging for Muz or the others.

'Do try a little, Fay,' Babs urged Muz (Fay was her first name). 'You'll find it very refreshing.' Muz tried a sip and nearly fainted as the brandy exploded in her mouth. Being teetotal, even the smallest amount of alcohol could give a powerful hit, added to which she had a lurking suspicion that Babs might be trying to poison her. For someone who never drank alcohol, a shot of brandy could seem like a potion of poison. With just this one sip making her sway and turn pale, Muz fled to her room, locking the door, which always happened sooner or later during Babs' weekend visits. After that, we would have to take food upstairs on trays to Muz and sit on the bed to calm her down until Babs left.

In later years Ros and I often discussed what Babs' strategy was during these visits. Was she genuinely concerned for Muz's welfare but so insensitive to the emotions stirred up that she was oblivious to the effect it caused? Or was she a scheming minx intent on reducing Muz to such a state of nervous exhaustion that she would crumble, and the marriage could be seen as void, allowing Fa to be free?

On this visit, among the numerous bags with their cargoes of strange food, were parcels of jumpers that Babs' mother had knitted for each of us from the hair of her pack of chows. The chows had dense hair, which Babs' mother carefully combed out, washing and spinning it into balls of wiry wool that could be knitted up. She was very proud of the results which she wore herself and outfitted her amiable, uncomplaining husband in a range of styles, but we noticed Babs never wore any of them and now we were to be recipients of the latest output. I was curious to find out whether the jumpers smelt of chow even after the washings in Lux flakes, and what the texture would feel like, so I volunteered to put one on and Ros tried one too. They were surprisingly light instead of heavy and thick, but very scratchy and the colour distinctly unflattering, a sort of dish-wash grey with liverish flecks. We looked like a couple of chows and Babs started laughing her tinkly schoolgirl laugh until we all joined in, clowning around, sniffing at the jumpers in a doggie sort of way. 'It's all right,' she said. 'I'll tell Mama they fitted beautifully, which they do, and she'll be delighted.'

Laughing about the weird dog-hair jumpers lightened the mood of the household and Muz upstairs, hearing the noise, came down to see what was going on, even joining in once she saw that the joke was on Babs.

Going back to the hospital after weekends at home had a new lilt for me now there were plans to be made and a wedding dress to be bought, which would not be a knitted one this time. Having missed a whole month of work, before being allocated a new ward or department I was given a stretch of 'study block' which was a regular part of training, sitting at desks in the basement classroom, taught by Sister Tutors preparing us for tests and exams. Always a bit of a swot I enjoyed these periods of study, which included plenty of social time catching up with friends who were scattered around various branches of the hospital. Also it meant our legs got a rest.

As we became more senior in our training, I noticed that we were treated with more respect by the Sisters and allowed to say what we thought about some aspects of technique. Times were changing with the onset of a new decade and the old rigid paths of nursing practice were being reviewed. Best of all, we went occasionally to lectures at the medical school in Russell Square, joining up with medical students and attending dissection rooms, where the internal anatomy of dead bodies was displayed for study.

The sickly smell (which came mainly from pungent preservatives) took some getting used to, as did the sight of those open bodies with so much exposure of grey morbid flesh; while my thoughts were of the person who had inhabited the flesh as a living spirit, with their own dreams and expectations like the rest of us.

From study block I was posted to the cancer ward (the title 'oncology' came later), where many patients arrived with tumours so advanced it was a wonder they could have allowed themselves to reach such a desperate state before getting help. There was still an ingrained attitude among the general public, used to hard times, of putting up with problems, not wanting to bother doctors, not wanting to make a fuss, and most of all, not wanting to think about cancer which generally carried a death sentence and was virtually a taboo subject outside hospitals. It was common practice among doctors not even to tell patients they had cancer, 'to spare them'. So the pretence would be kept up right to the end and they would die never knowing what had been wrong, still believing in many cases that they were getting better, regardless how obvious it was that they were dying. The power of the human spirit for delusion at these times seemed more than remarkable. Relatives would be told the truth by doctors and advised that it was kinder to keep it to themselves. Avoiding the word cancer, the ward was known simply as the Radiotherapy Ward. It was a mixed ward, with men and women in beds side by side, arranged in this way to encourage a sense of conviviality. In practice this worked very well, and of all the wards I worked on, radiotherapy had the most cheerful and relaxed atmosphere, which seems ironic as most of the patients were dying. Their lives were extended for varying lengths of time by radioactive treatment; no drugs were yet available for cancer treatment, except palliative ones.

Radioactive isotopes were delivered to the ward in heavy lead boxes on wheels that would be taken to the bedside for insertion into a cavity where a tumour was located; cervical tumours, in particular, were responsive to this form of therapy. We wore lead aprons to protect our own ovaries while we were handling the isotopes, and the processes involved were carefully controlled to avoid accidents. Some patients would be taken to a separate department for therapy, using radio waves or cobalt. Those with tumours too advanced for treatment came to the ward simply for terminal care, which they received with unlimited tender loving attention and compassion. One of these was a woman who had delayed seeing the doctor until her cancer had erupted from her chest like a rotten cauliflower, the smell so putrid it was necessary to apply layers of lint and gauze to smother it, while at the same time keeping her comfortable and snug. Her grace and calm acceptance of her situation I found poignant, while her gratitude for the kindness and care she received seemed to epitomise all the good things about the NHS at that time.

All patients on the ward received, on prescription, a pint of stout every day to boost their calories and morale. As a medicinal alcoholic drink it was unbeatable, lifting spirits and energy so they were able to enjoy their time on the ward in a happy sociable atmosphere that the staff enjoyed too. Pain-relieving drugs were not stinted and were given on the basis of need rather than arbitrary protocol.

Leaving the ward at the end of three months was the hardest part, with many tears on both sides, knowing we were unlikely to meet again after my transfer to maternity training at Liverpool Road in Islington.

This was a deprived area with some levels of poverty so dire that the wretchedness occasionally led to degradation, with young girls giving birth as a result of incest, usually linked to fathers. There was an explanation for this. We were advised not to judge but to try to understand how fathers in desperation could turn to daughters for comfort when their wives were worn out with childbearing and domestic labour. Nothing would be reported and the girls would sink into the same hopelessness as their mothers. Programmes of social reform, attempting to lift these families out of the cycle of inadequacy, met with little success, as they came from an attitude of mind rather than circumstances. As the old tenement buildings began to be demolished and replaced with new accommodation, families were moved and assisted, but were often unable to respond to improved living conditions. You could put the family into a new house, but you could not always make them into a new family, and the old ways tended to persist.

Babies born as a result of incest and others born illegitimately or from families too poor to support them were put up for adoption, and at any time in the nursery there would be a row of cots with babies waiting to be viewed. All these babies had to be perfect, certified by a doctor. If any defect was found, however small and seemingly insignificant, they were transferred to the children's ward after ten days to receive any treatment that might be necessary or possible, and later to an orphanage. Parents were not encouraged to keep handicapped babies as there was no State support apart from the health visitor, and it was thought best for the parents as well as the child that it should be placed in a home. In the case of Down's syndrome babies (at that time called Mongols) and others with disabilities that were thought untreatable or too unsightly to expose to general view, parents were advised it was better to 'put them away', out of sight in an institution, which seems harsh and cruel now in our more enlightened times. Parents had to be able to afford to keep their handicapped child at home, and be capable of providing the necessary care, in order to persuade professionals to let them do this.

At Liverpool Road the nurses' dining room was underneath the labour wards, so we had our meals accompanied by screams and yells from above, which put the more sensitive ones among us off our food. The loudest screamers were those women who were less culturally inhibited than English mothers, who were generally stoical. African women gave birth matter of factly with very little fuss at all, often preferring to squat on the labour room bed, which the midwives did not approve of, but had to admit was a much more practical position for delivery. I never became blasé about deliveries, however many I assisted; every birth was a miracle. The instant a baby emerged from such a fraught process and took its first breath was a moment of wonder for me as well as the mother. Dads were not allowed to be present as childbirth was thought to be 'women's business', and it took several years before this attitude changed.

Some of the midwives, having worked for years in such a tough area, had little time for niceties. One who was dealing with a nervous young girl arriving in early labour, was preparing to examine her when the girl wailed, 'God help me, I don't know how it's going to get out.'

'Same way it got in,' the midwife replied briskly.

It surprised me how ignorant many of the girls seemed, despite coming from large families where reproduction was, in effect, a way of life. The midwives explained this in typically forthright terms. 'The way these girls learn the facts of life is brutal. No facts. Just any man rough as dirt comes along soon as they's old enough, breaking and entering, that's all it is.'

Venereal disease was a problem and we were shown how to recognise signs of congenital syphilis in newborn babies. This was always distressing because the disease at this early stage included facial disfigurement and the baby would become one of those sent to an institution.

Most new mothers could not afford luxuries such as maternity bras and we improvised long strips of wide cotton fabric to make binders to support their breasts and keep them comfortable in between feeds. The binders were fastened with safety pins and were quite complicated to put on and take off, but the women were happy to be given a supply to go home with as these were washable and free. Bottle-feeding was generally unaffordable as powdered milk was expensive, so breast-feeding was the norm for cash-strapped families and first-time mothers were shown how to do it during their ten days' 'lying-in' time in hospital. This was the only holiday away from home that most mothers ever got.

The midwives were a mixed bunch, some of them having worked in the local area for years with all its abrasive edges, and others from abroad. Among these were two Nigerian midwives, nicknamed Deadly Nightshade and Rigor Mortis, due to their surprisingly slovenly and lazy ways. It puzzled me how the hospital with its insistence on high standards, would employ staff like these, but Sister Beddoes, a wonderfully tall, calm, kind and reassuring figure who was in charge of the maternity wards, said we must be tolerant to staff from foreign lands who had come to learn our ways and we must set an example for them to follow. This course of action was entirely lost on those two, who set their own rules, backed up by each other. We dreaded being on shift with them, being treated like skivvies while they sat regally in the office, barely moving a hand or a foot, except to ring the bell for us to wait on them. What really upset us, if they did move themselves to attend to a patient, was their attitude to routine procedures such as removing stitches. This was normally done with sterile instruments, but they used their fingernails, which were not even clean, and this so appalled us we devised a sweet system of revenge. Each time they sent us to make their cocoa, we used milk from the breast-milk bank, which they never seemed to notice, or figure out why we did so much giggling when we took the cups to them.

All this time Adam and I were exchanging letters as before, but now energised with the prospects ahead, our letters had a new focus. Taking the bus to Oxford Street also had a new focus for me, viewing shop windows from the top deck, looking at wedding dresses. I saw one for fourteen pounds in a small but smart-looking shop, which was at the top end of my budget, and Muz offered to contribute if the style was modest. She came on the train from Reigate to look at the model in the shop window and, agreeing it looked virginal enough to be suitable, she came into the shop with me to see if they had it in my size. I had a 22-inch waist and 32-inch bust and, amazingly, this was exactly the size of the one in the window. Muz helped me try it on, smoothing out the billowing organza until it all settled into place. It was a perfect fit, suiting me so well that my skinny shape was disguised by the long swirling skirt on top of a crinoline, bouncing as I walked up and down in front of the long mirrors. The bodice was plain with long sleeves and a rounded neckline, nothing too fancy, until the shop assistants produced a crystal coronet that sparkled and lifted the effect to a more dazzling level with a waist-length veil. Even Muz agreed it was just right and the whole ensemble costing less than twenty pounds secured her approval, so all this could be boxed up and taken back on the train to be kept safely at home. Everything seemed to be going well until one evening I found the mind-reading TV man loitering at the hospital gates, reminding me that I had agreed to go to one of his studio shows and have a drink with him afterwards. I was annoyed to find him still tailing me, but too tired to argue, and thought if I took a friend there could be no harm in going along. Susie was the perfect choice, being too streetwise to be fooled by anyone trying to pull a stunt. We arranged to go and join the studio audience at an evening show, meeting the celebrity guests afterwards, which sounded interesting. Susie sparkled with charm and eloquence during drinks with these people, entirely at ease with them, and going back by taxi to the hospital afterwards I asked her what she thought about the evening and my self-appointed new friend. 'A gas,' she said, 'but did you see the way he looks at you sometimes? Not a lean and hungry look, something else.'

'What do you mean?' I asked, alarmed. 'He has cold eyes,' was all she would say.

After that I used a different gate for going in and out of the hospital, hoping to avoid him if he reappeared, but he still had my phone number and it wasn't long before he started calling more frequently, trying to persuade me to meet him again. He was always very polite and charming on the phone, but I felt threatened by his persistence, which seemed like a campaign to wear me down. One evening a call came at about 6 p.m. when I was still in my dressing gown after sleeping during the day following night duty. My room was on the top floor of the nurses' home and the phone was on the floor below, where it would not disturb sleepers. One of the day nurses had come up the stairs to call me. Mobile phones were still the stuff of science fiction back then. I went downstairs, not wanting to miss one of the family calling, but dreading it might be him, freezing when his voice came through, cheery with compliments.

Without waiting for me to say anything, he went on, as if impatient to impress me, saying he could see me in his mind's eye. 'You are standing at the telephone in night clothes,' he said. 'I am not sure why you are wearing a dressing gown at this time of the evening, but I can describe it, and the night dress you are wearing underneath it, precisely, in every detail.' And he did. It was impossible for him to see me as there was no window he could be aiming a telescope at, and how could he know I had been on night duty as I'd been switched suddenly to fill in for a night nurse who was sick. He might have a spy inside the hospital, but why bother?

'Why are you doing this?' I said furiously, trying to stop panic rising in my voice. 'Why are you spying on me?'

'You know how this is happening,' he said smoothly. 'You yourself are communicating these images to me. I am simply relating this back to you, as you are the one sending the messages. We need to meet up to discuss the situation, as it is affecting me as much as you.' There was a slight pause. 'I think you will agree that you owe me that much.' He waited for me to reply, but I was still too angry and panicky to say anything. Seeming irritated by my silence, his voice turned slightly menacing as he went on, 'It could be dangerous for you if you go on denying that this is happening and refusing to see me.' That really scared me, so that I felt bold enough to shout down the phone, 'I have *not* been sending any messages to you and I don't want any of this. I don't believe what you are telling me. You are becoming a pest. Please go away, or I will call the police.'

Jamming the phone onto its hook made me feel better, as if this somehow symbolised a knockout blow, and I went on standing there for a few moments to steady my breathing and collect myself.

While I was doing this, the phone rang again and I knew it was him. I forced myself to pick it up, listening but not saying anything as he implored me to hear him out. I very quietly dangled the receiver on its long cord and left it hanging there, so he was talking to himself as I walked away.

I went to get dressed and got hold of Susie to come with me to the police station to make a report. To my surprise the police took it seriously and said, since a threat had been made about my safety, it was a criminal matter. They would caution the man (I had told them his name and where he worked) and would report back to me. After a few days I was contacted by the same policeman who had interviewed me, saying that I'd done the right thing by reporting the matter and he could now assure me that I would never hear from the man again. 'It is very surprising,' he said. 'This man is a respected member of his profession, well known in media circles. He seemed unable to account for his behaviour, which he said was completely out of character, and I was unable to obtain any explanation for it.'

Stalking was not something recognised as such then, but this must have been what it was. How the man got hold of so much private information about me remains a mystery. The policeman explained that now this person had been cautioned he would have to be careful not to repeat the offence or he would face prosecution the next time.

As this had been a police matter it had to be reported to Matron, with the result that I was transferred immediately to the hospital's Hampstead branch (thinking it might be safer). This was a complete contrast to Liverpool Road and a very welcome change of scene. The Hampstead branch was in Lawn Road, the very name suggesting summer gardens, an upmarket neighbourhood where the current out-of-date crumbling hospital buildings were due for demolition. Within a few years, the new Royal Free Hospital with all its branches under one roof, would rise from this site. Meanwhile the old wards were serviceable and I was sent to an acute surgical ward where patients were undergoing a form of radical brain surgery called hypophysectomy. This involved removal of the pituitary gland in female patients with certain types of hormone-sensitive cancers, in the expectation that cutting off the supply of pituitary hormone would inhibit the growth of the tumour. The drawback was that such drastic surgery caused extreme side effects, so that post-operatively the patients were often very ill and their condition unstable, requiring a lot of close care. These patients were looked after in a big thirty-bed Nightingale-style ward. Alongside the brain surgery cases, others undergoing major procedures were also needing a high degree of skilled care, so it was a busy pressurised ward and good experience for student nurses like me going into third year.

Enoch Powell was Minister of Health in the Conservative government of the time, full of zeal for reform of some of the old pre-war systems still persisting in this new age of the sixties. He wanted certain categories of mental patients to be looked after in mainstream hospitals instead of the primitive Victorian institutions where they were held as virtual prisoners without hope of recovery or release. If they were mixed in with 'normal' patients, he believed they would respond to this more congenial environment, which would be therapeutic for them. In theory, this was not such a bad idea as long as the selection of these patients was carefully done, making sure they were suitable for relocation, and the wards they were sent to were carefully selected as well.

A busy surgical ward might not have been the most suitable placement for seriously disturbed mental patients, but such was the enthusiasm and urgency for Enoch Powell's reforms that, following instructions from the Department for Health, empty beds were made available on our ward and psychiatric patients started arriving. We had thought only the most docile and non-violent cases would be sent to a ward like ours, but there seemed to be no logic or common sense to the selection process as the new arrivals were delivered by ambulance drivers glad to hand them over to us. These physically nimble and mentally cunning patients very quickly asserted themselves, taking charge of the situation, sizing up what they could get away with.

'They look like psychopaths,' we whispered to Sister, who was quickly sizing up the situation herself, as one very tall intimidating woman from the group roamed the ward in a threatening manner, bending over patients in their beds, hissing obscenities at them as they lay cowed and helpless. Hospital porters were called to advise on safety with methods we could use for restraint if it came to that. We were taught how to do arm locks and immobilise someone if they became violent, with instructions on how to 'talk them down'. The purpose was to encourage a positive response, but these were not tractable subjects and their response more generally produced volumes of abuse as a prelude to making a rush for the door or a window. The ward was on the second floor and one of these patients, during a manic episode, launched herself through an open window, wearing nothing but a pair of slippers. Landing heavily, she injured her ankle, but was still able to run like a hare out of the hospital gates and down the road to the tube station, causing onlookers to ring for the police at the sight of this mad woman streaking down Haverstock Hill.

The police, in due course, decided that apprehending escapees from the hospital on such a frequent basis could not go on. A conference was held with health officials where it was proposed to modify Powell's policy, so that only the most passive mental patients would be selected for transfer. This was agreed and the more severely disturbed ones were sent back to secure institutions, leaving our ward with just one very quiet, withdrawn woman whom I befriended since hearing her sad and strange story.

Chatting to patients was encouraged during quiet times in the afternoon, which were intended as a time for resting before teatime and visiting hour. This middle-aged woman said everything in her life had been completely normal until, suddenly, a few years previously, she had developed a compulsion to strangle her young daughter, who was her only child. The daughter had done nothing wrong and the mother loved her devotedly, but one day, without warning, to her absolute horror, she found herself putting her hands around the child's neck, trying to choke her. She said it was as if her hands had taken on a will of their own, outside her control. Luckily the girl was able to break free and run to a neighbour, who called the police. The mother was certified insane and committed to an asylum, where she was given various treatments, including electric shock, hoping that a time would arrive for her to be judged well enough to see her daughter again.

After some time had passed without incident and it was thought safe for the daughter to visit, this was arranged under supervision and both wept with joy to be reunited. All went well for a while until the extraordinary unbidden compulsion began to take over again; the mother describing to me how her hands, of their own accord, started trying to reach out to her daughter's neck, and she was so afraid of what might happen next she had to leave the room in a state of severe agitation. That was the last time she had seen her daughter, and was now reconciled to never seeing her again. She was an intelligent woman with an academic background, coming from a well-off family in Hampstead, but no amount of money spent on psychologists or psychiatrists had been able to help her.

Life at Lawn Road was less formal than the main hospital at Gray's Inn Road and I was beginning to enjoy more freedom and confidence as I went into my third year, with finals and the end of training in sight. Best of all, Beth was at Lawn Road and had a new boyfriend who was the son of an actress appearing on the London stage. All of us were fascinated by this celebrity connection. Beth never had ordinary boyfriends; they were always exotic and linked to the arts, their names sometimes appearing in the papers among those who led glamorous lives. I noticed how Beth was changing in subtle ways: affected by the disarming influence of this knowing set, she had taken on a worldliness that was unsettling for me. I felt uneasy with the new-style Beth who flashed a large ruby on her finger, laughing at the naivety of the rest of us and distancing herself from us as she moved into a circle of more sophisticated friends. I was very sad and miserable about losing her as a friend, but later, when her wedding photos appeared in a glossy magazine, I understood how her new life could never include me. I remember looking out of the window of my room at Lawn Road on a rainy day, watching rain drops sliding down the pane, thinking they were like tears, my tears for losing Beth, but consoled myself that my closest and dearest friend now was Adam, and my future with him was all that mattered.

Our letters took on a more urgent tone as the reality of getting married and creating a family together came closer with each month that passed. My enthusiasm for large families had to be curbed when I noticed Adam's response was less keen, and he suggested that we might postpone a family so we would be free to enjoy ourselves as a married couple, going on hunting safaris, lots of parties, and general socialising. It sounded too good to quibble about, so I stuck to discussing what kind of wedding we would have and where I would stay beforehand.

Moving onto night duty at this moment was a welcome change and any lack of spirits vanished in the intense routine on a busy ward with no time to sit down, except for a coffee break at midnight and 'lunch' at 3 a.m. Coffee breaks were lively as one of our night-call house officers was Rachel Miller, married to Jonathan Miller, who was currently appearing in a London review called *Beyond the Fringe*. After the evening show he used to come to the hospital to join Rachel and we would all have coffee together in Sister's office, discussing the latest theatre news and gossip.

Chapter 17

Extra pressure was piled on us in our third year, taking on new responsibilities ready to become staff nurses as soon as we qualified. After having settled into life at Lawn Road, I was not impressed at being unexpectedly moved again, back to the main hospital, this time to the ENT department (ear, nose and throat), which had its own theatres busy with operations such as 'nose jobs', that were messy and unpleasant. I was squeamish about procedures that involved digging about in people's faces or throats and did my best to avoid having to scrub for the surgeons or any other close-up assistance, and instead hung about in the background, hoping Sister might decide to get rid of me. Which she did. But it was come-uppance, as I was sent to join the Royal Free team of theatre nurses at Eastman's Dental Hospital, next door to our hospital on Gray's Inn Road. Here I had to assist and witness horrible gory surgery, reconstructing jaws and drilling into bone to extract impacted wisdom teeth, among the worst of my experiences during training, but worse for the poor patients who emerged with bruised and battered mouths, unable to speak or eat. Most traumatic of all was being there when a young man died on the operating table. He failed to start breathing on his own after the anaesthetic tubes were withdrawn, and his heart stopped. In an attempt to resuscitate him, the surgeon opened his chest to massage his heart manually, but nothing would bring him back. I have never been able to forget him and the desperate efforts made to save him. No one in the medical or nursing professions ever forgets such experiences.

This may have been a useful crash course for me in reacting quickly to extreme situations when I was given my next job, which was back in the main hospital as 'Relief Nurse'; an innocuous-sounding role that turned out to be more than usually demanding, as I was on call to be sent anywhere in the hospital where extra help was needed. This could be a seriously ill or dying person for one-to-one nursing, or laying-out someone who had died on a busy ward where staff could not be spared, or filling in for a nurse suddenly going sick, or assisting in Casualty if there was an emergency with large numbers of injuries. Despite the intensity of this kind of work, I found that I liked the variety and adrenalin rush, never knowing what was going to happen next, and being stretched was good for me, going into finals.

These final exams lasted over several days of written papers, oral questions and practical demonstrations, which were an ordeal and exhausting, but being with girls of my own set who were all going through the same stress relieved some of the tension. All of us had plans for what we were going to do after qualifying. Most were staying on as staff nurses, while others were going onto further training as midwives and some, like me, were leaving to get married. A girl I had become friendly with at Lawn Road with the unusual name of Nuala was joining the Queen Alexandra's Royal Army Nursing Corps, and I would have been tempted to join her if I had been staying on.

Another opening had presented itself the previous year, when Susie and I were riding a wave of optimism and each applied to BOAC to become air hostesses, just to see what would happen. We had to send full-length photos of ourselves with statistics of height, weight, bust and waist measurements. Susie was told she was too short, and I was told to wait until I had qualified, as being an SRN would make my contribution to the cabin team more valuable. Susie was furious to be turned down for being a midget, despite having breasts like melons, much too big for such a small person, I kept reminding her, and suggested she might have better luck applying to *Playboy* magazine.

Elaine was finishing her training and taking finals at the same time, and during this last year had been a diligent visitor to the dismal little house in Reigate which Muz was manning. I seldom seemed able or willing to spare enough for the train fare and was always short of money, but Elaine was exceptionally frugal and would never have allowed herself the extravagance of going to exhibitions and theatres like I did. After qualifying and then doing midwifery, she planned to go to Bible college in preparation for becoming a missionary, which followed the family tradition and pleased our parents very much.

Spindle was still at Netherne Mental Hospital, where he was not much more than a captive, kept calm on sedation, but at least this enabled him to go home for the occasional weekend. If I was home at the same time we had long discussions about his predicament, as he saw it – wasting his life mouldering away in a hospital, when at nineteen he should be thinking about being independent and having a career.

'What career would you like?' I asked.

'Studying space,' he replied straight away with conviction. 'I've been reading all the books. It's what I think about all the time, but no one in the hospital wants to talk to me about it. They think I'm mad.'

'You're not mad,' I said fiercely. 'You've got a very good brain and it's a terrible let down that some sort of chemical interference is blocking you from doing all the important things you need to do.'

'Yes, it's a block,' he said. 'I know what I want to do, but voices in my head won't let me. Sometimes I bang my head on the wall to stop them, but they still go on and on, saying wicked things, too horrible to tell you. The nurses say hearing voices is a sure sign of madness. Do you think a cure will be found before I get too old, so I can be normal and have a proper life?'

'You could read about all the research that's being done yourself, you know. Muz could find the papers for you; it would keep you in touch with what's going on. And you'll be top of the list when a cure is found. Then we'll make an enormous cake to celebrate!' I jumped up, spreading my hands wide, indicating the size of the cake and making him laugh.

At this point, without any warning, into what had seemed a stable world since the end of the war, a new and alarming threat was announced. Russia was sending nuclear missiles by ship to bases in Cuba, where these would be in range for firing at America. President Kennedy responded boldly, declaring that if the ships were allowed to proceed, American forces would have no hesitation in destroying them before they got across the Atlantic. He was able to adopt this uncompromising stance because he had secret intelligence from a double agent, Oleg Penkovsky, suggesting that Russia would back down if challenged, so Kennedy was able to call their bluff. Back in London we didn't know this, and memories of the last war remained fresh and frightening enough to put jitters into everyone, so we were all on red alert. If America sank Russian ships, Russia would retaliate, and Britain as an ally of America would be attacked first to neutralise any threat from us. Russian missiles loaded with nuclear warheads were not just in range, but already pointed and ready. Everyone knew this and tensions were so great that, when I was getting onto a bus at Holborn on the day of Kennedy's ultimatum, the conductor giving me my ticket, with cockney black humour, said, 'You won't get no refund, not getting to your stop this time, with all of us being blown sky high any minute.' Passengers looked at each other gripped with fear, thinking these might be our last moments, wondering how it could have happened so suddenly, with no way to prepare for it.

Within a day the Russians backed down and all of us who had been holding our collective breaths, gulped and carried on.

Just as my nerves were settling down again, a message arrived from Fa announcing that he was coming home. He had decided to leave Kenya for good, much to our surprise, after nearly twenty years of saying he would never live or work in England under the NHS. After selling everything he owned in Kenya, he returned with just a suitcase, and a letter of appointment to join a GP practice in Redhill.

The practice was owned by two middle-aged women doctors, occupying the ground floor of a tall Victorian red-brick building on a busy road in the centre of Redhill. The upper floors were living quarters, which Muz and Fa moved into, while the two ladies moved to another house in the town. Ros was at home and Spindle was there too, as well as Elaine, when I went for the first time to join them all together again in one place, after this very long time apart.

What was entirely unexpected when I arrived was finding Babs already installed, chirping away in high spirits as she flitted around the kitchen organising everyone. Except Muz, who wasn't there. Babs quickly explained, 'Your mother has got one of her heads and is lying down. I've made her a nice cup of tea. Here, you can take it up to her.'

'Muz doesn't get heads. She never has headaches,' I said, and wanted to add, *only when you're around*, but it wouldn't have registered. Babs knew she was in control now, with Fa back, and nothing any of us said could change anything. The only person who could do this was Fa himself, and he seemed oblivious to the tension in the household – or was choosing to ignore it.

I took the tea up to Muz and sat beside her on the double bed she and Fa still shared, which to her symbolised proof that Fa still loved her. Now, with Babs hovering, she clung to this evidence, patting Fa's side of the bed as if it offered consolation in the reassurance that his place was still there beside her. 'You remember me saying I would tell you all about Babs when you reached twenty-one,' she began, 'but then you went off to do your training and we lost the opportunity to talk about it.'

'Well, it's too late now,' I said. 'I remember you saying that to me when all this first started happening, and I asked you what was going on. I remember exactly where we were when I asked you. We were hanging up our coats in the hall after getting home from church one horrid day in Tunbridge Wells, when you were so unhappy with our family being split up it was making you ill. I knew something was wrong and it had something to do with Babs.'

'You were too young to understand. I was trying to spare you the worry of it,' Muz said, as if that excused her silence.

'I was at least twelve by then,' I protested, incensed. 'Why do adults always treat children as if they are morons and have no feelings of their own?'

Muz looked startled by this outburst, but I went on. 'I was quite capable of understanding and wanted to help you. When you said I had to wait until I was twenty-one, as if that was some kind of magic number, I felt my sympathy was being rejected, so instead of bringing us close through sharing the problem, it made me feel useless and shut out. Anyway, it's too late now. Babs has such a hold over Fa, the rest of us are just pawns.'

I knew this would start Muz weeping again but was determined to provoke her into feeling angry and militant, instead of sad and beaten, which seemed a much healthier reaction. I thought Fa would respect her for it, which might even lead to a readjustment of his behaviour.

'What are we going to do about it?' I said, pre-empting her tears.

'What *can* we do?' she said, sounding dejected, which was what I wanted her to overcome.

'We can go down together and show a fighting spirit, show Babs that this is your house and you are in charge of it. Put her in her place.' Muz was unconvinced. It was not in her nature to be assertive and Babs, she suspected, would see through it and call her bluff.

'She can do what she likes,' I said, 'but not on our turf, with our Fa.' Muz brightened a little and went to wash her face and put on some powder.

When we went downstairs, Babs was pouring tea into a Thermos beside a picnic basket on the kitchen table. 'Oh, it's lovely you've come down, Fay. Now you can come on the picnic with us.'

'You can go with Fa,' I said to her, 'and anyone else who wants to go with you,' thinking this would embarrass them both and expose the bare bones of the situation in front of everybody.

Fa looked nonplussed for a moment, then very casually picked up the basket and walked towards the door, saying over his shoulder,

'Who's coming then?' Babs followed with the Thermos, and, rather sheepishly, Elaine, Spindle and Ros trailed after her.

'Well, that didn't go exactly according to plan,' I said with a wry smile at Muz. 'Never mind, now they're all out of the way we can have a proper lunch instead of just sandwiches, and enjoy having the place to ourselves.'

Muz smiled back; the idea of being conspirators lightened the mood and she relaxed enough to laugh at my stories about the hospital and my friends. They fascinated her, with lives she saw as dangerously libertine and loved to hear all the romantic bits, but never suggested I might invite any of them home for a weekend. She had become withdrawn and insecure, losing confidence as a hostess, where once she might have enjoyed meeting and entertaining friends of all ages.

When the others got back, filling the kitchen with picnic debris and Babs' shrill laugh piercing the eddies of conversation as everyone milled about, I got Ros on one side to see what she thought about this latest move, living in a surgery house with Fa back home and Babs' star rising. This was not troubling Ros as much as I expected, since something else more disturbing had happened which she went on to tell me about.

She had been walking back from the station one evening after art college and saw in front of her, hurrying along the pavement, a woman weighed down with bags in each hand. Ros ran up, saying, 'Here, let me help you,' and was reaching for one of the bags when the woman turned and stopped, looking with horror at Ros, 'as if she had seen a ghost,' Ros said. The next moment the woman simply vanished right in front of her eyes, leaving Ros standing there with her hand still stretched out, waiting to take the bag. She went on standing there transfixed, unable to take in what had happened as it seemed impossible that the woman had disappeared just like that, with no trace, within an instant. There was no sign of her anywhere and the incident unnerved Ros, who was having flashbacks of the encounter, thinking she was losing her mind, seeing things that weren't there. We concluded that the woman must have been an apparition – while the woman herself had seemed to think that Ros was one!

It must have been a trick of the mind with Ros going through a fraught time since Fa's return and the move to Redhill. This was accompanied by gloom on all sides as everyone missed Kenya, and the family, instead of feeling happily reunited, remained fractured. Babs' reappearance was depressing enough, without the even more depressing prospect of my wedding taking place in the back garden of a doctor's surgery. But this was never going to be the springboard to marriage I had in mind, having already decided with Adam that a traditional Kenya wedding in the garden at Glanjoro was what we both wanted. Adam's sister Elizabeth had been married there with a reception in the garden, guests drifting about informally with children playing on the grass, a sunny day guaranteed.

Adam had to put up a cash bond to the Kenya government for my return as a non-resident. Where previously I'd had resident status as part of Fa's family, now I was going back to set up my own family with Adam, which was a dizzying prospect. It was a struggle for Adam to find the money for the bond, but a reassurance to me that he had not changed his mind.

Thinking about the family we had talked about and now planned to postpone so we could enjoy time alone together before being tied down, reminded me I better go to the local Family Planning Clinic to get advice on the latest devices, as the pill was still being trialled and was not yet available on prescription. The clinic was at Stoke Newington, in a run-down building where I queued in a line of fidgety women waiting their turn at the nurse's desk, contraception being an awkward subject; like sex, not mentioned in polite circles. The nurse's desk was at one end of a large scrubbed room where we waited, glancing nervously at the line of screens along one wall where some of the women had been sent to try on 'Dutch caps'. These were recommended by the clinic as the safest form of contraception, as long as they were an exact fit. Different sizes were available, with an internal examination performed first to assess the correct size. Condoms were not handed out at the clinic as these were judged to be 'men's business', purchased in barber's shops and referred to as 'rubber goods' or 'French letters'.

When it came to my turn, I was asked my name and address, and when the nurse said, 'Mrs Wendy Craddock?' I said, 'No, I'm engaged and getting married in Africa where there are no family planning clinics, so I need to get myself equipped before going back there.' The nurse gave me a sharp look and said it was against policy to advise unmarried girls. I would have to be wearing a wedding ring in order to register with the clinic.

That's easily solved I thought, as I left and went to Woolworths to get a cheap ring. With that on my finger I returned to the clinic the next week, and showing it to the nurse, it served as a passport to getting registered. After being measured for a cap, there was a comical process that took place, crouching behind the screen, trying to compress the rubber cap, which was like a mini jellyfish, into a shape that the nurse had confidently instructed was easy to slip into place once you knew how. It soon became obvious that, while being manoeuvred, the flexible caps had a tendency to shoot out of our hands like greased missiles. It was a technique not everyone had the patience to get on top of, as the stifled expletives, groans and giggles coming from behind the screens testified. I was determined not to be put off, and persisted with the struggles and contortions required to get the ridiculous thing under control, and at last was able to present myself to the nurse for inspection, having completed the task successfully. The prize was handed to me in a small Perspex box: my very own Dutch cap.

When the results of the Nursing Board final exams were pinned up in the classrooms, all of us had passed, except one girl. She was very stoical about it, saying she would stay on for another year so she could take them again. Going back to the nurses' home, waiting for the phone so I could tell Fa and Muz the news, a message came from Home Sister saying that Matron wanted to see me in her office immediately. I felt a pit opening at my feet after the elation of at last being able to add SRN to my name. A summons to Matron's office could only mean something dire had happened, especially if it was urgent. Maybe I hadn't passed after all, or had been reported to her for some offence that counted against my pass.

'Quick, get on a clean apron, and a duster to your shoes,' Home Sister said. 'Matron's waiting in her office now.'

Knocking at her door, my heart was beating so fast I felt faint and breathless. To my surprise, instead of hearing her voice saying briskly, 'Come in', Matron herself opened the door and showed me to a chair, where I sat gingerly, instead of standing to attention in front of her desk as usual. Even more surprising, she smiled and said, 'Congratulations!' She went on, 'I am pleased to tell you that you have been awarded a hospital prize.' I was speechless. 'The Jenner Hoskin prize. It is an honour for you,' she added, as I sat there stunned, unable to say a word. 'It is a prestigious prize and you should know also that you came out with high marks in the finals.'

She rose from her chair to shake my hand and all I could say in a weak voice was, 'Thank you, Matron,' as she showed me out.

A letter arrived a few days later confirming the award and all the family came to the prize-giving ceremony when our SRN certificates and badges were given out, along with hospital badges and awards. Mine was a silver buckle with the Royal Free emblem engraved on it, which I still have.

I left the hospital for the last time in November 1962, walking through the gates into the fumes and noise of traffic on Gray's Inn Road with my same old patched-up suitcase, and the train down to Redhill was the last time for me as well. I felt a chapter in my life closing and another one beginning as I was leaving the family behind – and with no regrets since that last uneasy weekend. I was glad to be escaping a situation that could have no happy outcome. But I felt guilty about Ros, who would be trapped without an ally after I had gone.

There was no talk of her or Elaine being bridesmaids for me, as Fa insisted it was too expensive for any of the family to fly out to Kenya for the wedding, since we had decided to have it there. But he conceded that he would contribute to the cost of it, if Adam's parents agreed to have the reception at the farm.

We were a subdued little group on a misty grey November morning at Redhill station when I went off on the train to Gatwick. My wedding dress was squashed into the same old suitcase, taking up most of the space in it, while my other possessions were to be dispatched by sea in my school trunk. Ros looked pale and strained, and so did Muz, while Fa stood tall and straight-backed like the army officer he had been in more glorious days, his face twitching a bit as he kissed me goodbye.

Printed in May 2023
by Rotomail Italia S.p.A., Vignate (MI) - Italy